In this collection of recent essays (several appearing in English for the first time), John Dunn brings his characteristically acute and penetrating insight to a wide range of issues facing politics – past, present and future.

In the first essay, 'The history of political theory', Professor Dunn argues for the importance of a historical perspective in political thought. Other studies engage with central concepts of political philosophy such as obligation, trust, freedom of conscience and property. A group of essays tackle specific contemporary problems and future dangers, for example racism and the dilemma of humanitarian intervention. The volume as a whole articulates the many dangers, but also the huge importance of contemporary politics, and provides a representative collection of work by one of the most astute political commentators writing today.

The History of Political Theory
and other essays

The History of Political Theory and other essays

John Dunn

University of Cambridge

CAMBRIDGE
UNIVERSITY PRESS

Published by the Press Syndicate of the University of Cambridge
The Pitt Building, Trumpington Street, Cambridge CB2 1RP
40 West 20th Street, New York, NY 10011-4211, USA
10 Stamford Road, Oakleigh, Melbourne 3166, Australia

First published 1996

Printed in Great Britain at the University Press, Cambridge

A catalogue record for this book is available from the British Library

Library of Congress cataloguing in publication data

Dunn, John, 1940–
    The history of political theory and other essays / John Dunn.
        p.   cm.
    Includes bibliographical references.
    ISBN 0 521 49707 8. – ISBN 0 521 49784 1 (pbk.)
        1. Political science – Philosophy.   2. Political science – History.
    I. Title.
    JA74.D86   1996
    320.1′1–dc20   95-18061   CIP

ISBN 0 521 49707 8 hardback
ISBN 0 521 49784 1 paperback

SE

For Heather
and in memory of Thomas

Contents

Preface

These essays, written over the last five years, reflect the pleasures (and I hope also in some measure the benefits) of thinking about the history of political theory in Cambridge in the intellectual atmosphere established over the last three decades, especially by Quentin Skinner, Richard Tuck and Istvan Hont, and steadily enhanced more recently by very many others. They also reflect the continuing stimulus of a remarkable range of colleagues and students who come to, or pass through, Cambridge from all over the world. It is a privilege to work in a setting of such beauty as that of King's College, and to work amongst such a rich and constantly changing array of friends and intellectual companions: a privilege which entails too many intellectual and personal debts for me even to begin to try to register them here. I should, however, like especially on this occasion to acknowledge what I continue to owe to my friends in Japan (above all to Professor Takamaro Hanzawa and Professor Takashi Kato and to their remarkable teacher Professor Kan'ichi Fukuda), to my King's colleague Istvan Hont, to my students over the last decade (Nick Taylor most of all), and to Silvana Dean and Helen Gibson who do so much to make the Department of Social and Political Sciences an endurable framework in which to work as a university teacher, even a decade and a half after the coming of Margaret Thatcher.

Acknowledgements

Chapter 2, 'The history of political theory', first appeared in Italian as a separate volume, *Storia delle dottrine politiche*, published by Editoriale Jaca Book, Milan in 1992 and was reprinted in this form in the volume *Politica* in Jaca Book's *Enciclopedia dell'orientamento* in 1994. It has also been issued in French as a separate volume by Editions Mentha, Paris in 1992. It is published here by permission of Jaca Book, who hold the copyright.

Chapter 3, 'Contractualism', was first printed in Italian in volume II of the *Enciclopedia delle scienze sociali* by the Istituto dell'Enciclopedia Italiana (Trecani) in Rome in 1992 and is published here by permission of the Istituto, who hold the copyright.

Chapter 4, 'Political obligation', was first published in *Political Theory Today*, ed. D. Held (Polity Books, Cambridge, 1991), and is republished here by permission of the editor and publisher.

Chapter 5, 'Trust', was first published in *A Companion to Contemporary Political Philosophy*, ed. R. E. Goodin and P. Pettit (Blackwell, Oxford, 1994), and is republished here with the permission of the editors and publisher.

Chapter 6, 'The claim to freedom of conscience: freedom of speech, freedom of thought, freedom of worship?' was first published in *From Persecution to Toleration*, ed. O. P. Grell, J. Israel and N. Tyacke (Clarendon Press, Oxford, 1991), and is reprinted here with permission of the editors and publisher.

Chapter 7, 'Property, justice and common good after socialism', was first published in a Festschrift for Ernest Gellner, *Transition to Modernity*, ed. J. Hall and I. Jarvie (Cambridge University Press, Cambridge, 1992) and is reprinted here with the permission of the editors and publisher.

Chapter 8, 'The dilemma of humanitarian intervention: the executive power of the Law of Nature after God', was initially prepared for a conference on the spirit of conquest in the Faculté des Sciences Sociales et Politiques, University of Lausanne, in the summer of 1993. It was first published in *Government and Opposition* in 1994 and is published here with the permission of the editors. It has also appeared in Italian in *Ragion Pratica* in 1994.

Chapter 9, 'Specifying and understanding racism', was first prepared for a conference on racism and its history organized by the Associazione Sigismondo Malatesta at the Rocca Malatestiana in the summer of 1992 and was first published in Italian in *Il Razzismo e le sue storie*, ed. G. Imbruglia (Edizioni Scientifiche Italiane, Naples, 1993). It was first published in English in *Government and Opposition* in 1993 and is published here with the permission of the respective editors.

Chapter 10, 'Political science, political theory and policy making in an interdependent world', was written for *Government and Opposition* and was first published in that journal in 1993. It appears here by permission of the editors.

Chapter 11, 'Democracy: the politics of making, defending and exemplifying community: Europe 1992', was initially prepared for a conference on the future of democracy in Asia at the Center for Asian and Pacific Studies at Seikei University, Kichijoji, Tokyo in April 1992 and was first published in Japanese in *The Future of Democracy in Asia*, ed. T. Kato (Tokyo University Press, Tokyo, 1993). It has also been published in Spanish in *Revista Internacional de Filosofia Politica* (Madrid) in 1993. It appears here by permission of Professor Kato and the Center.

Chapter 12, 'Is there a contemporary crisis of the nation state?', was initially prepared for a special issue of *Political Studies* in 1994, which is also published as a book, *Contemporary Crisis of the Nation State?* (Blackwell, Oxford, 1995). It appears here by permission of the editor of the journal, Professor Michael Moran, and the publisher.

Chapter 13, 'Political and economic obstacles to rapid collective learning', was initially prepared for a conference on responses to global ecological crisis at the Polish Cultural Institute, Portland Place, London, organized by Professor Janusz Kuczynski in March 1994. It was first published in *Philosophy and the History of Science* in Taipei and in *Dialectics and Universalism*, Warsaw, in 1995. It appears here by permission of Professor Kuczynski.

Chapter 14, 'The heritage and future of the European left', was initially prepared for a conference on the future of the left organized by the Fondazione Rosselli in Turin and was first published in English in *Economy and Society* (Routledge, London, 1993). It appears here by permission of the editor and publisher of the journal.

1   Introduction

Many people today have noticed that we do not really understand the political life of the world in which we live (or even that of the nation states of which we are citizens). Some who have noticed this are themselves students of politics by profession: political scientists, political sociologists, political economists, political or social theorists, even the more aspiring of journalists. Many who are in no sense professional students of politics (along with at least some who are) are certainly beginning to fear that this degree of incomprehension may be a source of danger in itself: not simply a (perhaps merciful) impediment to realizing quite how bad things already are, but a further aggravation of a range of hazards which are already acutely alarming. This book expresses just that fear. But it also attempts to show how quite archaic intellectual resources can help us to improve our judgement of the significance of recent political experience, and perhaps even (thereby) our prospects for securing a better rather than a worse political future for ourselves and our descendants.

All western universities which provide an opportunity to study politics offer, as part of their instruction, the study of a miscellany of major historical texts of political interpretation, usually of western provenance and stretching in time from Plato and Aristotle to Rawls and Dworkin. The virtual ubiquity of this practice, however, is far from matched by any corresponding commonality of judgement as to why such an offer is in any sense appropriate, let alone as to how the study of the texts themselves is best envisaged or conducted. 'The history of political theory' (chapter 2) seeks to show why this practice remains not merely intellectually defensible but educationally mandatory. It remains so not because the cultivation of a western canon is a due act of local piety or a preguaranteed exercise of presumptively cosmopolitan cultural authority, but because there is every reason to believe that this canon still holds strictly cognitive resources for a sound understanding of the politics of the world in which we all live, and resources for which there are no full surrogates in the insulated cultural heritage of other portions of the globe. To study this canon historically is not to embrace it uncritically or to defer to it passively. It is simply to view it as a sequence of experience in time, and to seek to wring from so viewing it a sharper apprehension of many dimensions of politics which the more recent and heavily scholasticized approaches of the modern social sciences and the continuing processes of ideological struggle and improvisation throughout the globe have singularly failed to provide.

In recent decades the canon has had many critics: political, cultural, epistemological, technical. Often these critics have been essentially right on the points on which they most wished to insist: right about its deformation at one point or another (by patriarchal or imperialist presumptions, by superstition, by parochialism, by inadvertent reification). Where they have been wrong, at least in their cumulative impact, has been in the quite unwarranted suggestion that in the face of modern world politics there is either no need for a coherent and strategic conception of what is really going on, or some other and inherently more reliable basis on which to form such a conception. Here there is really no case to answer: no public claimant on the field of battle with the slightest claim to meet the bill. But, of course, the judgement that the history of political theory does still offer the resources to do so is hardly one which can hope to prevail simply by dint of its own assertion. What I hope to show in this collection of essays, as in some earlier works (Dunn 1980, 1984, 1985, 1989, 1990a, 1990b, 1992), is why the history of political theory is still a key aid in understanding politics (yesterday, today and tomorrow), how that practical capacity bears on the issue of how it can most instructively be studied, and what sorts of illumination it can still provide. If this assessment of its utility is in any sense valid, the utility itself can only be convincingly shown in practice. But if it is indeed valid, then that in turn bears sharply and urgently on the question of how its history is best understood and how that history can most instructively be studied. A professional critique of the history of political theory as putative instance of historical knowledge can be crushingly effective without being especially discerning. After more than thirty years of reflecting on that history, the weightiest judgements about it now seem to me less often clear and negative than I used intuitively to suppose (compare Dunn 1969, Preface with Dunn 1990a, chapter 2). I do not believe that this conclusion is at odds with the analysis I originally offered in 'The identity of the history of ideas' (Dunn 1980, chapter 2; and compare the thoughtful essay by Tuck (1994)). But to be especially discerning, I now reluctantly acknowledge, may simply require a consideration of too intricate and too judgement-dependent a range of factors to permit decisive vindication or conclusive demonstration of command.

The ambiguous relation between academic elaboration and political illumination is explored further in chapter 3, in a study of the historical sources and intellectual upshots of the conception of a social contract. The most powerful movement in postwar political philosophy in the west, overwhelmingly dominated by philosophers from North America, has been a revived and transformed tradition of contractarianism, which seeks to deploy the idea of a free and rational agreement as clear and authoritative standard for assessing the entire public shape of modern political, economic and social life. The intellectual influence of this body of thought has been singularly at odds with its depressingly modest impact upon political struggle, not least in its own heartlands. This influence, however, is plainly an apt focus for historical understanding in its own right, and at least symptomatically of considerable political importance. It remains striking how little attempt has thus far been made to explain the imbalance between its considerable intellectual appeal and its exiguous political efficacy. As a prelude to such explanation, 'Contractualism' seeks to place the modern revival of the conception of a contract as foundation for political right in the context of its protracted prior history, underlining the sharp shift in analytic attention between its earlier users and its contemporary exponents. It argues that the subject matter which the idea of free and rational choice is now deployed to interpret is in some respects decisively less tractable than that which earlier contractarians volunteered to explicate, and that the further resources which its modern exponents (very reasonably) suppose themselves to have at their disposal are too jejune to give it any real chance of establishing the degree of imaginative ascendancy over countervailing ideological categories (let alone over the formidable congeries of opposed interests which they would also need to face down) to achieve any real political penetration. (Compare the report of the Institute for Public Policy Research's Commission on Social Justice (1994): a somewhat bowdlerized reading even of the implications of Rawls's viewpoint.)

Modern contractarian thought is centrally concerned with the issue of distributive justice. Its classical predecessor, by contrast, focused primarily on the question of political obligation, the validity or otherwise of the claims to political obedience levied by existing holders of political authority, and the basis (if any) on which such claims might be pressed legitimately. Classical contractarians, virtually without exception, saw this as a more fundamental question than the issue of distributive justice: indeed, as the key to understanding politics. Recent philosophers (with the exception of a handful of philosophical anarchists) have ceased for a variety of reasons to view the topic of political obligation as having any special and privileged importance for political understanding, and ceased, too, to presume that it can be rendered intellectually tractable enough for a treat-

ment of it to be either elegant or powerful. Chapter 4, 'Political obligation', locates the sources of this response and attempts to show how ill
judged it is (cf. Dunn 1980, Conclusion) and how enfeebling of political
understanding it was always bound to prove. Its central device is a
comparison throughout with the political theory of Hobbes, seen not as
an exemplar of theoretical success on its own (or any other) terms, but as
a more direct and potent address to the fundamental dimension of politics picked out by the problem of political obligation and (in notable contrast to the efforts of twentieth-century political theorists) as being as
sharply instructive in its failures and inattentions as in those elements of
the problem which it may reasonably be judged to have identified
successfully.

Chapter 5 complements this assessment of the superior political
illumination of classical contractarian treatment of the issue of political
obligation by underlining the greater frankness and political sensitivity of
classical contractarian treatment of the mutual trustworthiness or otherwise of human agents or agencies. Whilst once again seeking to register
what has motivated this drastic shift in intellectual and political judgement, and fully acknowledging the powerful forces which have prompted
it, 'Trust' attempts to right the balance by identifying the massive costs of
the disjunction between political and moral understanding which have
resulted from it (cf. Baier 1994).

Chapter 6 focuses on a key example of the depoliticization of the relation between issues of mutual trust and forbearance and the exercise of
political authority: the claim to freedom of thought and expression. In
contrast to a modern logic of individual moral entitlement unsullied by
considerations of political practicality, it underlines the consistently political handling of the issue of freedom of conscience in the master works
which emerged from Europe's lengthy and brutal experience of religious
warfare and persecution. The bowdlerized residue of this experience, as a
recipe for interpersonal fairness, has recently enjoyed some prominence
(cf. Rawls 1985 and 1993) as a grounding for contemporary liberal politics. But careful consideration of the uncensored originals makes it
evident that, however evocative it may prove as an expression of individual political or moral taste, this approach is too reluctant to confront the
brutalities of the struggle for political domination to offer sound guidance
on how we can hope to tame these in practice.

To register the full political sensitivity and intensity of these issues, the
fatwa against Salman Rushdie and the barbarities of the new Algerian civil
war offer a more instructive focus than the original position (Rawls 1971,
1993). In historical actuality the question of what shape we might freely
and rationally choose for a form of collective social and political life

already well entrenched within its own pre-existing political boundaries is appreciably less urgent (and substantially less clear) than the question of what terms we can reasonably hope to agree on for refraining from attempts to slaughter one another with more and more self-righteous zeal. (Compare: 'A Neighbour Country has been of late a Tragical Theatre, from which we might fetch instances, if there needed any, and the world did not in all Countries and Ages furnish examples enough to confirm the received observation, *Necessitas cogit ad Turpia*' (Locke [1689] 1975, II, xxi, 57: p. 272).) For those who favour a less hectic and more domestic focus, helpful contemporary examples might include the regulation of pornography or abortion (Dworkin 1993; Glover 1977; Kahane 1995; MacKinnon 1987, 1989; Sumner 1981; Thomson 1990, pp. 288–93).

A harsh view of the politics of modern liberalism, accordingly, would be that these are essentially unreal, founded on a simple refusal to acknowledge what is really going on in politics or economics (or indeed social life). But a fairer verdict might be that they, like all other reasonably morally ambitious styles of modern politics, have lost their strictly political nerve and exchanged the attempt to judge how moral purpose can be effectively inserted into the political world for the more comfortable topic of what that purpose would consist in if only it were to be so inserted.

Chapter 7 considers the political implications of contemporary liberalism on its own privileged terrain of distributive justice, pointing to the clear parallels in ethical taste over issues of distributive justice between socialists and contemporary liberals and insisting that the recent historical debacle of socialism must be seen primarily as a monumental failure to master practical causality and not as a loss in normative credibility as such. As yet, contemporary liberals have established no claim whatsoever to be able to realize their conceptions of distributive justice in practice, and therefore remain in this sense every bit as Utopian in their explicit political aspirations as their humiliated socialist adversaries. Neither has addressed the issue of effective political agency in a convincing manner, either at the simple formal level of the theory of collective action or at the messier contextual level of assessing contemporary political causality. It is not obvious at present whether this impasse reflects a common error in conceiving justice in distribution in terms of a relatively concrete but indefinite series of social outcomes (a real sceptical possibility in the light of Hayek's or Nozick's critiques), or whether it merely registers a temporary failure of political nerve and economic imagination. But in either case the impasse itself is palpably disastrous for what remain the dominant normative strains in the modern western vision of politics; and it is hard to see how anyone can reasonably hope to elude it without at least confronting it frankly and with some tenacity. (For a tentative start see Nagel (1991).) If it cannot in principle be so eluded, then the great bulk of *bien pensant* political opinion in the west today is either hopelessly confused or in grossly bad faith. (*Mal pensant* political opinion, we can be confident, we have ever with us. But it is grim for its hegemony to be essentially intellectually unchallenged.)

Chapter 8 exchanges a domestic focus on the practicality of embodying our moral sensibilities convincingly in the texture of shared social, political and economic life in a particular sovereign political unit for a more cosmopolitan focus on the prospects for averting conspicuously abominable outcomes in distant countries of which we now know more than we can hope to find agreeable. In many ways this issue offers a most illuminating (if unflattering) mirror for the preoccupations of contemporary liberal thinkers in the wake of the Cold War. In place of a Holy War against an adversary which could be confidently anticipated to act abominably but which had long also been plainly too powerful and dangerous for its freedom of action to be successfully restricted within its own territorial perimeter, the new configuration of political, military and economic forces plainly rendered it possible to intervene, with good (or less good) intentions, in a wide variety of settings (Iraq, Somalia, Bosnia, Rwanda, Haiti). Subsequent experience has dissipated any sense of ease and prospective efficacy in such interventions; but it has done little as yet to clarify quite what the balance of power to act, resistance, and political cost really means. 'The dilemma of humanitarian intervention' attempts to explain why this experience was bound to prove so discouraging, but also why it cannot readily be brought to a permanent end and replaced either by bland recognition of our comparative impotence or by self-righteous affirmation of our refusal to contemplate the costs of averting infamies of which we are distressingly well aware.

Chapter 9, 'Specifying and understanding racism', turns the mirror back on to some of the more intimate and discomfiting aspects of political and economic life in western societies today. It takes what is in many ways the paradigm case of political correctness and tries to show that the political perceptions embodied in the correct liberal response to this topic (one of fastidious but personally unruffled and imaginatively distant revulsion: *de aliis fabula narratur*) are predicated on a quite unwarranted self-righteousness, a very limited feeling for reasonably concrete social justice, and a refusal to acknowledge the limited capacities for effective political and economic agency on the part of what are still the most privileged states in the world. It underlines the political urgency of explaining the incidence of racism in the practical life of modern populations and the extreme unwisdom of assuming that we already know pretty adequately how to explain this. It is intended to disturb (perhaps even in some measure to offend), on the presumption that racist consciousness is indeed in many ways a political and social poison and that there is no chance whatsoever of checking its ravages unless we recognize more frankly just why it does spread so readily and so rapidly in the societies to which we belong.

The remaining chapters of the book turn more directly to the task of understanding aspects of modern political change and the effectiveness (or otherwise) of political action today. Chapter 10 considers how far contemporary political science or political theory have succeeded in capturing either the main determinants of response by policy makers to growing awareness of global interdependence or the effectiveness of their response to this recognition. It explains why neither professional practice is especially well equipped to identify each of these and why both practices ought nevertheless to be capable of making some contribution to doing so. Only an approach which contrived to combine a realistic conception of the causal dynamics of global economic interaction with a realistic conception both of the cumulative ecological impact of these dynamics and of the constraints on policy choice by contemporary state elites could hope to grasp each accurately. This, once more, is a collective task of some urgency, and one which will scarcely be discharged successfully merely by serendipity.

Chapter 11 turns to the role of democratic political choice and action in facing (or exacerbating) the problems of contemporary political life on the European continent. It was written late in 1991 for a conference in Kichijoji, Tokyo, concerned with the future of democracy in Asia, and reflects a range of judgements made at that time. I have refrained from modifying the phrasing in the (probably in any case futile) attempt to render its more incautious formulations less salient. It certainly did not anticipate either the degree of subsequent disruption in Japan's domestic politics or the hornet's nest stirred up by the Maastricht Treaty. In retrospect, I think it overemphasizes the role of the European Commission, following the terms of vulgar political debate in Britain then and since, and underemphasizes the degree of commitment of a succession of national political leaders in the major European states. But if it is potentially misleading about the determinants of the movement towards European integration and perhaps also overoptimistic about the extent to which this process has ingratiated itself with the electorates of the European Union (this still largely remains to be seen), there is less doubt than at the time of writing about the force of its central point. Whatever has caused the movement of European integration, it has certainly not been the conscious political choices and steady political will of its citizens at large. European citizenship, insofar as it has come and is still coming into existence, is a politically created identity. It may still prove a basis for effective agency over time which is clearly superior to the residues of more obdurately national tradition of which we still dispose. But then again, it may not. What I continue to wish to underline is that the force of democracy as a political value tells neither in favour of nor against the prospects for such an outcome. Democracy as a value qualifies the exercise of political authority. It does not and cannot serve to define the territorial scope of political membership.

Chapter 12 turns to the nation state as such as a political format and asks how far the growing sense of the inefficacy of political action in a wide variety of settings over the last decade and more can be attributed to real changes in the power and pertinence of this format. It seeks to distinguish the possible sources of such a sense which lie within the two key component concepts of the idea of a nation state from those which must lie (if they are to lie anywhere at all) in real shifts in the causal properties of economic or political or social structures in the world at large. Whilst the idea of a nation state has always been profoundly equivocal (and correspondingly vulnerable in political practice), it is not plausible that anything of decisive importance about either of its two main conceptual components has become apparent in the course of the last decade or two which would not have been equally clearly apparent for very much longer to anyone who cared to inquire into these. What plainly has changed in the world at large is the sharp compression in the economic discretion of individual national governments and the dramatic acceleration in the known damage (and the still more dramatic amplification of reasonably suspected damage) which human beings have inflicted and are continuing to inflict on their habitats. The first of these certainly threatens the ideological appeal of the nation state and might therefore eventually threaten its practical viability. (On any defensible analysis there is a consequential relation between the ideological appeal of the idea of a nation state and the viability in practice of putative instances of such states.) The second, on some constructions, is already an acute threat to the practical viability of all states and may yet prove to be an irresistible, and therefore in due course a terminal, threat. (This is a hypothesis to refute in practice, not one to rule out of court a priori by theoretical fiat or personal eupepsia.)

Chapter 13 inquires into the principal difficulties which contemporary societies are likely to face in warding off these threats, especially in their more eschatological version. In many ways this seems an unnervingly novel question. But it has a great deal in common with questions that have long preoccupied western interpreters of politics. Chapter 13 seeks to show, in the hastiest and most informal manner, quite how much a familiarity with the history of western political thinking can offer in formulating and deepening a strategic conception of how such threats might in the end be met successfully. Its main conclusion is the prospective centrality to this endeavour of very large-scale and rapid changes in popular attitudes and the extreme political peril of seeking to orchestrate and implement such changes of attitude principally by accumulating and directing coercive power.

The final chapter, on the heritage and future of the European left, argues that unless this increasingly loosely defined assemblage of political judgement and sentiment contrives to win a political future for itself, the surviving pride in their political heritage of its present bearers will prove to have been wholly unwarranted. To win such a future will require (amongst other things) a palpable intellectual mastery of key problems of practical life which the political left manifestly at present lacks and which they are in little danger of developing (or recovering) until they choose to recognize more frankly that this is indeed the case. There is always the possibility that intellectual mastery of such problems might rationally commit anyone who achieved it to fatalism (and indeed to despair). But a refusal to run this risk, while less hazardous to inane optimism, is as solid a recipe as lies within the reach of human agents for depriving the left of whatever chance of a future to be proud of they still in fact retain. *Sapere aude*.

REFERENCES

Baier, A. 1994. *Moral Prejudices*. Cambridge, Mass.: Harvard University Press
Commission on Social Justice (IPPR) 1994. *Social Justice: Strategies for National Renewal*. London: Vintage
Dunn, J. 1969. *The Political Thought of John Locke*. Cambridge: Cambridge University Press
　　1980. *Political Obligation in its Historical Context*. Cambridge: Cambridge University Press
　　1984. *The Politics of Socialism*. Cambridge: Cambridge University Press
　　1985. *Rethinking Modern Political Theory*. Cambridge: Cambridge University Press
　　1989. *Modern Revolutions*, 2nd edn. Cambridge: Cambridge University Press
　　1990a. *Interpreting Political Responsibility*. Cambridge: Polity Press
　　1990b (ed.). *The Economic Limits to Modern Politics*. Cambridge: Cambridge University Press
　　1992 (ed.). *Democracy: The Unfinished Journey*. Oxford: Oxford University Press
　　1993. *Western Political Theory in the Face of the Future*, 2nd edn. Cambridge: Cambridge University Press
Dworkin, R. 1993. *Life's Dominion*. London: HarperCollins
Glover, J. 1977. *Causing Death and Saving Lives*. Harmondsworth: Penguin

Kahane, D. 1995. 'Shared understandings'. Ph. D. thesis, University of Cambridge

Locke, John [1689] 1975. *An Essay concerning Human Understanding*, ed. Peter Nidditch. Oxford: Clarendon Press

MacKinnon, C. 1987. *Feminism Unmodified*. Cambridge, Mass.: Harvard University Press

    1989. *Towards a Feminist Theory of the State*. Cambridge, Mass.: Harvard University Press

Nagel, T. 1991. *Equality and Impartiality*. Oxford: Oxford University Press

Rawls, J. 1971. *A Theory of Justice*. Cambridge, Mass.: Harvard University Press

    1985. 'Justice as fairness: political not metaphysical'. *Philosophy and Public Affairs* 14, 233–51

    1993. *Political Liberalism*. New York: Columbia University Press

Thomson, J. J. 1990. *The Realm of Rights*. Cambridge, Mass.: Harvard University Press

Tuck, R. 1994. 'The contribution of history'. In *A Companion to Contemporary Political Philosophy*, ed. R. E. Goodin and P. Pettit, pp. 72–90. Oxford: Blackwell

All human efforts to understand rest in the end on some conception of what it is to understand something – of what understanding consists of. In the modern world the most powerful conception of what it is to understand something has long been drawn from the astonishingly successful historical career of the sciences of nature. It may not be easy (or, in the end, even possible) to specify clearly the sense in which these dynamic bodies of highly disciplined belief are in fact either genuinely cumulative or cognitively reliable. But it is certainly part of the thoroughly demotic consciousness of most inhabitants of industrial countries today to assume that the sciences of nature do offer genuine knowledge, and that they do so about a subject matter which can only be sanely understood as, in the last instance, independent of human preferences and preoccupations. For the sciences of nature, the universe, in a tradition which reaches back to Aristotle and beyond (Lear 1988), can only be accurately understood as consisting in the last instance of a vast assemblage of natural kinds: types of entity which exist apart from, and prior to, the vagaries of human interest – physical particles, chemical elements, biological species, stars and so on.

But the history of political thinking, like the history of other aspects of human thinking, while it is obviously located within the history of the natural universe, has a very different focus. Not only is it in itself, rather precisely, a history of the vagaries of human interest, it is also a history of those vagaries in relation to a subject matter – the circumstances and significance of politics – which is itself very far from independent of human preferences and preoccupations. This double immersion in the particularities of human attention (and even sentiment) make the history of political theory a somewhat frustrating intellectual genre for those who take their conception of what it is to understand something, at all literally, from the sciences of nature. To a modern natural scientist, a sustained preoccupation with distant intellectual origins is apt to seem an index of intellectual pathology: as inadvertently disclosing either personal intellectual neurosis or relatively calamitous collective intellectual failure. No modern physicist needs to be acquainted with the views of Democritus. So how can it be other than discreditable for a modern political theorist to brood so obsessively over the opinions of Plato or Aristotle or Machiavelli or Hobbes?

What is embarrassing about this question is not that the study of any aspect of human history should differ rather sharply from a study of the contemporary properties or historical evolution of cells or atoms or galaxies. It is simply that in the attempt to understand politics (unlike attempts to understand atoms or cells or galaxies) such a lengthy and disorganized history of human efforts at understanding should still be thought of such pressing relevance. The scandal is that our contemporary comprehension of politics, unlike our contemporary comprehension of physics or biology or chemistry, should still be so deeply mired in history as such: not that the history of political theory should differ appreciably from physics, but that political theory itself should still remain such an intractably and intensely historical subject. What I wish to do is to explain why this should still be so today (very much against the expectations of postwar American social scientists (Easton 1953) or British analytical philosophers (Weldon 1953; Laslett 1956)), why it is likely to remain so for the foreseeable future, and how it has affected the professional development of the history of political theory over the last quarter of a century.

In itself, this last question bears merely on the comparatively parochial record of recent academic inquiry. But it is neither grandiloquent nor analytically exaggerated to insist that the first two questions concern virtually every human being now alive, or indeed likely to live in the readily imaginable future. It is important to bear this contrast in relevance sharply in mind in considering what follows.

In the age in which we live, virtually all human beings are subjects of a particular nation state. The great majority of them depend for their material subsistence on the workings of an ever more complicated and deepening system of international trade, itself precariously sustained by the often highly confused decisions of a huge variety of political and economic agencies. Virtually every human being today, also, lives potentially at the mercy of barely imaginable extremes of destruction from the thermonuclear, chemical and biological weapons made possible by the progress of the natural sciences, the development of the world economy and the political construction of modern states. Whether there is still a viable human habitat on earth in two centuries' time or whether there is still a human species in three months' time will alike depend crucially on human political skill and insight. (In the last instance, mercifully, the odds have improved drastically over the last few years.) Politics has never been so important before in human history. But it cannot be said that the human understanding of politics has grown commensurately with its devastating importance.

If we ask why the understanding of politics should still be so intractably historical – why it should remain so in the face of a practical predicament which is in some ways so grimly novel – the answer lies in the fact that politics is a distinctive form of human activity – a space of human action, always conducted under very severe constraints and on the basis of restricted information, by creatures of limited skill and practical wisdom. It is the constitutive role of human agency in politics as a subject matter which renders it so radically exposed to the vicissitudes of human beliefs and of the ideas which organize and articulate those beliefs. All the central terms that organize modern political action (state, legislature, judiciary, citizen, subject, party, class, obligation, liberty, right, welfare, property, revolution and so on) have a history of their own behind them.

In each case that history combines in a profoundly untransparent fashion a dense context of economic, social and political experience with a vital and often highly inventive exploration of the implications of that context, in the attempt both to comprehend the context itself and to further or frustrate particular purposes within it. Political understanding is never simply a matter of comprehending the goals and potential means of well-considered action. It necessarily involves also the assessment of predicaments directly encountered and of the prospective consequences of given lines of conduct. (Only these can determine whether the pursuit of a given goal by particular means and on a particular occasion is in fact a well-considered course of action.) The history of political ideas or political thinking has relatively little to contribute to the identification and assessment of directly encountered political predicaments. It has somewhat more to offer, in some instances, over the prospective consequences of given lines of conduct (Dunn 1984b, 1992). (In these cases, it would be fair to say, its principal educative impact is in the forming or refining of political sensibilities and political judgement, rather than in the transmission of a definite set of findings.) Where the history of political theory remains of decisive significance, however, is in the clarification and assessment of political goals and in the appraisal of political action. (It has been in these two respects that the expectations of its obsolescence held by postwar American social scientists and British analytical philosophers have proved most obviously astray.)

These considerations have become increasingly salient in the recent development of the history of political theory; and we must return to them at a later stage. But before we do so, we need first to consider narrower and more comfortably academic features of that same development. As a genre, the history of political theory goes back a long way – at the very least to the history of Morality set out in the early eighteenth century by the distinguished Huguenot exile editor of the great natural law texts of Grotius and Pufendorf, Jean Barbeyrac. But the subject matter of the history of political theory, plainly, goes back decidedly further still. As a relatively self-conscious and continuous tradition of understanding, political theory in the west, for example, goes back at the very least to the civilization of ancient Greece and Rome. No one could hope to tell the history of that self-conscious continuity with any adequacy without dwelling at length on the world of the Greek city state (the *polis*) or the broader canvas of the Roman empire. But the view that the subject matter of the history of political theory has been essentially confined (at least until very recently) to the reflexive experience of Europe and its diaspora is not merely culturally offensive. It is also impossible to defend. Wherever there have been literate civilizations of any political scale and longevity (in China, in the Islamic world, in Japan, in India, in Indonesia, in nineteenth-century West Africa), there have developed traditions of understanding of prominent and undeniably important aspects of politics (Schwartz 1985; Hsiao 1979; Munro 1969; Metzger 1977; Gibb & Bowen 1950–7; Maruyama 1974; Najita 1974, 1987; Tambiah 1976; Geertz 1980; Wilks 1975). What separates these diverse and in many cases extraordinarily rich experiences most decisively from the dynamic continuity of the history of political theory in the west is not their comparative intellectual or moral depth and insight but precisely their historical and spatial discontinuities. More subtly, but perhaps in the end more profoundly, it is also the degree to which they, unlike the bearers of the political theory of the west, have been forced over the last few centuries to address the terrain of modern politics not just on practical terms set by intruding imperialist power and wealth, but also, increasingly, on intellectual terms set by the west and through categories forged in the west to interpret the demands and possibilities of a shared global habitat.

The superimposition of these two relations between the political experience of the greater part of the world and the history of political theory in the west poses today a singularly dramatic challenge to human understanding. A cosmopolitan vision of the history of political theory – like a cosmopolitan vision of human history in its entirety – would allot no arbitrary and inadvertent privilege to the experience of the west. It would see that experience as steadily and open-mindedly as the experience of any other area of the globe; but it would also see it no *more* eagerly and no *more* sympathetically than it would see the experience of any other area. As yet we are still very far from enjoying such a cosmopolitan vision; and it is hard to believe that anyone at present lecturing (or even studying) in a university has much conception of what such a vision would really be like. True, an occasional great scholar of the previous generation (perhaps Leo Strauss in the case of Islamic political philosophy) possessed a genuine scholarly knowledge of aspects of a tradition which certainly conceived itself as in some ways antithetical to the Christian west, while leading historians of the present generation, like John Pocock, have concerned themselves with the history of political ideas in China and Japan as well as in Europe, North America and the antipodes. As a result of the complicated and ambiguous history of western imperialism, there have long been profound western students of every great world civilization that has left extensive literary traces, both in the twentieth century (Dumont 1972; Gibb & Bowen 1950–7; Levenson 1958–65), and in some cases many centuries earlier (Pagden 1982, 1990; Marshall 1970). These attentions have not invariably proved ingratiating to their recipients or to the latter's descendants (Said 1985). But in the twentieth century, and of course increasingly, there have also been outstanding scholars of western political thinking in formidably alien societies, especially in the society that has proved most successful of all in first resisting and then in part reversing the intrusive pressures of the west – the ancient empire (and modern constitutional monarchy) of Japan. It would hardly be possible, however, for any single individual to master the range of historical traditions (or even the range of languages) needed to grasp the political thinking of the variety of the world's peoples. I know of nowhere in the world where the attempt to amass such an understanding could be said to be actively in train.

To concentrate on the professional historiography of western political theory, therefore, is in no way to seek to vindicate a preposterous western claim to monopolize political understanding, either now, in the future, or at any point in the past. It is simply to register two facts: firstly that the historical development of western political theory has been relatively continuous and self-conscious, and secondly that its relative continuity and self-consciousness have been subjected, in the present century, to increasingly rigorous and systematic historical analysis. For the moment at least, moreover, we may also be exceedingly confident that such a concentration *need* not be in any sense either narcissistic or self-indulgent. As matters now stand, no one thinking seriously and on any scale about political agency in the world in which we live can ignore for any length of time the legal, administrative and coercive apparatus of the modern state, the ideological and practical obliquities of the modern political party, or the recalcitrant dynamics of the world trading system. These are all historical realities that were first analysed with any rigour and profundity in the west; and it seems clear that, for a variety of reasons, they are still more intensively and deeply understood by thinkers who have chosen to adopt the categories of western political and economic analysis (with whatever amendment) for their own than they are by any traditions which have sought to insulate themselves as best they could from the imaginative pollution of western conceptions of value, purpose and causality. Upon these bluntly cosmopolitan practical realities, different historical societies bring very different cultural sensibilities and imaginative heritages to bear; and they do so, plainly, in the face of very diverse political and economic predicaments (Metzger 1977; Mottahedeh 1987), modifying the cosmopolitan realities very drastically indeed. But even the most blood-stained, obsessive and ignominious episodes in the last few decades of world history make it plain that no society in the world today can hope to live in cultural and political privacy for more than a decade or two. Modern politics may not be very agreeable or very edifying but, for the present, it is here to stay. The odds are still very much that it will last as long as any other single cultural feature of the world in which we live.

In considering the history of political theory it is helpful to distinguish three different types of question. Firstly, what is the appropriate (or historically given) subject matter of that history? (Just what is the history of political theory the history *of*?) Secondly, how is that history, whatever its precise contours (its scope and limits) should be judged to be, best understood? (What is the best method for, or approach towards, studying that history?) And thirdly, what is the broader human intellectual significance of that history? (Why is the history of political theory of the slightest importance to anyone who does not merely need to be able to discuss it fluently and accurately in order to placate some examiner?)

I shall discuss these three questions in turn. But it would be wise, even at this point, to underline the rather obvious judgement that the answers to these three questions are bound to be rather intimately connected with one another. A view about any of them will necessarily affect views about each of the others. Anyone who presumes that the history of western political theory (or indeed even the current content of western political beliefs, considered independently of the historical process of their formation) is in any sense – and however treacherously – a cognitive *resource*, rather than an instance of fated blindness or a purely affective condition, is certain to have quite strong feelings, however incoherently conceived, as to how that history is best understood. Disagreements about each of these three questions are often heated and not infrequently premissed upon very limited mutual comprehension. But if much of the academic squabbling about them lacks charm and comprehensively fails to enlighten, it should not be assumed that the intellectual pressures behind the quarrels are typically trivial or the emotional impetus towards them invariably obtuse. Amongst many other characteristics, to study, seek to understand, write or teach about the history of political theory are all themselves in some degree political activities – certainly a continuation of civic exertion, and in some instances, perhaps, even a continuation of military exertion, by very different (and, in the latter instance, distinctly more edifying) means.

The subject matter

The core subject matter of the history of political theory is, in a sense, relatively uncontentious. What are very contentious indeed, by contrast, are the grounds selected for endorsing the indispensability of that core for any sound understanding of the history of western political theory, the assessment of the moral and spiritual benefits or hazards of choosing to study western political theory at all, and the judgement of the range of peripheral materials that must also be studied if the core texts themselves are to be understood with any accuracy and reliability. The last of these heads of contention must be left until we come to consider the issue of appropriate methods or approaches. The second, by the same token, must be postponed until we come to consider the contemporary (and prospective) significance of the history of political theory. But the first requires immediate attention.

The core of the history of western political theory is a *relatively* determinate canon of works which have attained the status of classic texts (Condren 1985). It is an interesting (and very intricate) historical question how this canon came to be constructed, and an amusing (and recently popular) intellectual game to see how readily and decisively it can be deconstructed. But, for present purposes, what is important about it is simply its relative stability over the last century or so, and its resilience in the face of recent academic contumely. Any interpreter of this canon will compose it slightly differently from any other. But, as in the case of Ludwig Wittgenstein's famous analogy of family resemblance, no interpreter of it is likely to be in much doubt as to whether or not, on a given occasion, what they are confronting is indeed an interpretation of its constituent membership. The great figures who dominate it come from a wide variety of settings: the Greece of the fifth and fourth centuries BC (Plato and Aristotle); the Rome of the first centuries before and after Christ (Cicero, perhaps Seneca); the powerful intellectual leaders of the Christian church of late antiquity and the high Middle Ages (Augustine and Aquinas); the Italian city republics (Marsiglio of Padua, Machiavelli); the traumas of the French wars of religion (Bodin); the great natural law (or natural right) theorists of the European seventeenth and eighteenth centuries (Grotius, Hobbes, Spinoza, Locke, Rousseau); the classic constitutional deliberations of eighteenth-century North America and France (Montesquieu, Madison, Sieyes); eighteenth-century Scotland's profound analysis of the power and human significance of the new commercial society and of the world market constructed for its habitat (Hume, Adam Smith); the reception of this analysis in nineteenth-century imperial Britain (Bentham, Ricardo, John Stuart Mill); the searing challenge of revolutionary crisis (Burke, Benjamin Constant, Hegel); and the tangled history of nineteenth- and twentieth-century socialism (Marx, Lenin).

No canon is itself a strictly historical interpretation. What it purports to convey is the significance of a passage of history (sacred or profane), not a full account of the causal mechanisms through which that history has come about. (In the sacred case, any such account would run a high risk of impertinence.) The important question to ask about any specification of a canon is not whether it would be possible to add further figures who offer imaginatively striking or conceptually illuminating supplements to the insights contained in its specified membership, nor even whether some components of that membership truly are indispensable, or whether others might not be beneficially replaced by further favourites of one's own. Rather, it is whether anything truly indispensable has been omitted from it. Here, plainly, it is not possible to separate the issue of the canon's ideal (or even minimal) constitution from the issue of what truth it is deemed to disclose. So, to make any headway with the question of the felicity of its present composition (over and above noting its severely western confinement), we must return to the issue when we come to consider the broader human and intellectual significance of western political theory today. Let us, for the present, take the core subject matter (the canon) as given to us by history, and consider next the spirited disputes of the last three decades as to how that subject matter can best be understood.

Method

In contrast with sacred scriptures like the Koran, the Pentateuch or the New Testament, no one is likely to deny that the great texts of political theory, whether secular or devout, are essentially human artefacts: products of concentrated intellectual labour and imaginative exploration by palpably human agents (Dunn 1980, chapter 1). It is over the significance to be attached to this banal perception that the principal intellectual disputes about how best to approach the history of political theory have been fought out. The range of viewpoints adopted in these disputes has by now become very large; and much of the disagreement, predictably enough, has not proved especially instructive. But the extent and animus of the quarrelling has served by now to underline the continuing appeal of three very different approaches.

One of these, strongly associated with one of the most distinguished contemporary historians of political theory, Quentin Skinner of Cambridge University (Tully 1988; Viroli 1987), takes the historical character of the texts as fundamental, and understands these, in the last instance, as highly complex human actions, emphasizing especially the constitutive role of intention in human agency (though always firmly refusing to reduce the content of any human act to the agent's self-conscious intention). It treats, in effect, as the key to understanding every such text, the fact that it was the product of a human author (or set of authors) and focuses accordingly on the preoccupations and purposes that led that author to compose it at all and to do so just as they did. The second approach, best exemplified by scholars (like the late C. B. Macpherson) strongly influenced by one variety or another of Marxism, takes the historical character of the texts in question just as seriously as the first. But, unlike the first, it pays only the most perfunctory (or insincere) attention to the concerns of the author, and stresses instead the aspects of the historical society in which the text was composed, of which its author might well have been imperfectly aware but which, nevertheless, prompted him or her to think and express themselves as they did. By contrast, the third approach views the historical character of the texts with massive indifference, treating them, with varying degrees of attention and patience, simply as repositories of potential intellectual stimulation for a contemporary reader, and permitting themselves to respond, accordingly, just as the fancy takes them.

It does not take close intellectual attention to recognize that these three approaches involve no necessary intellectual disagreement with one another, but reflect, rather, more or less sharp divergences of taste and interest. (This point is well developed in Skinner's recent magisterial defence of the coherence of his pursuit of his own intellectual tastes and interests (Skinner 1988).) The three approaches plainly address different questions and, unsurprisingly, tend to offer different sorts of answers to these questions. But none need deny (and none would in fact be well advised to deny) the potential value of the others. Of the three approaches, however, it is the first, the self-consciously historical focus on authorial experience, intention and context, that has been pursued with most intellectual energy and panache over the last three decades. The ruling insight of this approach is that it is of profound intellectual and political (Tully 1988, Introduction; Ashcraft 1986; Dunn 1979) importance that political theory itself has a history. At first this judgement was expressed with relative caution, stressing the imaginative space opened up by a recognition of historical distance (Dunn 1969, Preface), and the resulting opportunities for more or less ironical self-detachment in political understanding (Skinner 1984, 1988). But more recently it has been pressed with more aggression and distinctly less caution (Hont & Ignatieff 1983; Dunn 1979, 1985, 1990a, 1990b; Pocock 1989). The potential force of this more intrepid phase in the historicist interpretation of the history of political theory depends as much on the degree of scepticism about the adequacy of contemporary political understanding that happens now to be apposite, as it does on the purely historical cogency of its analyses of past texts. Its evident temerity, therefore, may be charitably judged less absurd in the face of the effective collapse, both intellectually and practically, of Marxist understanding of a practical alternative to the capitalist world order (or disorder).

The historicist approach has beneath it the deep intellectual roots of the German historical movement (Herder, Ranke, Dilthey: Reill 1975; Meinecke 1972) and of German idealist philosophy. But its practical impact on the history of political theory probably owes more to the postwar professional standards of British historiography (Wootton 1986, pp. 11–12), as interpreted, particularly in Cambridge, by Peter Laslett, Duncan Forbes, John Pocock and Quentin Skinner. Skinner's own philosophical inspiration came principally from the Oxford idealist philosopher (and historian) R. G. Collingwood. But over the last quarter of a century he has defended the relevance and philosophical cogency of Collingwood's approach (Collingwood 1939) and of modern professional historiographical practice, with increasing rigour and assurance, in the terms set by Oxford linguistic philosophy and American pragmatism (Tully 1988). At least as much to the point, he has also practised what he has preached in a series of dazzlingly exemplary studies of the development of western political thinking (Skinner 1966, 1978, 1981, 1984, 1989).

This impressive oeuvre is neither offered nor advisedly received as a model for how all other students of the history of political theory should approach their subject. But its sheer force and brio has had the singular merit of sharpening the question of just what they suppose themselves to be doing, inviting thereby not merely abundant casual abuse, but also, if more intermittently, extended and relatively strenuous reflexive thought. The most prominent respondent over the last two decades has been an older scholar, from New Zealand, himself already far from averse to reflexive thought, J. G. A. Pocock, at present professor at Johns Hopkins University in Baltimore, USA. He shares, too, many tastes and concerns with Skinner – notably, like any true historian, a love of the past for its own interminable sake. But in some ways his key interests have always had a rather different ultimate focus. Like his scintillating first book, *The Ancient Constitution and the Feudal Law* (1957), his most famous and influential work, *The Machiavellian Moment* (1975), is centrally preoccupied with understanding the human significance of time. Both works, too, consider continuity and change in political belief and perception over a lengthy period, and in no way privilege the more searching or intellectually economical of the authors whose works they discuss. In contrast to Skinner's practice (but cf. Tully (1988) on his methodological precepts), Pocock is very much a historian of political thought, belief and language, rather than a historian of political theory: of highly self-conscious and energetic analytical argument, recoverable only by the closest analysis of given texts. For him, political thought is above all an aspect of the experience of a society in time; and the task of its historian is to recover that aspect of its experience as fully and faithfully as they can. This does not, of course, render him indifferent to contemporary political concerns. Both *The Ancient Constitution* and *The Machiavellian Moment* express a vivid scepticism about the historical trustworthiness of a Marxist approach towards the intellectual experience of past societies; and his subsequent writings have indicated an increasing dismay at many aspects of the American society and polity in which he has made his home and of the liberal ideology which, in his view, so distorts the understanding of its weaknesses and misdeeds.

Taken on its own, the principal impact of Skinner's work would probably have been to extend greatly the range of past thinkers whom historians of political theory chose to study with any intimacy, and to underline the indispensability of considering each of these with the utmost care in the dense and always somewhat opaque context which prompted their writings. Even Skinner's own more specific concern with the history of vocabulary focuses more upon the deployment of particular words and phrases in political dispute and on the constraints (ideological and political, as well as purely verbal) faced by a given historical disputant in defending their favoured line of conduct (Tully 1988). But authorial intentionality plays a far less prominent and structural role in Pocock's analyses; and the joint impact of their two oeuvres has now extended far beyond the history of what can aptly be described as political theory, into the history of political consciousness, expression and experience more generally.

There is no question of the historiographical value of this expansion. But it is less clear quite how important some of it is for the history of political theory itself. The constitutive role of language in human agency, and the fact that politics itself simply consists in human agency under constraints, together serve to guarantee that the history of political vocabulary must always be of great political importance: still more so, plainly, the history of the deployment and interrogation of the political concepts which that vocabulary is used to refer to and to convey. There has been much valuable work in the postwar decades on the history of the more analytically central terms in the modern vocabulary of social and political understanding, notably in Germany, under the editorial leadership of Reinhart Koselleck of the University of Bielefeld, in the preparation of the *Geschichtliche Grundbegriffe* (Koselleck *et al.* 1972– ; Koselleck 1985). In ethics, the continuing importance of the historical mutation of concepts has long been effectively stressed for British and North American philosophers by Alasdair MacIntyre (1967, 1981, 1988), Charles Taylor (1975, 1989) and Bernard Williams (1985). But only relatively recently has this approach been reapplied to the history of specifically political concepts, and applied in a way which reflects not merely the historiographical scruples of the new history of political thought, but also its vivid sense of the intensely political career of all concepts that feature prominently in political understanding (Ball *et al.* 1989; Ball 1988).

What is already clear, however, is that a history of political concepts or political vocabulary, which both succeeds in meeting the epistemic standards set by the historicist school and also fully engages with the political importance of the vicissitudes of the words or concepts that it studies, will be an extraordinarily demanding intellectual genre. In relation to this new (and as yet almost wholly unwritten) history, the history of political theory will be at least as much a grateful consumer as it will a proud contributor. What is certain, however, is that whether or not this new genre does make rapid headway, it could not under any circumstances serve as an effective alternative to, or replacement for, the distinctive forms of understanding provided by the history of political theory.

Questions and answers

To fathom the meaning of the canon of classic texts of the history of political theory cannot reasonably be thought of as a finite enterprise – as perhaps physicists, for example, might still hope will prove apt in the end with the project of identifying the fundamental particles (cf. Gadamer 1975; Collingwood 1939). But this absence of a reassuring cognitive destination does not mean either that the history of political theory cannot hope to be in some degree intellectually cumulative or that it cannot and should not be conducted by formulating clear and demanding questions and seeking to discover accurate and compelling answers to these questions. The historicist recognition of the heterogeneity of human purposes over time, and the sheer practical difficulty of identifying these purposes with any precision across great historical or cultural distances, is in no sense a sanction for intellectual licence: more a challenge to intellectual labour and imaginative energy than an excuse for indolence or complacency.

It is useful to distinguish four different types of questions that appropriately arise in attempts to understand the history of political theory. Three of these are unequivocally historical questions (which is not to say, of course, that they are unaffected by current human concerns). Only the fourth is asked not just from the present and for the present, but explicitly *about* the present. All four questions focus in the first instance on texts: but they do so with rather different purposes in mind. The first question asks simply what an author means by and in his or her text. (Only one woman, the late-eighteenth-century English radical, Mary Wollstonecraft, author of *A Vindication of the Rights of Women* (1792), has yet staked at all an effective claim for inclusion in the canon. But if the history of political theory endures for long enough to make this relevant, the same is most unlikely to prove true in another century's time.) As we have seen, this first question has been the central concern of the new history of political thought. Perhaps the main lasting intellectual contribution of that historical movement has been to show why the question itself cannot reliably be answered without the most intimate and searching exploration of the context within which the author in question lived, experienced and chose to express themselves as they did.

The idea of a context of authorship has proved, on closer consideration, remarkably elusive: less a cheap recipe for secure comprehension than a mockery of the hope ever to win through to an understanding that is at all complete. But the idea that authorship itself is a form of agency, despite the challenges of Michel Foucault, has proved comparatively robust. Once a text is conceived as an extraordinarily complex form of action, the issue of authorial intention forces itself intractably forward; and the full context of agency becomes, inescapably, of at least potential relevance. Not all historical studies of what an author means by and in their text disclose anything important that would not be apparent to a casual and historically ignorant, but mentally alert, reader. But any such study *may* well do so. It is hard to defend the view that, if you really want to understand what someone else far away and long ago has said, there is little point in bothering to ascertain who they were or what they were talking about. For anyone who has the slightest interest in the human beings whose strenuous lives made possible these great texts, and who condescends to consider them at any point as what they initially were and in the light of why they ever came to be at all, there is no possible case against a strictly historical approach to this first question. This is as much true for those, like the late Leo Strauss and his followers, who stress the slyness and secretiveness of some of the greatest theorists of politics, as it is for those scholars who think of themselves merely as professional historians practising their modern craft on a more or less arbitrarily chosen subject matter.

The second question may be treated more tersely, since it casts the light away from the texts of political theory themselves and towards the historical societies within which these texts were composed. What does the composition of a given text by an author (or authors) in a particular historical setting show us about that setting itself, or about the broader historical context within which it subsisted? This question is an invitation to read the history of political theory not directly but symptomatically: not for its own sake, but for what it can disclose about the historical milieu within which it was first enacted. Marxist scholars have laboured harder and more imaginatively at this genre than any other comparably determinate intellectual grouping (Goldmann 1970; Hill 1972; in some degree Macpherson 1962). But here, unlike in their efforts to explain aspects of authorial intention by features of the historical context of authorship not necessarily (or necessarily not) apparent to the authors themselves (Macpherson 1962), while the object of their study is plainly the history of political theory, its products are scarcely in themselves contributions to understanding that history.

The first question is perhaps best formulated as: 'What did its author mean by his (or her) text?'; the second, perhaps, as: 'What does that text show us about its author's own society?' Both of these queries have a clear initial focus, however much the field of view may eventually have to be widened out, if they are to be answered at all adequately. But the third question is more obviously centrifugal, even in the first instance: 'What has that text meant to others, reading it then or subsequently, and why has it meant that and not something else?' Every great text (like any other human action) has an occasion – something which prompted it. But, unlike most human actions, great texts also have a protracted and wildly differentiated fate. That fate often stands (indeed perhaps always stands) in a somewhat ironical relation to its author's original intentions. But its very scope and variety are themselves a tribute to the unsteady but urgent power of the text itself. Studies of the fate of great texts could be immensely fascinating, as well as exceptionally illuminating. But they are also dismayingly demanding, not simply for the range of imaginative sympathy and the degree of intellectual control for which they call, but also for the sheer quantity of grubby and often unrewarding archival labour which they necessarily require (cf. Dunn 1980, chapter 3; Kelly 1989). It is an unsurprising index of human frailty that there should be so few studies of real ambition on the historical fate of the great texts of the history of political theory, and perhaps none, as yet, which fully realize the intellectual promise of the genre. From the viewpoint of professional historiography, it has to be said, this is probably the most intimidating – the most brutally labour-intensive – of all three of the genres which we have considered.

Only the last of these four questions is not a question about the past (though it is certainly a question about the present and future relevance of a set of human creations fashioned in the past): 'What do the great texts of the history of political theory mean today, and mean for us?' ('And what will they mean *tomorrow*, or for human generations to come?') That question has been waiting for us at the end of the corridor throughout. If it does not have an answer, none of the other questions could even refer to anything very definite, let alone arise with any urgency. It is that question, effectively, which has constituted the history of political theory as a subject for university education in Europe and North America, from the seventeenth or eighteenth centuries up to the present day, and since extended it, not just to the remainder of the European diaspora or the former colonial or imperial territories of European powers, but to those few world societies which were never really subjugated by the west.

The great scholars of the history of political theory since the Second World War have mostly not thought of themselves as essentially historians, though they have all perforce had to get to know a great deal of history and many have had considerable respect for history as a form of knowledge: in North America, Carl Friedrich and Judith Shklar at Harvard University, Sheldon Wolin at Berkeley or Princeton, Leo Strauss at Chicago, Charles Taylor at McGill; in Britain, John Plamenatz at Oxford, even Michael Oakeshott at the London School of Economics; in Italy, Norberto Bobbio at Turin; in France, Robert Derathé at Nancy, and Raymond Polin at Lille. True, in Oxford, Isaiah Berlin had deserted philosophy purposefully for the history of ideas by the time that he took up the Chichele chair of social and political theory; and in the dizzily prestigious law faculty of the University of Tokyo, Maruyama Masao and Fukuda Kan'ichi both saw themselves in part as intellectual historians. But it was only in Cambridge that the emphasis on the historicity of the history of political theory became overwhelmingly dominant. It would be nice to believe that Cambridge has been simply right, and everywhere else has been wrong. But it would be a shade ingenuous.

What is more likely to be true is that one aspect of the Cambridge emphasis of historicity, language and authorial intention does possess a real prudential force even when it comes to considering solely the current or future significance of the great works of political theory. It is not a necessary truth that a lengthy text can be best understood by reading it the right way up. But it remains an eminently sound practical judgement. By the same token, and however ironical the relation between the fate of a text and its author's own initial intentions may sometimes prove to be, it would be very odd if a great work of analytical argument were not in general best understood by considering in the first instance what the person who composed it intended it to convey. In their justifiably rising intellectual excitement at the discovery of how complicated and difficult it can often be to answer that question at all adequately, the new historians of political theory have sometimes allowed their attention to wander a little far from the blunt force of this simple admonitory commonplace. To understand what its author meant could never be sufficient for assessing the current significance of a great text's arguments. But it is both impertinent and ludicrous to assume that it is not in general a wise preliminary to trying to do so. As theorists of literature have shown us so amply over the last few decades, it is possible to use any text whatsoever as the equivalent of a sort of imaginative Rorschach test, on to which to project the interpreter's fancies. But, since the great texts of political theory are, amongst other characteristics, works of urgent analytical thought, and since their being so is a substantial part of the grounds for continuing to study them, the Rorschach blot approach to these texts, however assiduously applied, is not a promising recipe for fathoming their current significance.

Significance

Politics, as we have already noted, is not a clearly demarcated or self-identifying segment of the history of nature, but a huge, diffuse and very hazily located space of human action, experience and interpretation. The human attempt to understand politics, accordingly, not only has no clear boundaries – as the new historians of political theory have so compellingly insisted – it also has no uncontentiously given core. Hence the acute post-modern suspicion that the canon of great works, which virtually all practitioners of the history of political theory still identify as lying at the centre of an understanding of politics, must be a ludicrously devout (or flagrantly discreditable) index of parochial complacency, rather than a real cognitive resource.

This suspicion is naturally reinforced by observing (if not always with great hermeneutic delicacy) the existence of an intimate historical connection between many of the components of this canon and the history of western imperial power or patriarchal exploitation. But in this last version the suspicion rests on a very crude *non sequitur*. To recognize that an instance of human understanding has cognitive limits (that it is imperfect), and to recognize, correspondingly, that it may well be less than wholly trustworthy, is no ground for supposing it devoid of cognitive force. To acknowledge that an instance of understanding is indeed simply human is itself to register that, for many possible purposes, it cannot be wholly trustworthy (that it cannot be, like Caesar's wife, above suspicion: Rorty (1980)). The study of the canon, then, is best seen not as an inherently chauvinist exercise in Durkheimian secular piety but as an exploration of the most continuous and systematic tradition of analytical inquiry that bears on modern political predicaments. To study Plato or Aristotle, Hobbes or Rousseau, is not to finger gloatingly over the jewels of an intellectual treasury which offers, in the luminous phrase of the Greek historian Thucydides, 'a possession for ever', it is the struggle to win from often inaccessible and refractory seams, the materials for grasping the possibilities and dangers of the human world as this still confronts us.

That tradition goes back to the world of the Greek city state, the *polis*, and to the political and intellectual practices developed in that historical setting, above all in the fifth and fourth centuries before Christ: most notably, the practices of democracy, philosophy, logic and a miscellany of sciences of nature. The word 'politics' itself was essentially given us by the fourth-century philosopher Aristotle in his great lecture course which now carries that name. Aristotle's *Politics* begins with the claim that 'all associations aim at some good; and ... that the particular association which is the most sovereign of all, and includes all the rest, will pursue this aim most, and will thus be directed at the most sovereign of all goods. This most sovereign and inclusive association is the *polis*' (Aristotle 1946 edn, p. 1: 1252a).

It is the practical power of the political unit and the sheer scale of its human ambition which mark it out against all other types of human association. Used for lower and more private purposes (appropriation, destruction), the power itself would not be sufficient to mark a political unit (a kingdom or empire, the mightiest of robber bands: *latrocinia*) out in this way. But the *polis* was (or liked to think of itself as being) a highly distinctive form of political unit: one which consisted, in the last instance, of a set of human beings deliberating and acting together for their own best interests. With the very gift of the term 'politics' itself, Aristotle passed on the equivocal but intensely seductive claim that good human communities must be communities of agents thinking and acting together for a common good, and that politics (the collective life of communities genuinely engaged in this activity), was therefore deeply involved in the search for, and the attempt to realize, the human good.

Aristotle himself was emphatically not a fool. It did not escape his attention that public deliberation, listened to with any care, is always in large part impatient, obtuse and mutually deaf, nor that most action intended to affect political outcomes is prompted by narrower and more insistent motives than a concern for the public good. But he did contrive to link together, in a way which has still not been effectively dissolved, three profoundly important elements. The first of these was the elusiveness and urgency of the goods which human beings require if they are to live well. The second was the prominence amongst these goods of those which they can only hope to enjoy by cooperating effectively with one another on a relatively large scale. The third was the intense practical difficulty of such cooperation.

It is the conjunction of these three elements which still makes politics both so overwhelmingly important and so extraordinarily hard to understand. All of the great texts which have staked a durable place in the canon have something of real importance to say about one or more of them. But it is an open question whether any of these texts (let alone the collective mind of modern professional political science or contemporary public administration) has ever developed a sounder or more illuminating conception of the relations between the three than Aristotle himself contrived to offer.

What is certain, however, is that the world in which we have to live is very different from the world which he inhabited. In comparison with the *polis* (certainly in comparison with Athens, about which we know so much more than we do about any other Greek *polis*: Finley (1983)) it is a world whose public deliberation is awash with moral sententiousness. But it is also a world in which the relations of coercive power and economic force extend over immensely greater distances than they did in the Hellenic *oecumene* of the fourth century BC, and in which these relations of power and force are often palpably no longer under the control of any single geographical site of human choice, let alone any process of public deliberation (Dunn 1990a). It is an important doubt about the tradition of western political theory, especially urgent in relation to the economic domain, whether it does not absurdly privilege the conceptions of sovereign choice and moral purpose at the expense of causal understanding. (This is one reason why segments of professional political science most closely involved with the analysis of aspects of this causality – like the practitioners of international political economy – are so apt to see the history of political theory as a fantasy world well lost. But compare Keohane in Dunn (1990a).)

It is still a question of the keenest intellectual interest quite how the distinctive character of Greek social and political life (above all its division into small self-governing communities, but also, for example, its extensive dependence on slave labour) shaped both its extraordinary intellectual dynamism and the astonishing power of its imaginative legacy. If Bernard Williams is right to insist that the legacy of ancient Greece to western philosophy is western philosophy (Williams 1981, p. 202), it is important to ask how far its legacy to modern politics is simply modern politics (or perhaps, as the late Moses Finley and the German historian Christian Meier have both insisted, if in sharply different ways, the very conception of politics itself (Finley 1983; Meier 1990)). One link between these two questions which has been explored with some subtlety in the last few decades is the possible connection between the political organization of Greek society (above all, the place of public deliberation in shaping sovereign decisions about war and peace, law and justice) and the development of highly systematic bodies of self-critical thinking: logic, philosophy, medicine, geometry, astronomy (Lloyd 1979, 1990).

The most dazzling of ancient philosophical moralists, Plato, was an unsurpassably savage critic of democracy; and even Aristotle was, at best, a decidedly muted enthusiast for it. But modern historians of Greek thought and political practice have shown very clearly that Greek communities did not merely invent the term 'democracy', but also consciously devised an extremely complex and painstakingly conceived system of collective self-rule (Finley 1983), of the point and significance of which they were very fully aware (Farrar 1988; Meier 1990). On the whole, the causal understanding of the working of modern democratic institutions goes at least as uncomfortably with their effusively offered moral self-advertisements as anything that came the way of Thucydides or Plato. If ancient Greece has bequeathed to the modern world, albeit somewhat off-handedly, both the idea of democracy as a uniquely compelling candidate for a legitimate political regime and an intellectual practice of the causal analysis and moral appraisal of political regimes that can hardly avoid casting the most disturbing light at regular intervals on the practical achievements of democratic regimes, it has certainly left us a legacy which we would be well advised to try to understand as an internally related unity, and not as an assemblage of discrete elements, which can safely be taken up or cast aside, as the fancy takes us.

Understanding politics: values, practices and institutions

To see politics, as Aristotle presents it, as a partly cooperative and partly conflictual effort by the members of a given community to identify and realize in their collective life a good which they can truly share is to view it with sympathy and conceive it fundamentally in terms of agency rather than fate. Neither of these perspectives is in any sense cognitively mandatory. Each can readily be repudiated without the necessity of either intellectual error or dishonesty. Taken either individually or collectively, human agents are seldom unequivocally reassuring, and never above suspicion. Sympathy with their current purposes is often imprudent, and sometimes not even morally decent. (Adolf Hitler, one should remember, effectively won the German elections of 1933.) Not infrequently, indeed, it is simply psychologically out of the question: beyond the emotional or imaginative capacity – let alone the active inclinations – of another individual or group. To consider politics in terms of agency is to focus attention in the first instance on the intentions embodied in it. But most political actions which have any effect at all have at least some unintended consequences; and many stand in the most distressing relation to the outcomes which they prove to deliver. (When the Archduke Ferdinand travelled to Sarajevo in the summer of 1914, he did not intend to cause the First World War.)

In understanding politics, consequences are always at least as important as intentions. Indeed, it is reasonable to insist, as Max Weber in effect did (Weber 1948), that they are invariably of decisively greater importance. But to understand political consequences it is necessary to grasp social, political and economic causality: to understand how institutions and practices work, and how and why they generate the kinds of outcomes that they do. In the modern academy, this task has been energetically shouldered by the social sciences (political science, sociology and economics); and a concern with values, purposes and intentions as such relegated increasingly to custodians of the history of political theory and more or less urgent contemporary moralists. Political scientists study what is politically the case, and seek to understand why it works as it does, while historians of political theory, political philosophers and social critics deplore the sorry realities so revealed (or occluded), stressing how far short these realities fall of the better world we can all so readily imagine. It would not be difficult to describe this state of affairs with greater sympathy. But since the intellectual division of labour which it evinces has such lamentable effects on the understanding of politics (Dunn 1990b), sympathy in this instance is scarcely in order.

It is probably the single greatest merit of the history of political theory today that it resists so tenaciously the modern academic reduction of political understanding to a purely positive (or normatively perfunctory) analysis of political causality on the one hand, and a frictionless and emotionally self-indulgent recycling of cherished political pieties on the other. To an adept of the history of political theory, what it offers is both a stimulus and a challenge to moral intelligence. But it is certainly not a justification (nor, indeed, even an excuse) for causal ignorance or stupidity. Uniquely within the present academic world, a study of the history of political theory must view with settled animosity (and barely concealed contempt) the presumption that either of these two lines of inquiry into the nature of politics might be defensibly pursued by an adult and civically responsible human being, independently of the other. But no student of this history has any good reason to try to obscure the intellectual and imaginative strain which is inseparable from the effort to combine the two, and which is also, in the light of the historical record, intrinsic to the very attempt to understand politics.

Many of the great historical texts of political theory are deeply concerned with political causality; and some (Aristotle, Machiavelli, Grotius, Montesquieu, Burke, Kant, Marx) are still extremely instructive over how particular aspects of that causality can best be understood. But it is as the carrier of the deepest and most politically intelligent probing of the place of human values within the historical reality of politics that the tradition stakes its more commanding claim on modern attention. To seek to understand politics without energetic reflection on the nature and force of human values is to condemn oneself to a more superficial and inadvertently conventional level of understanding. (Even the most nihilist of the great political thinkers – Machiavelli, Maistre, conceivably Nietzsche – drew their imaginative force and insight largely from the vehemence of their desire to deny – to refute theoretically, as well as obliterate rhetorically and practically – prevailing moral assumptions.) But it remains extraordinarily difficult to form a steady and well-considered view of the place of human values in politics. Ever since Plato composed his *Republic*, it has been reasonable to suspect that an especially intense concern with the elusiveness and urgency of human values (with the sad fragility of human goodness: Nussbaum (1985)) will prove in the end to be deeply anti-political: either crisply irrelevant to the practical dynamics of political conflict, or a careless stimulus to (or dishonest cloak for) political actions of a character very different from those which it advertises. In the great revolutionary movements which have made so much of the modern history of world politics, that suspicion has often proved hideously compelling (Dunn 1989; Dunn 1990a, chapter 6). But ever since Plato, too, there have been just as powerful grounds for a countervailing suspicion: that a more comfortable acceptance of prevailing political practicality and current political belief involves complicity in unacknowledged structures of power and oppression which run through every remotely civilized human society, mocking the vulnerability and misery of their hapless victims. Few more painful fissures run through human consciousness. But it is a condition of intellectual, moral and political health that we remain able to feel this fissure, and do not opt instead for some simple analgesic. It is the permanent task of the history of political theory to remind us of that pain: to force it bluntly upon our attention and prevent it from beginning to dull. And all the more so since the professional study of philosophy chose to abnegate the responsibility.

This is assuredly the most austere and puritan contribution which that history can offer; and it is an offer that those with stouter spiritual nerves (or coarser sensibilities) can readily decline to take up. But, in addition, the history of political theory offers many other intimations of the continuing presence of historical values in the texture of modern political ideologies and practices, which are more immediately serviceable and less harshly disconcerting. It illuminates, for example, the continuing presence of categories drawn from the christianization of Europe in features of modern political ideology which now often appear irreproachably cosmopolitan: notably the secular transposition of the rights of man and the citizen first constructed from the duties each individual human agent owed to all their fellow human beings, in the light of a common subjection to the purposes of their divine Creator (Dunn 1984a; Dunn 1990b, chapters 2–4; but cf. Tuck 1979). It illuminates, too, the drastic tension between the central normative category of modern political legitimacy, democracy, premissed on the shared agency of all the members of a given populace (Dunn, 1979, chapter 1), and what is still its most prominent practical reality, the modern state, carefully constructed as a concept for the express purpose of denying the claims of any populace to be itself the continuing locus of political authority (Skinner 1989). It was a natural (though not, perhaps, a necessary) consequence of this ingenious construction that the primary duty of citizens should leave them free to act only on the sufferance of their political masters, and frequently in practice confine their agency virtually to purely private life.

Most serviceably of all, perhaps, the history of political theory is unique in offering a truly strategic perspective on the tangled and often singularly opaque history of modern political ideologies. It cannot, of course, explain the detailed history of their adoption by different groupings in different settings, or the finer nuances of their historical mutation across space and time. But, unlike the (for this purpose) epically inappropriate methods of positivist social science, it does show how to identify the conceptual elements out of which these ideologies have been composed, the internal lines of intellectual force (of understanding, as well as sentiment and prevarication) which hold them together, the main features of the practical and imaginative challenges which they were devised to meet, and the more decisive sources of their enduring intellectual frailty and instability. By this demonstration, to speak optimistically, it renders modern politics intelligible (open to active and informed understanding). But it offers no cheap and lazy substitute for active and informed understanding. And in some respects its most important practical lesson is precisely to underline the sharp contrast between the various milieux of human existence in which it first took shape, and the very differently organized practical world in which all human beings now live: the contrast, in particular, between a human habitat which could helpfully be thought of in the first instance as though it were potentially autarkic (and therefore genuinely autonomous), and one of pervasive and locally uncontrollable interdependence – economic, ecological, even cognitive.

The history of political theory, therefore, certainly cannot serve on its own to define what precise conclusions we should reach about modern politics, let alone what allegiances we should take up or sustain within this. What it can indicate, however, is a series of sharp and as yet very poorly recognized disjunctions. One of these disjunctions, plainly, lies between the territory of Benjamin Constant's modern liberty (the pleasures of personal choice and private existence (Constant [1819] 1988, pp. 313–28)) and the residual public sphere of the modern constitutional republic, forged to guarantee that liberty (Fontana 1985, 1991). A second falls between a national system of (increasingly slender and erratic) political responsibility and accountability, with its own legal assignment of property rights (Dunn, 1990a, chapter 5), and an international domain of market exchange and productive organization (Dunn 1990a; Hont & Ignatieff 1983). A third falls between a world of mutually recognizing nation states and conscientious agencies of putative international beneficence, created, funded and defended by those states, and a world of brutally unequal suffering and enjoyment in which vast masses of the poor have little, if any, prospect of a happier existence even for their children's children.

None of these themes is simply going to disappear. But the great historical movement which for the last two hundred years has volunteered most evocatively to cause them to do so (the project of egalitarian social revolution, or of socialist transformation) has foundered, with historically unprecedented speed and conclusiveness, in the course of the last few years. That movement, too, is unlikely simply to disappear. But, for some time to come, we can be confident that its offers will be distinctly tamer and more modest, and that the movement itself will pay a wary regard to the intractability of the practical problems that have caused it to founder, and to the severely cognitive limitations (Dunn 1984b; Dunn 1985, chapter 6) which it has never managed to transcend. The history of political theory does much to explain the vulnerability and the humanly undependable consequences of this great movement. But it offers little distinctive insight into why it should so suddenly and devastatingly have collapsed. (To understand that, we need above all to consider the distinctive vulnerabilities of empires (Dunn 1980, chapter 9), and the contradictions which have emerged at the very heart of the socialist conception of a rationally planned modern economic order (Brus & Laski 1989).)

What we can be confident of, however, is that the disjunctions at the centre of modern political understanding will continue to pose a critical challenge to what the Chinese leader, Deng Hsiao Ping described as the 'bourgeois liberal republic', or, as we might more generously express it, to the current political victor of modern world history. That political form – the modern constitutional representative democracy and its precarious socio-economic accompaniment, the welfare state – has certainly established itself as a uniquely serious practical claimant to modern political legitimacy. But it still has no claim whatever to be a sufficient institutional realization of the values which professedly inspire and legitimate it: democracy, the rights of man (let alone woman), justice, security, as yet an even minimal prudence in the human use of non-human nature (Dunn 1991).

To understand the political condition of the world in which we live – and still more, to learn how to meet the human challenges which that condition presents – we need bolder, clearer, imaginatively more searching, and humanly more engaging insight than any now offered by the modern social sciences or the current practices of professional politicians or bureaucrats. In the face of that need, it is both intellectually inept and humanly profligate to an unforgivable degree to view the canon of the history of political theory just as an impressive (or sinister) cultural fossil, or an occasion for narcissistic chauvinism. These great texts may often elicit an indolent and smug devotion. But what they invite, indeed what, taken together, they *require* from us, is a brave and active response: that we should learn to understand modern politics less shallowly, and act more effectively to improve its outcomes.

REFERENCES

Aristotle. *The Politics*, trans. Ernest Barker (1946). Oxford: Clarendon Press
Ashcraft, R. 1986. *Revolutionary Politics and Locke's Two Treatises of Government*. Princeton: Princeton University Press
Ball, T. 1988. *Transforming Political Discourse*. Oxford: Blackwell
Ball, T., J. Farr and R. Hanson 1989 (eds.). *Political Innovation and Conceptual Change*. Cambridge: Cambridge University Press
Berlin, I. 1976. *Vico and Herder: Two Studies in the History of Ideas*. London: Chatto and Windus
    1978. *Russian Thinkers*. London: Hogarth Press
    1990. *The Crooked Timber of Humanity*. London: John Murray
Bobbio, N. 1965. *Da Hobbes a Marx*. Naples: Morano
    1971. *Una Filosofia militante: studi su Carlo Cattaneo*. Turin: Einaudi

Bobbio, N. and M. Bovero 1979. *Società e stato nella filosofia politica moderna.* Milan: Il Saggiatore

Brus, W. and K. Laski 1989. *From Marx to the Market.* Oxford: Clarendon Press

Collingwood, R. G. 1939. *An Autobiography.* Oxford: Clarendon Press

Condren, C. 1985. *The Status and Appraisal of Classic Texts.* Princeton: Princeton University Press

Constant, B. [1819] 1988. *Political Writings,* ed. B. Fontana. Cambridge: Cambridge University Press.

Derathé, R. 1970. *Jean-Jacques Rousseau et la science politique de son temps,* 2nd edn. Paris: J. Vrin

Dumont, L. 1972. *Homo Hierarchicus.* London: Paladin Books

Dunn, J. 1969. *The Political Thought of John Locke.* Cambridge: Cambridge University Press

1979. *Western Political Theory in the Face of the Future.* Cambridge: Cambridge University Press

1980. *Political Obligation in its Historical Context.* Cambridge: Cambridge University Press

1984a. *Locke.* Oxford: Oxford University Press

1984b. *The Politics of Socialism.* Cambridge: Cambridge University Press

1985. *Rethinking Modern Political Theory.* Cambridge: Cambridge University Press

1989. *Modern Revolutions,* 2nd edn. Cambridge: Cambridge University Press

1990a (ed.). *The Economic Limits to Modern Politics.* Cambridge: Cambridge University Press

1990b. *Interpreting Political Responsibility.* Cambridge: Polity Press

1991. 'Political obligation'. In *Political Theory Today* ed. D. Held, pp. 23–47. Cambridge: Polity Press

1996. 'Western political theory and the understanding of Third World political experience'. In *Culture and Polity in the Developing World,* ed. T. A. Metzger. Stanford: Hoover Institution Press

Easton, D. 1953. *The Political System.* New York: Alfred A. Knopf

Farrar, C. 1988. *The Origins of Democratic Thinking.* Cambridge: Cambridge University Press

Finley, M. I. 1983. *Politics in the Ancient World.* Cambridge: Cambridge University Press

Fontana, B. 1985. *Rethinking the Politics of Commercial Society.* Cambridge: Cambridge University Press

1991. *Benjamin Constant and the Post-revolutionary Mind.* New Haven: Yale University Press

Forbes, D. 1975. *Hume's Philosophical Politics.* Cambridge: Cambridge University Press

Friedrich, C. J. 1958. *The Philosophy of Law in Historical Perspective.* Chicago: University of Chicago Press

Gadamer, H.-G. 1975. *Truth and Method.* London: Sheed and Ward

Geertz, C. 1980. *Negara: The Theatre State in Nineteenth-century Bali.* Princeton: Princeton University Press

Gibb, H. A. R. and H. Bowen 1950–7. *Islamic Society and the West,* 2 vols. London: Oxford University Press

Goldmann, L. 1970. *The Hidden God*, trans. P. Thoday. London: Routledge and Kegan Paul

Hill, C. 1972. *The World Turned Upside Down*. London: Temple Smith

Hont, I. and M. Ignatieff 1983 (eds.). *Wealth and Virtue*. Cambridge: Cambridge University Press

Hsiao, K.-C. 1979. *A History of Chinese Political Thought* 1, trans. F. W. Mote. Princeton: Princeton University Press

Kelly, P. 1989. 'Perceptions of Locke in eighteenth-century Ireland'. *Proceedings of the Royal Irish Academy* 89, 2, 17–35

Koselleck, R. 1985. *Futures Past: On the Semantics of Historical Time*, trans. K. Tribe. Cambridge, Mass.: MIT Press

Koselleck, R., O. Brunner and W. Conze 1972– (eds.). *Geschichtliche Grundbegriffe: Historisches Lexicon zur Sprache in Deutschland*, 5 vols. (to date). Stuttgart: Klett-Cotta

Laslett, P. 1956 (ed.). *Philosophy, Politics and Society, First Series*. Oxford: Blackwell
  1960 (ed.). *John Locke, Two Treatises of Government*. Cambridge: Cambridge University Press

Lear, J. 1988. *Aristotle: The Desire to Understand*. Cambridge: Cambridge University Press

Levenson, J. 1958–65. *Confucian China and its Modern Fate*, 3 vols. London: Routledge and Kegan Paul

Lloyd, G. E. R. 1979. *Magic, Reason and Experience*. Cambridge: Cambridge University Press
  1990. *Mentalities Demystified*. Cambridge: Cambridge University Press

MacIntyre, A. 1967. *A Short History of Ethics*. London: Routledge and Kegan Paul
  1981. *After Virtue: A Study in Moral Theory*. London: Duckworth
  1988. *Whose Justice? Which Rationality?* London: Duckworth

Macpherson, C. B. 1962. *The Political Theory of Possessive Individualism*. Oxford: Clarendon Press

Marshall, P. J. 1970 (ed.). *The British Discovery of Hinduism in the Eighteenth Century*. Cambridge: Cambridge University Press

Maruyama, M. 1974. *Studies in the Intellectual History of Tokugawa Japan*, trans. Mikiso Hane. Princeton: Princeton University Press

Meier, C. 1990. *The Greek Discovery of Politics*, trans. D. McKlintock. Cambridge, Mass.: Harvard University Press

Meinecke, F. 1972. *Historism: The Rise of a New Historical Outlook*, trans. J. E. Anderson. London: Routledge and Kegan Paul

Metzger, T. A. 1977. *Escape from Predicament: Neoconfucianism and China's Evolving Culture*. New York: Columbia University Press

Mottahedeh, R. 1987. *The Mantle of the Prophet*. Harmondsworth, Penguin

Mukherjee, S. N. 1968. *Sir William Jones: A Study in Eighteenth Century British Attitudes towards India*. Cambridge: Cambridge University Press

Munro, D. J. 1969. *The Concept of Man in Early China*. Stanford: Stanford University Press

Najita, T. 1974. *Japan: The Intellectual Foundations of Modern Japanese Politics*. Chicago: Chicago University Press
  1987. *Visions of Virtue in Tokugawa Japan*. Princeton, Princeton University Press.

Nussbaum, M. 1985. *The Fragility of Goodness*. Cambridge: Cambridge University Press

Oakeshott, M. 1946 (ed.). Thomas Hobbes, *Leviathan*. Oxford: Blackwell

　1975. *On Human Conduct*. Oxford: Clarendon Press

Pagden, A. 1982. *The Fall of Natural Man*. Cambridge: Cambridge University Press

　1990. *Spanish Imperialism and the Political Imagination*. New Haven: Yale University Press

Plamenatz, J. 1963. *Man and Society*, 2 vols. London: Longman.

Pocock, J. G. A. 1957. *The Ancient Constitution and the Feudal Law*. Cambridge: Cambridge University Press

　1975. *The Machiavellian Moment*. Princeton: Princeton University Press

　1985. *Virtue, Commerce and History*. Cambridge: Cambridge University Press

　1989. 'Edmund Burke and the redefinition of Enthusiasm: the context as counter-revolution'. In *The French Revolution and the Transformation of Political Culture 1789–1848*, ed. F. Furet and M. Ozouf, pp. 19–43. Oxford, Pergamon Press

Polin, R. 1953. *Politique et philosophie chez Thomas Hobbes*. Paris: Presses Universitaires de France

　1960. *La Politique morale de John Locke*. Paris: Presses Universitaires de France

Reill, P. H. 1975. *The German Enlightenment and the Rise of Historicism*. Berkeley: University of California Press

Rorty, R. 1980. *Philosophy and the Mirror of Nature*. Oxford: Blackwell

Said, E. W. 1985. *Orientalism*. Harmondsworth: Penguin

Schwartz, B. I. 1985. *The World of Thought in Ancient China*. Cambridge, Mass.: Harvard University Press

Skinner, Q. 1966. 'The ideological context of Hobbes's political thought'. *Historical Journal* 9, 3, 286–317

　1978. *The Foundations of Modern Political Thought*, 2 vols. Cambridge: Cambridge University Press

　1981. *Machiavelli*. Oxford: Oxford University Press

　1984. 'The idea of negative liberty'. In *Philosophy in History*, ed. R. Rorty, J. Schneewind and Q. Skinner, pp. 193–221. Cambridge: Cambridge University Press

　1988. 'A reply to my critics'. In *Meaning and Context: Quentin Skinner and his Critics*, ed. J. Tully, pp. 231–88. Cambridge: Polity Press

　1989. 'The state'. In *Political Innovation and Conceptual Change*, ed. T. Ball, J. Farr and R. Hanson, pp. 90–131. Cambridge: Cambridge University Press

Strauss, L. 1953. *Natural Right and History*. Chicago: Chicago University Press

Tambiah, S. J. 1976. *World Conqueror and World Renouncer*. Cambridge: Cambridge University Press

Taylor, C. 1975. *Hegel*. Cambridge: Cambridge University Press

　1989. *Sources of the Self*. Cambridge: Cambridge University Press

Tuck, R. 1979. *Natural Rights Theories: Their Origins and Development*. Cambridge: Cambridge University Press

　1987. 'The "modern" theory of natural law'. In *The Languages of Political Theory in Early Modern Europe*, ed. A. Pagden, pp. 99–119. Cambridge: Cambridge University Press

Tully, J. 1988 (ed.). *Meaning and Context: Quentin Skinner and his Critics.* Cambridge: Polity Press

Viroli, M. 1987. '"Revisionisti" e "ortodossi" nella storia delle idee politiche'. *Rivista di Filosofia* 78, 121–36.

Weber, M. 1948. 'Politics as a vocation'. In *From Max Weber*, ed. H. H. Gerth and C. W. Mills, pp. 77–128. London: Routledge and Kegan Paul

Weldon, T. D. 1953. *The Vocabulary of Politics.* Harmondsworth: Penguin

Wilks, I. 1975. *Asante in the Nineteenth Century.* Cambridge: Cambridge University Press

Williams, B. 1981. 'Philosophy'. In *The Legacy of Greece: A New Appraisal*, ed. M. I. Finley, pp. 202–55. Oxford: Clarendon Press

1985. *Ethics and the Limits of Philosophy.* London: Fontana

Wootton, D. 1986 (ed.). *Divine Right and Democracy.* Harmondsworth: Penguin

3 Contractualism

Introduction

The idea of a contract or agreement has played a central role in the political thinking of the western world over two main periods and in relation to two principal issues. In the first of these periods, the epoch of early modern natural law thinking, the idea of a contract served as the main intellectual device for analysing the grounds, scope and limits of political obligation: the duty of subjects to obey the constituted authorities of the political community to which they belong. In the second, in the American political philosophy of the last three decades, it has served instead principally to analyse the standard of justice in the distribution of the costs and benefits of social membership. The precarious bridge between these two preoccupations was provided by the eighteenth-century German philosopher, Immanuel Kant.

Behind the first of these two intellectual episodes there lay the cultural and social heritage of medieval Europe. The social element of this heritage was furnished by the hierarchical relations of European feudalism with their intimate dependence on mutual commitment (the pledge of personal allegiance) and their heavy emphasis on the social virtue of trustworthiness (*fides*). Its cultural components were distinctly more complex. But they reflected at least two profound imaginative impulses: the Greek commitment to the critical power of human reason and the Christian stress on the significance of human intention and consciousness and on the equality of individual human souls. In the course of the last seven centuries the steady imaginative pressure of these cultural elements has increasingly eroded the hierarchical self-assurance of the very different social setting in which they first began to exert themselves together. The egalitarian thrust of Christianity and critical rationalism has sapped the ideological foundations of feudal hierarchy and left the modern beneficiaries of social, economic and political inequality to justify their powers and privileges by an increasingly shifty and implausible range of instrumental arguments (Unger 1987). In the course of the last century its impact has extended far beyond the territorial limits ever established in practice by Christianity as a majority faith. Over most of the world, the formal standard of political equality, however travestied in practice, is now no longer subject to explicit public challenge (Dunn 1993, chapter 1). But the substantive standard of economic equality cannot be conceded in a purely formal manner; and economic inequality has therefore proved a markedly more robust ideological antagonist. A constitutional order which provides for civil liberties and representative government chosen on a basis of universal adult suffrage is a convincing (if insufficient) interpretation of the requirements for subjecting political power to individual will and reason. But the very muted economic egalitarianism of the western welfare state or of residual communist regimes is an altogether less cogent interpretation of the requirements for subjecting economic distribution to the same standard; and, even so, the compatibility of either with the preconditions for effective economic development is still under severe challenge both in theory and in practice across the globe (Dunn 1990). There is no intellectually convincing modern assessment of the degree to which economic process can in principle be subjected to human will or choice, and abundant practical experience of its recalcitrance to such subjection.

The idea of subjecting political authority and economic allocation to the normative criterion of a contract or agreement is an ambitious and historically important intellectual project. It has taken a very wide variety of forms and enjoyed very varying degrees of intellectual success and political influence. After a lengthy interval it has recently reappeared at the very centre of intellectual dispute about the significance of modern politics and is likely to retain this centrality for some little time to come. It cannot either be understood coherently or assessed accurately without due attention to this variegated and intricate career.

Types of contract

The idea of a contract or agreement has been applied to society and politics in two broadly distinct ways: categorically (or, as it is sometimes expressed, historically) and hypothetically. In its categorical application it has been used to provide a historical explanation for the very existence of human social relations and to offer an analysis of the fundamental character of these relations. Why do human societies exist at all? Why is man a social animal? What is it about human beings which leads them to live in association with other human beings and, in most instances, to live as members of social groupings that extend beyond the limits of a single nuclear family? How are the relations between human beings and these broader social groupings within which they make their lives ultimately to be understood? In the classical natural law theory of the social contract it was these structures of extended cooperation that were referred to as the true social contract (*pactum societatis*). But the idea of a contract or agreement has also been used categorically to give a historical explanation for the existence of government and to interpret, in accordance with this explanation, the political duties and rights of those subjected to its authority. Why do governments exist at all? Why is man a political animal? What is it about human beings that leads them to subordinate themselves (or causes them to find themselves subordinated) to the organized authority of rulers or governments? How are the relations between human beings and those who govern them ultimately to be understood? In classical natural law theory this second (and sometimes quite distinct) application of the idea of agreement was known as the contract of political subjection (*pactum subjectionis*). In a less ambitious fashion the idea of contract or agreement has also been freely applied in the history of Christian and post-Christian Europe to the relations of right and duty between particular governments and their subjects, usually with the explicit intention of restricting the arbitrary scope of governmental power and rendering it in some measure responsible to those whom it governs.

In its hypothetical form the idea of contract is naturally less well adapted to provide a causal or historical explanation for the existence of human societies or polities. But, unlike the categorical or historical usages of the idea, hypothetical contracts do not depend for their force on the acceptance of a universally valid structure of law prior to any particular human practices or projects, nor do they rest on contentious and often highly implausible claims about the past. They are therefore decidedly easier to reconcile with the canons of modern historical scholarship or the scientistic presumptions of the modern social sciences of sociology, economics or political science. The recent revival of the theory of the social contract, accordingly, has interpreted the idea of contract overwhelmingly in hypothetical terms: not as a matter of historical fact or conjecture but, in the words of Immanuel Kant, as 'an idea of reason' (Kant [1781–97] 1971, p. 79). It has also prompted its exponents to vigorous (and sometimes illuminating) efforts to reinterpret even the great seventeenth-century contractarian theorists like Hugo Grotius, Thomas Hobbes and John Locke, as intending a purely hypothetical understanding of the nature and status of the contracts which they invoked. In its hypothetical form the social contract serves principally to analyse what types of social, economic and political arrangements human beings have good reason to accept. On the basis of such assessments it has by now offered grounds for criticizing and rejecting or justifying and defending virtually the entire range of existing human practices.

Both in its categorical and in its hypothetical uses, the idea of contract or agreement has proved over time to be remarkably plastic in its social and political implications. It is not difficult to see why. Historical agreement or contract might reasonably be thought (other things being equal) to validate any human practice that members of a particular society find it in themselves to believe has arisen from or been subsequently sanctioned by such an agreement. Hypothetical agreement or contract (other things being equal) could reasonably be thought to validate any human practice to which members of a particular society can believe that they would, under some appropriate circumstances, have freely agreed. Since judgements of historical plausibility and moral cogency are seldom unanimous in any society where the legitimacy of a particular social or political practice has come under question, it is difficult to apply either a historical or a hypothetical interpretation of the social contract to any serious dispute with conclusive results. Both the clarity and the determinacy of historical fact and the universality and force of an 'idea of reason' have to accommodate themselves, as best they can, to the vagaries of human belief across the vast array of societies of which we are now aware. The most important question about the idea of contract or agreement in modern political understanding is whether this idea can in itself validate or refute the normative status of any human practice, the validity of which is not already independently identifiable. Is the idea of contract or agreement simply a dispensable device for expounding independent conceptions of value? Or is it in fact a distinct source of evaluative insight or a separate ground for critical judgement?

The ancient world

Most human communities attach some weight to the sharing by their members of a range of common values. But in Europe, from ancient Greece onwards, the view that human agreement is of central importance for the understanding, explanation or justification of society or government has been explored in a uniquely searching and elaborate manner. The political life of the Greek *polis*, especially in its democratic form, depended directly upon public reasoning for the taking of major political decisions. This condition led to dramatic intellectual developments in many different fields: notably mathematics, natural science, logic and the analysis of argument (Lloyd 1979). It also prompted systematic critical inquiry into the nature of human values and what some historians have seen as the invention of politics itself (Finley 1983). Greek thinkers disputed at length how far human society, law and government were products of human choice and convention (*nomos*) rather than natural necessity *(phusis)*. The principal aim of Plato's moral and political philosophy was to defend the rational force of moral values against the conventionalism and moral scepticism of Sophists like Glaucon and Thrasymachus. But his pupil Aristotle took a less sardonic view of the political significance of human agreement. For Aristotle, what makes human beings unique amongst animals is their perception of good and evil, justice and injustice, and their power, through language, to articulate and deepen this perception (Aristotle 1946 edn: 1253a). The shared experience of these values is what makes a *polis* what it is. Outside its common experiences and commitments a human being is as dramatically truncated in nature and significance as a severed human hand or a stray counter from a board game like draughts (1253a). Human beings are not naturally compelled to live in a *polis*. Earlier and more primitive forms of association, sexual, domestic and monarchical, all have their roots in nature and in human need (1252a–b). But only in a *polis* can men realize fully their most distinctively and admirably human characteristics. That is why man is by nature a political animal (a *polis*-dwelling animal). For Aristotle, political association is the triumphant product of human intelligence: wholly conventional in its origins, but answering many of the deepest needs in man's nature. His *Nicomachaean Ethics* and *Politics* gave the richest contemporary analysis of the Greek political experience.

But it was Plato's brief dialogue, the *Crito*, that furnished the most dramatic Greek interpretation of the political significance of human agreement. In it, Plato's teacher Socrates explains why he sees himself as obliged to accept the death sentence passed upon him by the court of his native Athens, even though he judged the grounds of the court's verdict utterly unjust. His arguments offer what is still the simplest and most eloquent expression of the view that the obligation to obey the authority of a free community is absolute. Political obligation, he argued, is an obligation, in the first place, of gratitude for benefits received. But there were two further grounds why Athenian citizens had a duty to obey the laws. The first was the entirely practical right of each citizen to emigrate, along with all his property. Anyone who chooses to remain in Athens 'has thereby, by his act of staying, agreed' with the laws to do whatever they demanded of him (Plato 1979 edn: 51d–e). As a free and democratic community, Athens gave every citizen the opportunity to persuade it to alter any law that they regarded as wrong (51e–52a). Socrates himself had chosen to be an Athenian citizen in a peculiarly strong way by the life which he lived and by raising a family within the city. It would be ignominious for him now to desert it.

The belief that the obligation of its members to the community to which they belong is deeper and more sacred than even their duties to parents and kinsfolk was common in ancient Greece, as it has been in many other civilizations. The interpretation of the grounds of this duty in terms of gratitude for benefits received is correspondingly widespread. It has been revived in the less devout and more compelling form of a duty of fairness to fellow members of the community by the modern British legal philosopher Herbert Hart (1955). But the force of the conception of political obligation set out in the *Crito* depends less on its portrayal of Socrates' attitude towards the duties of the moral life than on two key preconditions for seeing his relation to the laws of Athens as one of conscious agreement: the fact that he had indeed had every opportunity over many decades to leave Athens with everything he owned and make a new life elsewhere and the fact that the political institutions of Athens fully entitled its (invariably male) citizens to argue for themselves in its sovereign assembly for the alteration of any law of which they disapproved. It is, to say the least, questionable whether both of these conditions hold for the majority of the adult population of any modern state.

Medieval Europe

At the heart of European feudal society in its classic form lay a single relation: the personal tie of feudal subordination of a vassal to his lord. In the act of homage the vassal pledged aid and service to his lord in return for the latter's protection, sealing his pledge physically 'by hand and by mouth' and consecrating the resulting duty of fealty by an oath (Bloch 1965, pp. 145–7, 219–30). It was a conditional exchange of obedience for protection, secured by a binding promise: a genuine bilateral contract voided by the failure of either party to discharge their engagement. As the great historian of feudalism Marc Bloch noted, it was inevitable that this conception should be transferred in due course to the political sphere and that its eventual influence upon this sphere would be immense (Bloch 1965, p. 451).

Here it merged with a miscellany of other independent sources that stressed the significance of human agreement for a sound understanding of political authority. Some of these came directly from writers of classical antiquity: the Roman orator Cicero's insistence that a genuine political order (*civitas*) is essentially a human association founded upon law, echoed in St Augustine's *City of God*, Aristotle's *Politics*, echoed in the writings of St Thomas Aquinas. Others derived from the heritage of Roman law, as interpreted by medieval civil or canon lawyers. The most important civil law text was the alleged *Lex Regia*, by which the Roman people, by freely transferring its own rule to the emperor was held to have conferred upon him all the power and authority that he enjoyed (Gierke 1900, pp. 39, 147). By the twelfth century it had become a commonplace of European civil law that this act of alienation was still the foundation of the authority of the law of the empire and a natural inference that any valid claim to political authority anywhere must therefore be traceable ultimately to the agreement of the ruled. The claim of the papacy to draw its authority over the church immediately from God himself presented a greater obstacle to seeing the church simply as a voluntary association of individual human beings deriving its authority over its members from the latter's voluntary submission. But the intricate balance of civil and ecclesiastical power in medieval societies and the variety and complexity of ecclesiastical institutions themselves prompted intensive inquiry into the principles of legitimate organization within the church also (Tierney 1982). In the course of these inquiries, canon lawyers transformed the narrowest technicalities of Roman private law into far-reaching principles of political legitimacy. The maxim *Quod omnes tangit ab omnibus approbetur* ('what touches all should be approved by all'), a precept of the private law of co-tutorship, had been converted by the Decretists by 1200 into a justification for the authority of general councils of the church over the Pope himself. In the course of the next century it figured as the ground for summoning civil representative bodies in kingdoms from Sicily to England (Tierney 1982, pp. 24–5). In the later Middle Ages it came to serve also for political thinkers as different from one another as William of Ockham, Marsiglio of Padua and Nicholas of Cusa as an evidently valid principle of political order.

As early as 1085 the Alsatian monk Manegold of Lautenbach, defending Pope Gregory VII against the partisans of the emperor who had sacked his own monastery, insisted trenchantly that a tyrannical ruler deserves to be deposed: that 'his people stand free of his lordship and subjection, when he has been evidently the first to break the compact (*pactum*) for whose sake he has been appointed'. Under these conditions, as John Locke insisted six hundred years later (Locke [1689] 1960, II, pp. 226–7), it is the ruler and not his subjects who have broken faith. To remove such a monarch from his throne is as fitting, just and reasonable as it would be for the employer of a swineherd who had stolen or neglected the pigs in his care to reproach and discharge him without even paying his wages (Lewis 1954, I, pp. 164–5; Gierke 1900, p. 146).

Manegold himself was defending the authority of the pope against the emperor in the bitter conflicts of the investiture controversy. But the political significance of consent as the foundation of governmental authority was soon affirmed by writers of a more intractably secular allegiance. The great Bologna civil lawyer Azo in the late twelfth century interpreted the

Lex Regia not merely as the formal expression of a popular authority permanently alienated to the emperor, but as an index of the continuing political entitlements of the people. The people, he claimed, 'never transferred this power except in such a way that they were at the same time able to retain it themselves' (Skinner 1988, p. 393). It is only as individuals that the people have surrendered their power to make law: as a corporate whole (a *universitas*) they still hold this power, even against the emperor himself (Skinner 1988, p. 394). Azo developed this doctrine quite openly as a justification for the autonomous political authority of European kingdoms like England or France and for the political independence of the city republics of Italy. Later commentators on the *Lex Regia*, like Bartolus of Sassoferrato in the fourteenth century (Skinner 1978, I, pp. 62–5) and the Roman patrician Mario Salamonio in the early sixteenth century (Skinner 1978, I, pp. 148–52, II, pp. 131–4), reiterated and amplified the same conclusion. For Bartolus the citizens of an independent city republic 'constitute their own *princeps*' and any right of judgement exercised by their rulers or magistrates 'is only delegated (*concessum*) to them' (Skinner 1978, I, p. 62). For its transmission to be valid at all, jurisdiction 'must always be voluntarily transferred' (Skinner 1978, I, p. 63).

The impact of the Reformation

When the Reformation of the sixteenth century split the western church into a range of competing claimants to religious orthodoxy, these medieval and Renaissance conceptions of popular sovereignty were put drastically to work in practice. In the sixteenth-century wars of religion, the duty (and in due course the right) to resist unjust political authorities on behalf of deeply felt religious convictions became a matter of acute urgency, above all in Germany, France, Scotland and the Netherlands. It was amongst the legal advisers of the two principal Lutheran Electors, Philip of Hesse and John of Saxony, that the constitutionalist theories of the civil law commentators were first applied to justify resistance by individual Protestant rulers to a Catholic emperor who was deemed by them to have violated the duties of his office and thus reduced himself to the status of a private person (Skinner 1978, II, pp. 194–206). Despite his earlier emphasis on the duty of passive obedience, even Luther himself chose to endorse the private law entitlement to repel force with force; and Philip Melanchthon and Martin Bucer reaffirmed it with greater care and elaboration.

Calvinist theologians at first found it more difficult to repudiate the duty of passive obedience which they, like the Lutherans, had drawn from the classic formula of the thirteenth chapter of St Paul's epistle to the

Romans: 'The powers that be are ordained by God' (Rom. 13:1). But the direness of the Huguenot predicament in France in face of the repressive energies of an orthodox and increasingly absolutist monarchy soon likewise prompted a more inventive exploration of the potential justifications for rebellion. It was the leading Huguenot resistance theorists of the 1570s, the famous Monarchomachs François Hotman, Philippe Duplessis-Mornay and Theodore Beza, writing in the aftermath of the massacre of St Bartholomew, who first turned a contractarian conception of the origins of political obligation into a fully fledged doctrine of the right to resist unjust rulers (Skinner 1978, II, pp. 323–37).

Hotman's *Francogallia*, published in 1573, defended the full subjection of the French crown in the last instance to the political will of the people, expressed in the authoritative decisions of the three Estates (Skinner 1978, II, pp. 312–13). As a professional teacher in the self-consciously 'historical' style of French legal education, he developed his case in the guise of a history of the French constitution from its Frankish origins onwards, insisting that, since the Estates and the people had conferred the crown in the first place, they retained full power not just to transfer it but to take it away as they judged fit (Skinner 1978, II, p. 312; Hotman [1573] 1972, pp. 234–52). Theodore Beza's *Right of Magistrates over their Subjects* of 1574 and Philippe Duplessis-Mornay's famous *Vindiciae contra Tyrannos* ('Defence of Liberty against Tyrants') of 1579 offer the fullest version of Calvinist resistance theory. The people's right to resist, on their interpretation, derives from two very different sources. In the first place it stems from the duties imposed by the sacred covenant or oath (*foedus*) which both they and their rulers have independently sworn to God himself (Skinner 1978, II, pp. 325–6, 331–2). The duty of the people to sustain this covenant in face of its violation by their rulers had already been presented as grounds for revolutionary action by the English Calvinist Christopher Goodman and the Scottish Calvinist leader John Knox. But for Beza and Mornay the right of popular resistance also stems from the contract (*pactum*) through which the people establish a properly constituted political order and confer royal power upon their monarch. The terms of this contract establish the duties of the king as a minister of the political order (*servus reipublicae*) (Skinner 1978, II, p. 333) and they subordinate his authority to that of his inferior fellow magistrates, who likewise derive their authority from its true proprietors, the people themselves, and who have equally sworn a solemn oath to protect and defend the people against tyranny and oppression, domestic or foreign (Skinner 1978, II, p. 335). As single individuals the people and their magistrates remain firmly subordinate to their lawful monarch; but as a collectivity they are just as decisively his legal superior.

A still more decisive vindication of the right of the people to resist unjust rulers was developed by the Scottish humanist George Buchanan in his *De Jure Regni apud Scotos* ('The Right of the Kingdom amongst the Scots'), published in 1579. Buchanan conspicuously ignores the religious covenant and interprets the contract that creates governmental authority in far more individualistic terms than his French co-religionists. Before the establishment of government, human beings lived a solitary and wandering life. When they established government they did so by a simple contract between their chosen ruler and the people as a whole. It was therefore the people as a whole (and not merely their inferior magistrates acting on their behalf) who had the right to 'shake off' the authority of a government whenever they judged fit (Skinner 1978, II, p. 343). The right to kill or depose a tyrant, accordingly, rests at all times 'not only with the whole body of the people' but 'even with every individual citizen one by one'. Two decades later, the same radically individualist theory of the origins of political society was endorsed by the Spanish Catholic Juan Mariana in his *De Rege et Regis Institutione*. Like Buchanan, Mariana also drew from this view the clear implication that even a single private person (*cuicumque privato*) had every right to punish a tyrant on behalf of his injured fellow citizens.

The seventeenth century

It was in the seventeenth century that the idea that the basis of political authority is best understood in terms of a contract or agreement received its fullest and most striking development. A remarkable array of political theorists: the Germans Johannes Althusius and Samuel von Pufendorf; the Dutchman Hugo Grotius and his Jewish fellow countryman Benedict de Spinoza; the Englishmen John Selden, Thomas Hobbes and John Locke; all organized their interpretations of politics around the idea of a voluntary transfer of power and liberty from the individual members of a particular society to its ruling authority. The theories which they constructed on this foundation took sharply different forms and sanctioned dramatically contrasting political conclusions. Some writers, like Selden and Hobbes, insisted that the initial natural freedom and equality of human beings was alienated decisively and permanently by the establishment of political society. Others, like Althusius and Locke, denied that human beings even possessed the right to alienate their freedom and equality unconditionally, and insisted that they could never have sufficient motive to do so and could therefore never be validly presumed to have done so. Some, like Spinoza, eventually concluded that the idea of a contract itself was an unnecessary and confusing element in the structure of their theories (Spinoza [1670–7] 1958, pp. 22–32). But even Spinoza firmly retained the human individual's voluntary transfer of natural power as the practical basis of political authority and the model of a 'union of minds' *(animorum unio*, p. 288) as the central feature of a commonwealth.

The most important seventeenth-century innovation in the understanding of natural law concerned the nature of the entitlements that men and women hold under that law: their natural rights (Tuck 1979). Grotius, Selden, Hobbes, Spinoza, Pufendorf and Locke all developed theories which rested political authority on the surrender of a varying proportion of these rights, on varyingly strict conditions, as a means for retaining the largest total endowment of rights possible. They interpreted these rights not objectively (as intrinsically licit actions or states of affairs) but subjectively (as moral powers and practical liberties which individual persons enjoy to act in determinate ways – in particular the power of each human adult to exclude others from what is truly their own, their *suum*) (Haakonssen 1985). Interpreted through the category of subjective right in this way, the novel version of natural law continued to specify an ideal natural order but an order of an increasingly minimal kind. The principal impetus behind it came from a combination of intellectual discomfort and political anxiety. The intellectual discomfort stemmed initially from an urgent moral scepticism, grounded in the growing awareness of cultural relativity expressed in such writers as Charron or Montaigne; but it was reinforced in due course by the more purely epistemological scepticism of the great philosophical interpreters of the implications of the scientific revolution, from Descartes to David Hume. The political anxiety stemmed from the grim experience of a century of fanatical confessional struggle within and between the European states. It culminated in two classic defences of the human indispensability of peace, internationally in Grotius's *De Jure Belli ac Pacis* of 1625 and civilly in Hobbes's *Leviathan* of 1651.

The two principal theoretical issues which divided seventeenth-century contractarians were the character of the natural powers and rights of individual human beings and the nature of the political entity constituted by the conditional transfer or absolute surrender of these powers and rights. Some writers – notably Hobbes and Spinoza – equated individual rights with individual physical powers. From this equation they drew the conclusion that the natural relations between human beings are ones of enmity and that the condition of mankind in the absence of government is one of war. The need for rule is therefore of pressing urgency and the rights of rulers over their subjects are correspondingly draconic. Other writers – notably Locke – insisted that nature was ruled by the authoritative law of its divine Creator, and that any rights which human beings enjoyed were given to them by that law and remained bounded by its requirements: above all the duty to treat one another peacefully. The need for rule amongst human beings depended upon the circumstances of their association with one another; and in any economically developed community it would necessarily be pretty acute. But even where governments were most evidently indispensable, the rights of a ruler over his subjects remained closely confined by the law of nature.

The new theories of natural rights furnished a powerful tool for analysing the nature of governmental authority. Already in the sixteenth century Jean Bodin had been prompted to devise a decisive doctrine of sovereign power as sanction for the absolutist claims of the French monarchy in the face of religious civil war. Early in the seventeenth century, the Spanish Dominican theologian Francisco Suarez responded to the radical populist resistance theories of the previous century with an equally drastic doctrine of the transfer of rights from individual to ruler: *non est delegatio sed quasi alienatio* (Skinner 1978, II, p. 183). For Suarez, a political community acting in self-defence retained every right to resist even its own ruler, since the right of self-preservation cannot be surrendered voluntarily (Skinner 1978, II, pp. 177–8). But it retained this ultimate power as a constituted political community and could exercise it solely for self-defence, while the ruler acquired, through the contract which established his initial authority, 'absolute power, to be used by himself or his agents in whatever manner he may think fit', unconstrained by legal sanctions (Skinner 1978, II, pp. 183–4). In addition, Suarez combined this robust defence of absolute power with a subtle analysis of the features of human agents which alone rendered them able to establish a genuine political community in the first place. Free and rational men with power over their own faculties are not simply a random aggregation. They are also potentially 'a single mystical body', capable through their moral powers of exerting 'a special will or common volition' and agreeing together to form 'a single unified whole' (Skinner 1978, II, p. 165).

Hobbes

The strongest defence of the authority of the state as a single will, created by its individual citizens through the contractual alienation of their private right of judgement, was formulated by Thomas Hobbes. In his two remarkable books, *De Cive* ('On Citizenship', 1642) and *Leviathan* (1651), Hobbes attacked what he saw as the two greatest sources of self-righteous dissidence that threatened the political stability of the English state. The first of these was the conception of citizen liberty as free and independent political agency, inherited from classical Greece and Rome. The second was the Protestant insistence on the right of each believer to interpret for himself the religious duties imposed by the Christian scriptures. For Hobbes, each of these powerful ideologies grossly accentuated the already formidable dangers to one another which lay in the most fundamental and ineliminable features of human nature.

Human beings pursue their own conception of good and shun their own conception of evil. Above all they shun that supreme evil, death; and they do so in every instance compulsively: 'by a certain impulsion of nature, no lesse then that whereby a Stone moves downward' (Hobbes [1642] 1983, p. 47). Because of these compulsions all men have a natural right to do whatever they judge will best preserve their lives and a consequent natural right to everything which they see as necessary to that purpose (Hobbes [1642] 1983, I, x, p. 47), even 'one another's body' (Hobbes, [1651] 1946, I, xiv, p. 85). Because they often conflict with one another over the objects of their desires (material goods, honour, eminence), and because they can never be sure of realizing their desires in the future, their natural relations with one another are profoundly hostile. The State of Nature is a State of War and the life of man within it is not merely deprived of the comforts of civilization but dominated by continual fear and danger of violent death: 'solitary, poor, nasty, brutish, and short (Hobbes [1651] 1946, I, xiii, p. 82). This condition, Hobbes conceded, may never have been general 'over all the world'; but it still held good in most of America and all independent rulers continued to confront one another in this fashion (Hobbes [1651] 1946, I, xiii, p. 83).

To escape these perils, human beings need peace and for peace they need government. To establish government they have a single key resource. They can bind themselves voluntarily and rationally to alienate their individual will and judgement to a single unified will and judgement: to the artificial reason of the commonwealth – *Leviathan*. Civil societies are not mere meetings. They are *bonds* (Hobbes [1642] 1983, I, ii, p. 44) that depend upon contracts and the keeping of faith. A contract is a mutually binding promise to act in a given way on a future occasion. The capacity to make contracts is a natural human power and the duty to observe them (where they are binding) is a natural human duty. But contracts bind only where the contracting parties individually judge that it will be physically safe to observe them. The natural necessities of man's nature preclude him being obliged by any contract to submit to death or physical hurt (Hobbes [1642] 1983, II, xviii, p. 58). Without peace and the effective enforcement which peace requires, men's natural passions will make them wholly untrustworthy observers of their contracts. Covenants 'without the sword, are but words, and of no strength to secure a man at all' (Hobbes [1651] 1946, II, xvii, p. 109).

A commonwealth is '*one Person*, whose *will*, by the compact of many men, is to be received for the *will* of them all' (Hobbes [1642] 1983, V, ix, p. 89). It is through its sovereign power alone (the soul of the common-wealth) that the latter has a will at all. The sovereign is therefore entitled to will and judge on behalf of each of its subjects and these have no right to dispute or resist its judgement on any issue whatever (even the most inflammatory questions of religious interpretation). Only where it levels an immediate physical threat at particular individuals does their obliga-tion to obey and support it cease. The conjunction of men's natural rights is indispensable to sustain the coercive power of the sovereign. But it is the alienation of their individual judgement which is the most urgent and painful of the preconditions for establishing civil society. The covenant which establishes the sovereign power is a mutual undertaking by its sub-jects with one another, to surrender their rights to it. They appoint a single authority to 'bear their Person': to represent them by willing and judging on their behalf. They authorize all the subsequent acts of this authority as their own acts. This is more than 'consent, or concord; it is a real unity of them all, in one and the same person' (Hobbes [1651] 1946, II, xvii, p. 112). It can arise by deliberate agreement. But it can also arise, just as validly, through 'natural force', by conquest and the submission of the conquered in exchange for the chance to remain alive. In Hobbes's eyes there is not the slightest inconsistency between fear and liberty. Peace is man's supreme need. Only government can meet that need; and every effective government is therefore fully entitled to the obedience of its subjects. *Leviathan* sets out 'the mutual relation of protection and obedience; of which the condition of human nature and the laws divine, both natural and positive, require an inviolable observation' (Hobbes [1651] 1946, Rev. and Conc., pp. 467–8).

In his own view, his theory thus establishes that all subjects are fully obliged on all occasions to obey the commands of an effective political authority, except in the single case of a threat to their own body. Here the obligation of the compact on which political authority is founded effec-tively lapses, just as the constraining force of the laws of nature can lapse in war itself. This is why, in Hobbes's view, unlike that of Grotius (Tuck 1988, pp. 261–2), physical fear precludes a criminal from being obliged to endure even the justest of punishments. In the last instance human polit-ical authority is a rational response to the overwhelming motivational power of human fearfulness. It rests practically upon a systematization of the passion of fear and its scope and limits are both best understood in terms of the rational grounds for that passion.

Modern interpreters of Hobbes have disagreed sharply over the nature of his theory of political obligation. Some have seen it as a classical natural law theory, in which the laws of nature oblige human beings deontologically: as genuinely moral laws and perhaps even as laws of Nature's God (Warrender 1957). Others have seen it as a purely secular prudential doctrine, advocating the pursuit of individual self-interest but seeking to explain as clearly as possible what that self-interest consists in (Brown 1965). But the most compelling recent interpreters have shown that Hobbes's uniquely determined attempt to meet the challenges of moral and epistemological scepticism yielded a theory which fits neatly with neither of these models (Tuck 1988). Hobbes's modern moral science accepts a minimal schedule of universal rights and duties dependably identifiable by human reason, deeply grounded in the human passions, but directing these unfalteringly towards the peace which is the deepest human need. The obligation to obey the sovereign rests, like all binding relations between human beings, on a commitment of the will. But this is a logical truth about the nature of obligation, not a historical claim about the origins of governmental authority. The laws of nature oblige human beings to obey governments established by conquest just as clearly and decisively as they do those generated by men's most carefully and dispassionately considered choices. The categorical duty to obey effectively eclipses, at least for subjects, every other political value or preference. It is unsurprising that subsequent commentators have found Hobbes's argument less than compelling (Hampton 1986).

Locke

It was essential for Hobbes that men should alienate totally both their will and their judgement to the sovereign, except in the final instance of imminent hurt to their own body. But even in the seventeenth century other contractarian thinkers doubted whether they either could or should do anything of the kind. Those who doubted whether they could (like Spinoza, whose psychology was in this respect more consistent than Hobbes's) did not necessarily regard human beings as any less of a natural threat to one another than Hobbes supposed them to be. But those, like John Locke, who merely disputed whether they should do so, were distinctly less inclined to attribute men's capacity to live peacefully with one another solely to terror of the magistrate's sword.

In contrast with Hobbes, Locke deployed the idea of a compact as foundation for governmental authority not to explain men's capacity to live with one another in peace at all but to set clear and decisive limits to the degree of their rightful subjection to any possible human ruler. His two great works, the *Two Treatises of Government* and the *Letter concerning Toleration* (both first published in 1689), provide the most powerful seventeenth-century statement of the restrictions on the legitimate authority of human rulers over the religious and secular rights of their subjects. These restrictions are defined by the divine law of the Creator of the world and by the peculiar religious requirements of the Christian revelation. Under the law of nature human beings have not merely a right against each other to do their best to preserve themselves, but also a duty to their Creator to do the same and to preserve each other also, insofar as they safely can, to the best of their ability. Under the Christian revelation they have a still higher and more pressing duty to worship their Creator as they judge He would wish them to do, in order to save their souls from eternal extinction. Since worship requires the full belief of the worshipper, no imposed religious practice can save an individual's soul; and no human power can possess a right to dictate the content of belief or worship.

For Locke the contractual basis of political authority was essential to the understanding of each of these restrictions. Like Aristotle and the classic Anglican theologian Richard Hooker (and also like St Peter: I Pet. 2:13), he saw political authority as an human contrivance (ἀνθρωπίνη κτίσις), not a given fact about the created order of nature (Locke 1768, p. 423). His *Two Treatises of Government* defend this judgement not against Hobbes (who fully shared it) but against the distinctive absolutism of Sir Robert Filmer's *Patriarcha* (which trenchantly denied it). For Locke neither political authority nor private property derived, as Filmer supposed, from God's gift of the world to Adam. Instead each arose from the efforts of individual men and women to confront the practical challenges of the world which He had given them in common to enjoy. Filmer had in fact accepted Hobbes's agreeably absolutist conclusions, whilst firmly rejecting the grounds on which Hobbes based them. He had also criticized damagingly Grotius's use of the universal consent of mankind to explain the right to private property, presenting this as a ludicrous and incoherent fiction. In response, Locke set out to refute Filmer's absolutist political conclusions and to combine his refutation with an independent and more robust explanation of the right to private property.

Property he saw as arising from human labour – the impact of men's intelligence and effort upon the natural world. Over time property rights changed in character and in structural complexity, with the invention of money as a means of exchange, and with the creation of separate political authorities and the steady division of the world between these. But like other rights of human beings within the created order of nature, its source remained independent of political authority and could never simply be withdrawn at will by the latter.

The state of nature for Locke was not, as it had been for Hobbes, a dramatic representation of what human beings are really like; rather, it was a model of the relations of right which hold between them under the law of nature. In Locke's view, the practical character of relations between human beings outside a legitimate political authority could be extremely diverse. He was far from supposing that it could be inferred from the concept of the state of nature. What could be inferred from that concept was simply the nature and scope of human entitlements. Because of their partiality, human beings may well quarrel at any point in their history over the interpretation of their mutual rights and duties. But the occasions for quarrelling increased dramatically as they moved from an economy of hunting and gathering to one of agriculture, sophisticated handicrafts and monetized international commerce. Money was a human invention, its value resting simply on consent. Through its durability and its capacity to serve as a permanent store of value, it provided a motive for the creation of an entirely new system of production and exchange, vastly augmenting the productivity of nature but at the same time massively extending the private appropriation of nature's goods and in particular of the land itself, and widening immensely the economic and social inequalities within and between human populations. Insofar as this appropriation preserved entitlements derived from human labour and the voluntary exchange of its products, and insofar as it did not entrench on the preservation of any human beings, it was fully compatible with the natural rights of all. But it intensified the threat of human partiality to a point that rendered a genuinely legitimate political authority (a set of known standing laws and a power dependably committed to their impartial administration and enforcement) not an intermittent convenience but a permanent necessity. Political authority itself could be either a matter of right or a blunt fact of power. Over most of the world it was still very much the latter. But where it had been brought into existence by the consent of a group of human beings and had continued to serve the purposes for which they had initially established it, they owed it a genuine duty of obedience. Legitimate governments were distinguished from illegitimate governments by their origins in popular consent. But even in the former, the obligations of subjects continued to rest upon their own individual consent to its authority. Locke had considerable difficulty in explaining how this consent was in fact given, either by explicit expression or by voluntary conduct which might reasonably be judged to carry the obligations which flowed from it (Dunn 1980, chapter 3). For most of its population, residence in seventeenth-century England was an altogether less convincing index of commitment than it could have been for a citizen of Socrates' Athens.

Legitimate polities (what Locke called 'civil societies') drew their authority from their own subjects and fully recognized the latter's rights of political choice and agency. Governments which refused to recognize these rights simply could not be civil societies. But even the most legitimate polity, like England itself, could lose its legitimacy by threatening these rights. Then the body of the people could judge for themselves that their consent had been abused and that their fundamental rights to life, liberty and personal possessions stood in jeopardy. Under these conditions the body of the people, and even single individuals acting on its behalf, could take back into their own hands the right to execute the law of nature's God and protect themselves and each other, as best they could, against the menace of their rulers.

The eighteenth century

Locke's radical Whig doctrine was the classic contractual assertion of the right to resist unjust power. It was deployed most memorably by American colonial pamphleteers in vindication of the American struggle for independence. But in the century following Locke's death in 1704, its foundation in a theocentric conception of natural law made it increasingly vulnerable to more reflective and less radical critics. David Hume's mordant essay *Of the Original Contract* (Hume [1741–7] 1985, pp. 465–87) pilloried the absurdity of grounding the obligations of subjects to obey their government, recognized in every civilized country, obligations which no one but the victims of fashionable philosophical doctrines had ever thought of attributing to a promise, to undertakings which none of them was even aware of having given. In his view, the continued residence of a poor peasant or artisan in the country of his birth provided no better evidence of his free choice than the failure of a man who had been carried on board ship whilst asleep to leap overboard and drown immediately gave of his free consent to the authority of its captain (Hume [1741–7] 1985, p. 475). Even by mid-century Hume saw Locke's Whig contractarianism as absurdly parochial as well as potentially subversive. Instead, he argued, political obligation should be grounded firmly in utility. In face of the French Revolution, Edmund Burke and Georg Wilhelm Friedrich Hegel laid even stronger emphasis on the potential arbitrariness of grounding political authority in individual will and judgement and on its disruptive and even murderous implications.

It should, however, be noted that both of the two greatest contractarian thinkers of the eighteenth century, the Genevan Jean-Jacques Rousseau and the Königsberg philosopher Immanuel Kant, had already done their best to address these potential weaknesses. Each saw the free commitment of the individual will as an indispensable but insufficient basis for legitimate political authority. As Rousseau asked: 'what more certain foundation can obligation amongst men have than the free agreement of him who obligates himself?' (Rousseau [1755–1915] 1962, II, p. 200). But Rousseau's *Discourse on the Origins and Foundations of Inequality amongst Men* portrayed the voluntary acceptance first of private property and then of political authority as a source of immense harm, since it 'irretrievably destroyed natural liberty, fixed for ever the law of property and inequality that a skilful usurpation had made an irrevocable right, and, for the profit of a few ambitious men, subjected the whole human species thereafter to labour, slavery and misery' (Rousseau [1755–1915] 1962, I, p. 181). He was, therefore, even less inclined than Locke to see most political authority as legitimate at all. In the *Contrat Social* (1762) he set himself to answer the question: what could make such authority legitimate? Convention is certainly the basis of political authority; and it is the opposition of private interests which makes the establishment of societies necessary (Rousseau [1755–1915] 1962, II, p. 39: Bk I, chapter 1). But society can only be governed justly on a basis of common interests; and only in a justly governed society can political authority be truly legitimate. In such a society, and in such a society alone, 'each, whilst uniting himself with all, might still obey himself alone, and remain as free as before' (Rousseau [1755–1915] 1962, II, p. 32: Bk I, chapter 6). Each citizen subjects their will completely to the General Will (which is merely their own will when they will the common good); and they exercise their collective sovereignty together in interpreting the content of this General Will. Where this content happens to clash with the particular wills of individual citizens, these are to recognize that they have made a factual error in assessing the purposes of their fellow citizens (II, pp. 42, 50–1: Bk II, chapters 3 and 6). The State is a moral *Persona Ficta*; but any citizen who hopes to enjoy his civic rights without fulfilling his duties as a subject towards this moral person is to be compelled to obey it: to be forced to be free (II, p. 36: Bk I, chapter 7). The creation of such a political community is an immensely complex political achievement, calling for propitious initial conditions, skilful institutional design and unrelenting attention to the cultural formation of its citizens. Rousseau himself was understandably pessimistic about the prospects for realizing it in the sophisticated and highly commercialized Europe of his day.

Rousseau thus fully accepted the classical contractarian presumption that government originated historically in human agreement; and he insisted that legitimate political authority required the continuing right and opportunity for self-commitment on the part of its subjects. But he also strongly doubted whether most political power was in fact legitimate and set the most demanding criteria for reaching and maintaining a genuine political legitimacy. Seeing economic progress and the social institutions which secured this as often profoundly malign in their human consequences, he set himself fiercely at odds with Hume and Adam Smith (and even with Burke) in refusing to rest political authority practically upon its proven capacity over time to improve the economic conditions of the great majority of a given population (Hont & Ignatieff 1983). The true social contract that grounded political legitimacy for Rousseau was therefore not merely severely hypothetical; it was also very infrequently encountered in practice.

In marked contrast with Rousseau, Immanuel Kant denied the entitlement of the subjects of any state at any time to resist their legal sovereign (Kant [1781–97] 1971, pp. 81–4), though unlike Hobbes he also insisted that the people have inalienable rights against their sovereign, underlined the need for a 'spirit of freedom' in every commonwealth, and proclaimed trenchantly that 'freedom of the pen is the only safeguard of the rights of the people' (pp. 84–5). For Kant the original contract which furnishes the foundation for political legitimacy 'requires freedom, equality, and *unity* of the will of all the members' (p. 77). All human beings are free to seek their own happiness as they see fit, provided only that they do so in a way that recognizes the freedom of others to do the same (p. 74). All are equally subject to the authority of the sovereign, blending their coercive rights together to support his authority and surrendering these absolutely in relation to him (pp. 74–5). This civic equality is fully compatible with extreme inequalities in the ownership of property, though not with hereditary privilege in the allocation of rank or economic opportunity (pp. 75–6). Even in the case of citizenship rights the freedom and equality of all human beings 'requires no less than the will of the entire people (since all men decide for all men and each decides for himself)' (pp. 75–6). But the equality of citizen independence which is a precondition for political legitimacy does not extend into the continuing legislative process of the commonwealth (pp. 77–8). Here, only adult males who are their own masters (*sui juris*) and who hold property are qualified to be citizens at all; and the actual history of property rights (particularly in land) is often in distressing tension with the demands of right (p. 78). This original contract is not a matter of historical fact, to be ascertained by inspecting historical records or legal documents. It is 'merely an *idea* of reason, which nonetheless has undoubted practical reality'. It demands that every legislator 'frame his laws in such a way that they could have been produced by the united will of a whole nation' and provides 'the test of the rightfulness of every public law' (p. 79).

As a negative test, this is luminously clear: 'if the law is such that a whole people could not possibly agree to it … it is unjust'. But as a positive criterion it is harder to disentangle in a convincing form from the idiosyncrasies of Kant's views about the priority of right over good and about the universality of the imperative of political subjection: 'if it is at least *possible* that a people could agree to it, it is our duty to consider the law as just, even if the people is at present in such a position or attitude of mind that it would probably refuse its consent if it were consulted' (p. 79). For Kant, basing the political choices either of sovereigns or of subjects on the quest for happiness is a recipe for moral and practical chaos. Sovereigns lose the clarity of the 'infallible a priori standard' of an original contract and are left to the vagaries of their own judgement over the prudence or otherwise of political measures (p. 80). They are also very apt to become despots, intent on rendering the people happy in accord with their own conception of what should make them so, while the people themselves cleave to the universal human desire to seek happiness in their own way and feel entitled (in Kant's view, quite unjustifiably) to resist their sovereign accordingly (p. 83). The idea of the original contract is the fulcrum of a 'theory of political right to which practice must conform before it can be valid' (p. 86). It stands in the starkest contrast to 'precepts on how to be happy' (p. 72), which may have some admonitory force but 'cannot give laws to the free will' and therefore always leave human beings free to choose what they think best and to take the consequences.

In some respects, Kant's political theory represents the acme of the social contract tradition (Riley 1982, chapter 5). No previous writer had placed such emphasis on the distinctive dignity of the human will, seeing in its capacity to legislate for itself the foundation of all value for human beings in the world: as what makes each of them an end in themselves. The original contract, in Kant's eyes, establishes the sole possible standard of right for the shared public life of creatures who are ends in themselves. It establishes their individual freedom, equality and independence under coercive public laws that guarantee to each their due, secure each against its invasion by others, and restrict their freedom solely to the degree required to make it harmonize with that of their fellows (Kant [1781–97] 1971, pp. 73–4). It was its unforgettably public proclamation of this standard of right which led Kant to respond with such enthusiasm to the French Revolution and led him to hope for the eventual extension to mankind at large of constitutions which genuinely embodied it and promised a new era of international peace (pp. 184–9).

But the contract, as Kant conceived it, remained severely hypothetical. Not merely was it in no way a historical occurrence; he also fully acknowledged its exceedingly hazy relationship to the political realities of his day. More importantly still (in contrast with Locke, Rousseau and in the last instance perhaps even Hobbes), Kant himself stressed that the contract offered political subjects no title whatever to resist even the gravest abuses on the part of their rulers (p. 145). The duty of political subordination is the first duty of every human individual who acknowledges the concept of right at all (p. 137). It does not preclude the frankest criticism of public authority. But it in no way justifies or excuses the least attempt to coerce the public authority or to defend the independent judgement of a private citizen against the coercive public judgement of the magistrate. The trenchancy of Kant's proclamation of human equality as the universal standard of public right and the feebleness and vagueness of his treatment of the means for realizing this standard in political practice were each highlighted in the equivocations of his response to the French Revolution (Beck 1978, chapter 10). Taken together, they foreshadow both the intellectual convenience of the hypothetical contract as a device for analysing human value and its extremely limited capacity to furnish clear and convincing direction for political actions.

The twentieth century revival

In its classic seventeenth-century versions, contractarianism fell a ready victim over the two succeeding centuries to a sequence of formidable intellectual adversaries: the utilitarian realism of Hume, Smith and Jeremy Bentham in Britain; idealist philosophy and the historicist critique of rationalist pseudo-history in Germany; and the historical materialism of Karl Marx and his successors over a large part of the globe. In the last quarter of a century, however, contractarian theories have recaptured a considerable degree of attention, especially in North America. But today such theories are little, if at all, concerned with questions of political obligation. Instead they focus overwhelmingly on issues of distributive justice, particularly in the allocation of economic goods.

Seventeenth-century contractarians aspired to show their readers when and why they were obliged to obey the governments which they directly encountered. Their twentieth-century descendants, by contrast, aspire to demonstrate what it would be for a set of human social institutions to meet the criteria for justice. In place of a stern address to historically given circumstances of political choice, they offer a more academic and debilitated reverie on the internal instabilities of the conceptions of social justice with which modern history has endowed us, and on how (and how far) these motley conceptions can still be brought into a condition of 'reflective equilibrium'. The leading figure of the contractarian revival is the Harvard philosopher John Rawls, who explicitly sees his approach to moral and political theory as modelled on that of Kant.

Rawls's interpretation of the social contract is set out most elaborately in his *A Theory of Justice* (1972); but see also now Rawls (1993). Along with most other contemporary contractarians, he envisages the contract not as historical but as purely hypothetical. A voluntary relation between the wills and judgements of individuals is not the cause of social and political relations between human beings. Rather, it is a standard which these relations should aim to meet. (Rawls is in fact at least as disinclined as his Marxist critics to attribute full causal responsibility for their own 'achievements' to individual human agents, seeing the claims of merit in economic distribution in most instances as blatantly ideological.) The contract which defines the content of justice is a hypothetical agreement amongst the members of a given society, made under carefully defined circumstances: in what Rawls refers to as 'the original position'. In this setting, human agents are deprived of all particular knowledge about their own social circumstances and their personal dispositions, capacities and tastes. They thus lack most of the features which any actual human being brings to bear in making a choice. For all practical purposes they are in fact identical. Rawls renders them identical in this way, quite deliberately, for two reasons. In the first place he regards the incapacity to bargain on behalf of particular interests as a precondition for equality of power between the choosers and the equality of power between the choosers as a compelling principle of fairness in itself. In the second place, he believes that only such drastic deprivation of relevant information could guarantee that the choosers arrive at any definite outcome. (His critics, unsurprisingly, have seen the first of these reasons as viciously circular and the second as imposing an evidently inappropriate constraint on the content of justice.)

In the original position, Rawls's contractors endorse two strong principles of social order: broadly, that each should have as much individual civil and political liberty as is compatible with a like liberty for all, and that inequalities in income, wealth, power and other resources should be accepted only where they directly benefit the worst-off members of society (the famous 'maximin' principle). Critics have questioned whether it would in fact be rational for persons in the original position to choose either of these principles, arguing especially that the second implies an arbitrarily extreme aversion to risk and that the first option is less attractive than the choice to maximize their average individual utility.

But the most important doubt about Rawls's theory concerns not the prospective outcome of decisions made in the original position but their real force for human beings who find themselves elsewhere. The master conception of classical contractarianism was the capacity of individual human beings to bind their own future actions by making a promise. The unique clarity of fidelity, the duty to keep faith, came from its being self-imposed. This was why its obligatory force could be and was, as John Locke insisted, quite independent of the rules of any particular society: 'Truth and keeping of Faith belongs to Men, as Men, and not as Members of Society' (Locke [1689] 1960, II, 14: p. 295). But hypothetical contracts, as Ronald Dworkin has pointed out, cannot in this way 'supply an independent argument for the fairness of enforcing their terms. A hypothetical contract is not simply a pale form of an actual contract; it is no contract at all' (Dworkin 1977, p. 151). In this sense Rawls's contract is doubly hypothetical. In the first place it is an attempt to specify not what anyone has in fact agreed to, but simply what the human beings in one very particular circumstance would agree to. But, more importantly, it carries no categorical implications for all human agents, but depends for its obligatory force upon the prior acceptance by particular human beings of the criterion of antecedent voluntary agreement as the appropriate standard to govern all human institutions. Rawls himself now stresses this dependence (Rawls 1985), not merely because the priority of personal liberty over economic betterment is a privilege of relatively prosperous societies, but also because the emphasis upon antecedent voluntary acceptability is a characteristic of some political cultures and not of others. (It is, for example, markedly absent from the political tradition of pre-Meiji Japan.)

For a political culture, like that of the United States, which centres on individual rights, Rawls's theory offers an evocative method for specifying a public standard of social justice. It is a standard which clashes extensively in its implications with the loosely utilitarian ideology of economic expansion, founded upon private ownership and appropriation minimally impeded by fiscal redistribution, which is an equally prominent characteristic of American political culture. Even within its own relatively parochial milieu it is therefore at present of fairly muted political efficacy. But in a political setting in which capitalist ownership rights are more deeply contested, it may still provide a more promising basis for clarifying the entitlements of citizens in a modern pluralist state (Veca 1982; Barry 1989).

As a purely political theory its greatest importance lies in its challenge to the adequacy of utilitarianism as an account of the nature of human value. In Rawls's view, utilitarianism fails to do justice to the most fundamental fact about human beings: that they are profoundly separate creatures all of whom define happiness for themselves. But his own theory has been attacked in its turn by Robert Nozick for failing to respect the separateness of persons by redistributing the economic (and other) advantages that flow from their own physical and mental capacities to those whom nature has endowed less generously. It has also been attacked by modern admirers of Hegel (Sandel 1982) for seeing individual consciousness and preference as the sole source and site of human value and for failing to acknowledge the dependence of individuals on the societies and cultures which form them.

But the two principal limitations faced by Rawls's theory would face any other contemporary interpretation of contractarianism and perhaps any other normative theory that aspired to direct political power today. The first of these is purely philosophical. Where contractarianism has been philosophically compelling in the past, its force has always come from a robust and well-integrated theory of practical reason: of what human beings have good reason in practice to do. Because of the distinctive separateness of human persons – because all of them who are capable of acting at all experience and judge and choose for themselves – the conflicts between their judgements and choices are as central a concern of politics as their very evident mutual dependence. Modern western philosophy offers nothing analogous to the rich and precise theories of practical reason advanced by Aristotle or by early modern natural law writers. But in the absence of such a theoretical frame to define its force for it, any normative theory enters the domain of politics simply on a par with the judgements and choices of all existing political participants. Under these circumstances, unsurprisingly, such theories have the greatest difficulty in establishing a solid political footing.

This is especially important today since there is at least one overwhelmingly powerful influence upon modern governments and political actors that is notably recalcitrant to normative preferences. The perceived requirements for economic expansion dominate the political concerns of every modern state which is governed with the least pretension to competence. Modern subjects can be said to consent to the activities of their governments only in the thinnest and most marginal of senses. But very few of them can still sanely contemplate dispensing with the profoundly ambiguous services of some government or other. The most drastic hypothetical contract in modern history has been the commitment of most of the world's population to the inscrutable rhythms of the world economy. As they work through the domestic politics of every modern state, these rhythms impose the starkest of practical limitations not just to Rawls's theory of justice but to the entire western tradition of political understanding (Dunn 1990).

REFERENCES

Aristotle. *The Politics*, edited and trans. E. Barker (1946). Oxford: Clarendon Press
Barry, B. 1989. *Theories of Justice*. Hemel Hempstead: Harvester-Wheatsheaf
Beck, L. W. 1978 (ed.). 'Kant and the right of revolution'. In *Essays on Kant and*

Hume. New Haven: Yale University Press

Bloch, M. 1965. *Feudal Society*, trans. L. Manyon. London: Routledge and Kegan Paul

Brown, S. K. 1965 (ed.). 'The Taylor thesis: some objections'. In *Hobbes Studies*. Oxford: Blackwell

Dunn, J. 1980. *Political Obligation in its Historical Context*. Cambridge: Cambridge University Press

1990 (ed.). *The Economic Limits to Modern Politics*. Cambridge: Cambridge University Press

1993. *Western Political Theory in the Face of the Future*, 2nd edn. Cambridge: Cambridge University Press

Dworkin, R. 1977. *Taking Rights Seriously*. London: Duckworth

Filmer, Sir R. [1648–80] 1949. *Patriarcha and Other Political Writings*, ed. P. Laslett. Oxford: Blackwell

Finley, M. 1983. *Politics in the Ancient World*, Cambridge: Cambridge University Press

Gierke, O. 1900. *Political Theories of the Middle Age*, trans. F. Maitland. Cambridge: Cambridge University Press

1950. *Natural Law and the Theory of Society 1500 to 1800*, trans. E. Barker. Cambridge: Cambridge University Press

Gough, J. 1957. *The Social Contract*. Oxford: Oxford University Press

Hampton, J. 1986. *Hobbes and the Social Contract Tradition*. Cambridge: Cambridge University Press

Hart, H. L. A. 1955. 'Are there any natural rights?' *The Philosophical Review* 64, 175–91

Hegel, G. W. F. [1821] 1942. *The Philosophy of Right*, trans. T. Knox. Oxford: Clarendon Press

Hobbes, T. [1642] 1983. *De Cive: The English Version*, ed. H. Warrender. Oxford: Clarendon Press

[1651] 1946. *Leviathan*, ed. M. Oakeshott. Oxford: Blackwell

Hont, I. and M. Ignatieff 1983 (eds.). *Wealth and Virtue*. Cambridge: Cambridge University Press

Hotman, F. [1573] 1972. *Francogallia*, ed. R. Giesey. Cambridge: Cambridge University Press

Hume, D. [1741–7] 1985. *Essays Moral, Political and Literary*, ed. E. F. Miller. Indianapolis: Liberty Classics

Kant, I. [1781–97] 1971. *Political Writings*, ed. H. Reiss. Cambridge: Cambridge University Press

Lessnoff, M. 1986. *Social Contract*. London: Macmillan

Lewis, E. 1954. *Medieval Political Ideas*, 2 vols. London: Routledge and Kegan Paul

Lloyd, G. 1979. *Magic, Reason and Experience*. Cambridge: Cambridge University Press

Locke, J. [1689] 1960. *Two Treatises of Government*, ed. P. Laslett. Cambridge: Cambridge University Press

1768. 'Second letter concerning Toleration'. In *Collected Works* II, 7th edn. London: A. Woodfall *et al.*

Nozick, R. *Anarchy, State and Utopia*. Oxford: Blackwell

Plato . *The Crito*, trans. A. Woozley. In *Law and Obedience*, ed. A. Woozley (1979), pp. 141–56. London: Duckworth

Rawls, J. 1972. *A Theory of Justice*. Oxford: Oxford University Press
    1985. 'Justice as fairness: political not metaphysical'. *Philosophy and Public Affairs*, 14, 223–51
    1993. *Political Liberalism*. New York: Columbia University Press

Riley, P. 1982. *Will and Political Legitimacy*. Cambridge, Mass.: Harvard University Press

Rousseau, J.-J. [1755–1915] 1962. *The Political Writings*, ed. C. Vaughan, 2 vols. Oxford: Blackwell

Sandel, M. 1982. *Liberalism and the Limits of Justice*. Cambridge: Cambridge University Press

Skinner, Q. 1978. *The Foundations of Modern Political Thought*, 2 vols. Cambridge: Cambridge University Press
    1988. 'Political philosophy'. In *The Cambridge History of Renaissance Philosophy*, ed. C. Schmitt and Q. Skinner, pp. 389–452. Cambridge: Cambridge University Press

Spinoza, B. de [1670–7] 1958. *The Political Works*, ed. A. Wernham. Oxford: Clarendon Press

Tierney, B. 1982. *Religion, Law and the Growth of Constitutional Thought 1150–1650*. Cambridge: Cambridge University Press

Tuck, R. 1979. *Natural Rights Theories: Their Origin and Development*. Cambridge: Cambridge University Press
    1988. 'Optics and sceptics: the philosophical foundations of Hobbes's political thought'. In *Conscience and Casuistry in Early Modern Europe*, ed. E. Leites, pp. 235–63. Cambridge: Cambridge University Press

Unger, R. 1987. *Politics: A Work in Constructive Social Theory*, 3 vols. Cambridge: Cambridge University Press

Veca, S. 1982. *La Società Giusta*. Milan: Il Saggiatore

Warrender, H. 1957. *The Political Philosophy of Hobbes*. Oxford: Clarendon Press

4   Political obligation

In its paradigmatic form, political obligation is the duty incumbent on any person or set of persons legitimately subject to a legitimate political authority to obey the legitimate commands of that authority (cf. Hobbes [1642] 1983, p. 32). Every human agent now alive is held by at least one particular state to be subject to such obligation, in very many respects and usually for life. Stateless persons, diplomats or officials of international agencies such as the United Nations, at least at the time, hold somewhat different schedules of entitlements, immunities and responsibilities. But there is no part of the world today in which a human being can confidently expect to escape from the presumption of political subordination. The state of nature may subsist, for some purposes, between the jurisdictions of particular modern states; but nowhere, not even in the unappropriated polar territories or the far recesses of the great common of the oceans,[1] is there habitable space on earth which lies simply beyond the jurisdiction of state power. Virtually everyone in the modern world, accordingly, is claimed as subject to political obligation.

In itself this universality of the claim to political subordination is simply a fact of power – and one with widely varying degrees of practical significance. What has produced it is the omnipresence in the world of the late twentieth century of a single political form: the modern nation state. As an ideological concept the modern state was constructed deliberately in the late sixteenth and early seventeenth centuries as a decisive repudiation of the classical republican theory of citizen self-rule (Skinner 1989, esp. pp. 116–22). But since the collapse of the French *ancien régime* in 1789 it has come to be fused, in the great majority of

---

[1] Rights to use the ocean are defined legally today, in the last instance, by agreement between states; and opportunities to do so are secured principally in practice by the capacities (and inclinations) for enforcement of the naval, air and land forces of the great world powers. Consider, for example, the commercial practices of the international drug trade or the ghastly vicissitudes of maritime refugees from Vietnam. Japan, to take a prominent example, may own a remarkably large proportion of the world economy; but it lacks the capacity to protect physical access to the great bulk of the raw materials used by its own domestic industry.

instances, with a claim to democratic legitimacy (or popular sovereignty) which sits very awkwardly with its practical realities (Dunn 1993, chapter 1). As a strictly political pretension, therefore, the universality of political obligation is more than a little strained. But its evident moral precariousness can be readily diminished by reverting to the conceptual contrast between the legitimate commands of a legitimate political authority, at one extreme, and the illegitimate commands of an illegitimate political authority or private coercion by particular groups of men or women, at the other.

Etymologically, the problem of political obligation is a nineteenth-century name for a typically seventeenth-century problem. Every modern state, naturally, presumes itself to be legitimate and thus presumes the question to have a valid answer, at least in its own case. But since modern states are less consistently charitable (as yet) in their views of each other, they are distinctly less confident that political obligation must either plainly hold or fail to hold in other instances also. Defence agreements, rights of extradition, and even structures of international commercial law link many modern states in effective solidarity and cooperation. But the universality of political obligation itself cannot (at least as yet) be sustained merely by a complicity between all existing state powers.

Seen in this way, the universality of the claim to political obligation in the modern world is essentially a disreputable contingency of ideological history; and there is no pressing reason why it should be perceived as the site of a single distinctive puzzle of understanding, let alone one which might yield a clear and intellectually authoritative solution by the application of scientific method or in the light of the authority of a transcendent moral truth. This comfortable conclusion is reinforced by the more purely theoretical fact that the problem of political obligation, so conceived, is difficult to state at all incisively within a number of major twentieth-century traditions of political reason and yields, within the terms of these traditions, only weak and relatively trivial solutions (compare Hare (1967) and (1976) with Dunn (1980)). This leaves the problem of political obligation at (or beyond) the periphery of the intellectual interests of the two main classes of theorists who still aspire to reduce modern politics to ethical order. Those whose principal interest lies in political practice focus their energies on the question of what makes modern contenders for political authority genuinely legitimate (Marxists are an important example), while those whose principal interest lies in the nature of human value concentrate instead on the design and intellectual elaboration of general theories of that nature and apply these, on completion, more or less ingeniously (and ingenuously), and very much from the outside. Both of these approaches remove most of the urgency and much of the distinctive content from the classical problem of political obligation, implying not merely that it is a problem that has no general solution, but also that it cannot be aptly understood as constituting a distinct and coherent problem at all.

Even if this last judgement were plainly correct, the problem of political obligation would retain some intellectual importance, because of its deep historical impress upon modern conceptions of political legitimacy. If we do not understand the genesis of our political ideas we shall be compelled to remain their prisoners rather than enabled to become their masters.[2] But it is, in any case, to mistake the nature of human understanding to suppose that this judgement could be authoritatively *correct*. Judgements about the integrity and weight of particular intellectual problems are necessarily relative to particular cognitive concerns. The reasons for the comparative neglect or disavowal of the problem of political obligation may be apt enough in relation to the intellectual preoccupations of particular schools of modern political strategists or ideologists (or indeed, of modern moralists or philosophers), but they do not guarantee any universal human felicity to these preoccupations; and, in relation to politics at least, it is far from evident that the styles of understanding and perception which they have fostered do represent an enhancement in the profundity and accuracy of our understanding.

I shall argue, in effect, that the classical problem of political obligation does isolate a range of considerations which need to be seen in relation to one another if politics at any time is to be understood as clearly and accurately as it can be understood. I shall also argue, more hazardously, that, while the problem itself certainly does not permit a universal and authoritative solution, the great seventeenth-century formulations of it still offer in many respects a strategically bolder and sounder approach to political understanding than any of their historical successors and an approach, in particular, notably bolder and sounder than any more recent and more palpably extant tradition of political reason.

The problem of political obligation was best stated – and perhaps most nearly resolved – by Thomas Hobbes in the middle of the seventeenth century. In Hobbes's view it was intrinsic to human existence that vulnerable, greedy, self-righteous and, above all, judgemental or opinionated creatures[3] or groups of such creatures should be apt to clash over the

---

[2] See, for example, Skinner (1984, esp. pp. 193, 218–19). This is a consistent theme in Skinner's writings.

[3] It is important that these groups can include states themselves; and, since states are the remedy for the clashes between other groups, the threat of clashes between states is profoundly significant. This has always been a serious limitation to Hobbes's theory: something more perturbing than a mere boundary condition. In the nuclear age, its importance has become overwhelming.

requirements for meeting their entirely objective need for security, their (often considerably less realistic) aspirations to ensure the way of their future felicity (for which security is a necessary but an evidently insufficient condition) and their still flightier conceptions of how other human beings should be permitted to live their lives.

The sole rational common basis for resolving these clashes was the recognition of the priority of security over all other human values. What made it rational and common was not a simple matter of biological or cultural fact – that all individual human beings or groups of human beings set the goal for self-preservation steadily above all their other goals (Hobbes came eventually to recognize fully that there was no such sane and reassuring structure of priority to appeal to within human preferences); rather it was a matter of right – that no human being could rationally deny to other human beings the natural right to do their best to preserve their own lives and to judge what actions such preservation required.[4]

In Hobbes's view, security for individual human beings, at least in a crowded and civilized society like that of seventeenth-century England,[5] could be guaranteed (or even made reasonably probable) in one way and one way only: by the radical subordination of individual or group will, judgement and capacity to threaten or endanger, to the unified will and judgement and the effectively imposed coercive authority of a sovereign power.

Two features of Hobbes's view combine to render it the best statement of the reasons for according the duty to obey a sovereign a special priority in the schedule of human reasons for action. The first is its sharp focus upon human vulnerability and on those human qualities which most endanger the vulnerable in practice. The justification of state power, if it is to rest anywhere stable at all, must depend finally upon the peculiar urgency for every human being of meeting this particular need: on a mutual relation between protection and obedience. The degree of modern philosophical preoccupation with distributive justice, from this point of view, reflects a confident, and often somewhat careless, presumption that the problem of protection has been solved definitively. (It is unlikely, for example, that Hobbes would have been impressed by the levels of security offered to the populations of great American cities, and especially unlikely that he would have been so in the case of their poorer

---

[4] This point is particularly well developed in Richard Tuck's studies of Hobbes. See now most conveniently Tuck (1989).

[5] It is a moot point how concerned Hobbes was about the fate of capitalist property rights. But it is clear that he set some store (and was confident that his contemporary readers would also set some store) on 'commodious' living.

black citizens.)[6] This focus has rendered modern Anglo-American political philosophy peculiarly unilluminating in relation to the politics of any
country in which the structure of the state is in active political jeopardy.

The second feature of Hobbes's views which make them an especially
powerful expression of the priority of political obligation over contending
claims of human duty is his strong and imaginative synthesis of a radically
objective perspective with a full recognition of the omnipresence and
force of human subjectivity. This comprehensive acknowledgement of the
force and refractoriness of human subjectivity was a characteristic
response among early modern natural rights theories to the challenge of
moral relativism (Tuck 1987, 1988): an acceptance that good reasons for
human agents must be addressed to them as they actually are and not as
scholastic or humanist moralists would have preferred them to be. What
makes it so effective in the hands of Hobbes is its stark apposition to an
especially strongly imagined and analysed conception of nature as a
whole, seen as a single mechanical order. The device which links the two
perspectives – the rational calculation of the implications of pursuing
given human desires within an objectified natural order – is an intricate
and precarious intellectual construction. But it is also remarkably well
conceived as an instrument for analysing the distinctive character of politics, yielding a very strong representation of a universe of causal constraints, but treating the reasons for action of human agents operating
within these constraints with an unselective realism. No twentieth-
century thinker has contrived to represent the context of political agency
(or inertia) in such a steady and comprehensive manner.

The principal reason for this comparative failure is not difficult to
identify. Twentieth-century philosophy has been at its least commanding
in its understanding of the nature of practical reason. There are at least
three distinct perspectives on the human predicament (and thus on the
force and character of human reasons for action) open to modern thinkers. The first is radically objectified and determinedly non-anthropocen-
tric, seeking an absolute conception of the universe and of the place of
human beings within it. When first conceived with any clarity, what gave
it conceptual determinacy and stability was a framework of theological
assumptions: the universe seen in the steady gaze of its Creator. With the
fading away of this framework of assumptions, contemporary philosophers have come to disagree fundamentally on whether the conception
itself still makes sense. But even the most ebulliently anthropocentric
among them (cf. Rorty 1980, 1982) hesitate to deny the analytical gains

---

[6] For the importance for Hobbes himself of a preoccupation with the predicament of the
least secure, see Baumgold (1988).

that have come from its protracted exploration. Taken in its entirety, the
radically objectified perspective on the human condition may simply
erase the perspective of practical reason and is certainly hard to articulate plausibly with the latter. But it does effectively dramatize the dense
and oppressive significance of political causality: of what can and cannot
be caused to occur at any time or place through political action. Anyone
with serious and relatively autonomous political purposes must feel at
best ambivalent about the significance of political causality. But it takes
a bold (or blatantly frivolous) thinker, over three centuries after the scientific revolution, openly to challenge its significance for political
agency.[7]

The second modern perspective on the human predicament envisages
it through the texture of social relations viewed essentially as a structure
of imagination: through intersubjectivity (see Taylor 1985; cf. Dunn
1990a; Walzer 1983). It is a diffuse (and perhaps necessarily diffuse) idiom
of understanding, with little internal dynamism. Within it, individual
identities are seen as precommitted to social roles and responsibilities,
not as an external burden but as a constitutive feature of what they most
fundamentally are. The problem of political obligation, accordingly, loses
both its starkness and its relative urgency. It becomes hard to distinguish
human individuals from their social or cultural obligations; and political
obligation is either a logical extension of, or an impertinent competitor
with, these other more central and deeply insinuating bonds.[8] This
modern communitarian emphasis on intersubjectivity has many attractions. But it is important to recognize how feebly and sentimentally it
addresses the problem of political obligation. For Hobbes, the social or
cultural contours (most especially the *religious* contours) of such
identification, so far from offering a cogent and general answer to the
problems of practical reason, were precisely what presented these problems in their most acute and perilous form. Religious and social solidarity, so far from being the solution to the problems of political instability,
were virtually the source of that instability. The point of political obligation was precisely to contain, to bring under rational and humane control,
the diffuse but vivid menace which these wider imaginative bonds represented.

The third modern perspective on the human predicament is, in the
first instance, radically subjective. What establishes it is simply the
content of the consciousness of individual human agents: how the world

---

[7] Cf. however, albeit a trifle elusively, Unger (1987).

[8] Marxism provides an interesting example of these difficulties – at least one reason for its
notable infelicity as an approach to the understanding of many aspects of politics.
Compare Miliband (1977), Thompson (1978), Anderson (1980) and Lukes (1985).

is from each of their points of view. While it is hard (if not impossible) to link the objectified perspective on the world with the viewpoint of individual agency, it might well seem that no such problem could arise in the case of individual subjectivity. Intentions, purposes, goals and concerns – the categories which establish the point of agency – are all obtrusively present in individual consciousness. There may be ample doubt as to what individual subjects would be best advised to do. But it can scarcely be doubted that they do possess reasons for acting which are genuinely their own.[9]

Modern western thinkers have made extensive efforts to systematize each of these three perspectives, in no case with complete success. But they have certainly made greater progress, at least until very recently, in systematizing the first and the third. The characteristic modern approach towards practical reason is an attempt in some way to unite these two: to fuse science with subjective preferences and factor out intervening social relations either by treating these as a feature of the causal environment of individuals or by reducing them to purely numerical accumulations of individual subjectivity. Hobbes's approach can be seen as an early and peculiarly trenchant example of this modern strategy. But, perhaps because he devised it more single-mindedly to resolve a particular problem of practical reason, his approach also yielded a far more explicit and orderly address to the issue of good reasons for action than his modern successors have contrived to muster.

There is every reason to suppose that all three of these modern perspectives are still indispensable for specifying the field of politics. But it is far less clear how the balance between them is to be struck. Each can readily be rejected, from the viewpoint of at least one of the others, as being essentially fictional: as not a given aspect of an indefeasible reality, but a contingent cultural projection, an artefact of the human imagination. For most purposes, however, this contrast is singularly uninstructive. The critics of each approach are clearly right to reject a claim from their competitors to a monopoly on understanding of the human predicament. There is evident force in Hegelian or Marxist attacks on the imaginary substantiality and normative self-sufficiency of the discrete right-claiming individual – just as there is in utilitarian or libertarian insistence that human value is always value for particular individual human beings. It is not necessary to endorse any of the dilapidated positivist programmes for the conduct of the social sciences to recognize that human beings subsist within a material universe, that they are themselves in many respects incontestably material creatures, and that they can be

[9] This is a normative, not a descriptive, claim. Cf. Louis Althusser.

accurately understood only as subject, in at least these respects, to material causality. Each perspective, however, imposes its own constraints on how reasons for human action can be systematically understood, privileging some conceptions of the nature of these reasons and virtually outlawing other conceptions of what it could be to have a good reason to act. In particular, the characteristic modern reading of practical reason – the fusion of a scientific understanding of the natural world with a humane acknowledgement of the presence and motivational force of subjective human preferences – yields an especially disobliging approach to the understanding of politics (Dunn 1980).

One way of posing the problem of political obligation today arises naturally out of this minimalist conception of individual subjectivity and its significance. It is hard to explain, on the basis of this conception, how any unfelt obligations can be good reasons for individual action (Williams 1981) or how any individuals can have good reason to see the space of politics as a site of obligation (of duty to determinate others) rather than an arena of enjoyment or suffering or a series of opportunities for investment or occasions for insurance (Dunn 1980). But although this approach does address real difficulties in modern understanding (and more especially in modern academic understanding), and although it certainly can after a fashion take account of more practical menaces to human existence today, it has two important disadvantages. In the first place, it poses the problem in a form which in principle palpably precludes its being given any clear and general solution. In the second place (and more crucially), it elides the unique character of the claim to, and the grounds for, political obedience, and does so in a world in which that claim is pressed very hard on virtually every adult human being.

Among modern thinkers, only philosophical anarchists like Robert Paul Wolff have been anxious to isolate and underline the unique character of the claim to political obedience; and they have attempted to do so, naturally, in order to challenge (or demolish) the force of these grounds. Wolff's own major premiss for his rejection of these grounds (Wolff 1976) is the general duty of every human agent to retain to the fullest degree her or his own autonomy – to refuse in any way and for any period of time to alienate any element of their will or capacity for judgement to any other agent. He makes no attempts to justify this extreme but evocative ethical theory,[10] simply assuming both its validity and its incompatibility with the view that the general duty of autonomy might itself give an agent obligatory grounds for alienating their will and judgement in more specific

[10] Wolff (1976, p. viii): 'To put it bluntly, I have simply taken for granted an entire ethical theory.'

respects. It is worth contrasting the structure of this view with that of Hobbes's, in which the capacity to alienate their will[11] through a promise is a key practical resource which human beings possess for accommodating their mutually destructive qualities in relative harmony. Hobbes himself scarcely regarded autonomy as a moral virtue or a cultural merit, let alone as a dominant and universal moral duty. But he did think that all human beings had at least some duties – the duties specified (whatever the significance of the nomenclature) in his laws of nature: notably the duties to seek peace and to observe covenants made. It is instructive, as critics have pointed out (Green 1988), that Wolff's theory is unable to give a clear account of the obligation of promises and is at least arguably incompatible with recognizing any such obligation. But, for the understanding of politics, it is even more important that within his ethical theory the general formal duty to judge normatively for oneself is in no way offset by any more concrete duties to others (or indeed even to oneself): such, for example, as the duty to seek peace by the most effective means currently accessible.

It may thus still prove instructive to consider the problem of political obligation in Hobbes's stark rendering, concentrating hereafter on the issue of how far Hobbes himself mustered a successful solution to this problem. As the titles of his two greatest works (*De Cive* and *Leviathan, or the Matter, Forme and Power of a Commonwealth Ecclesiasticall and Civil*) suggest (Hobbes [1742–51] 1946), Hobbes considers the problem of political obligation from the twin viewpoints of the natural individual (and potential citizen) and of the effectively alien entity, the state, to which that individual is properly obliged (Hobbes [1742–51] 1946, p. 32; Skinner 1989). Within this structure, the obligation of every citizen is plainly self-incurred (a product of an act on the part of the citizen himself);[12] but it is also plainly externally enforced. What is less immediately evident but at least equally important is that the obligation itself is constructed not through the authenticity or compulsiveness of individual sentiment or the cognitive dependability of individual judgement, but through a theory of individual good reasons for action. (It cannot, in Hobbes's view, be constructed through the necessary presence or compulsion of sentiments or the guaranteed validity of individual judgement, since the unavailability of appropriate sentiments and dependable judgement is precisely what constitutes the problem in the first place.) In Hobbes's view, his is therefore a firmly normative theory, but one

---

[11] There were, of course, good reasons why this happened not to be Hobbes's own vocabulary. But it serves to map the structure of his theory on to that of Wolff.

[12] This is not plausibly true of the female half of the population, who are not envisaged as citizens and with whose political obligations Hobbes is little concerned.

adjusted with the greatest care to the properties of human agents as he is confident these really are.

How far is its construction successful? How far does it contrive to identify good reasons for all human adults to constitute an effective sovereign power where none yet exists or to see and feel themselves bound to its authority wherever one is already present? A plausible general answer to this question (and one which consorts comfortably with such modern political ideology) is that it is relatively successful in isolating good reasons why all human adults (especially within an advanced commercial society) (Hobbes [1742–51] 1946, pp. 82–3) would have good reason to constitute an effective sovereign power if (or wherever) none was present at the time, but that it is distinctly less successful in establishing (or fails comprehensively to establish) good reasons for them to see themselves as bound to its authority wherever a state power currently subsists. There are plenty of decisive reasons for questioning the latter claim on particular occasions and in particular places: Belsen, Hiroshima, Kampuchea under Pol Pot, Equatorial Guinea, the Soviet Union under collectivization and during Stalin's purges, China during Mao's Great Leap Forward, much of Central America for most of the twentieth century. (It is important, however, to notice that the more decisive the reasons for questioning the normative authority of the state, the less plausible it is that Hobbes himself would have regarded his theory as validating that authority.) But the modern instances exemplify a timeless point, memorably expressed by John Locke:[13] if the *raison d'être* of the state is the provision of protection, no state which actively menaces its own subjects can have a sound claim to their dutiful obedience. There has been much careful and instructive recent analysis of the clarity and internal stability of Hobbes's account of individuals' good reasons for actions (for example, Warrender 1957; McNeilly 1968; Gauthier 1969; Hampton 1986; Tuck 1989), not all of it particularly sensitive to the political context to which Hobbes addressed himself (Baumgold 1988; Tuck 1979, esp. chapters 4–6; Skinner 1966). But what has been less effectively captured is just why Hobbes should have been so much more successful in explaining the grounds for welcoming the construction of an effective sovereign in the state of nature than in justifying the scope of unrestricted sovereign power within civil society. (Contrast, however, the careful analysis in Hampton (1986).) The principal reason for this notably uneven success, however, is not elusive. Whereas Hobbes's model of the individual human agent

---

[13] Locke [1689] (1960, II, p. 93, II, pp. 30–2): 'this is to think that Men are so foolish that they take care to avoid what Mischief may be done them by *Pole-cats* or *Foxes*, but are content, nay think it Safety, to be devoured by *Lions*.'

yields clear (and illuminating) results in the simple counterfactual instance of a stateless but highly civilized habitat (compare metropolitan New York), the same model yields no clear results at all in the opaque and extravagantly complicated space of potential contention for the control of sovereign power in any particular civilized habitat over a more or less protracted period of time (Dunn 1980). His approach is paralytically feeble in its treatment of the criteria for and implications of political legitimacy, principally (if not exclusively) because it offers no theoretical facilities whatever for the systematic analysis of political possibilities or political causality.

This last limitation is extremely important. If Hobbes's formulation of the problem of political obligation is still the sharpest available, and if his solution to this problem cannot be brought validly to bear on particular problems of political choice within a seriously contested political space (and if all modern political spaces are in some measure seriously contested), the implications for the claims of modern political authority are acutely sceptical (Dunn 1988a). They certainly do not imply that claims to such authority cannot and do not vary drastically in merit. But what they do imply is that the rather evident expediency of some form of effective political authority within a modern economy cannot by itself serve to vindicate the legitimacy of any particular claimant to such authority, incumbent or otherwise. Nor, more pressingly, can it readily serve as a decisive refutation of the legitimacy of a considerable range of such claimants, some of whom at this time may carry little superficial political plausibility.[14] One reasonable, if mildly indolent, inference that might be drawn from all this is that the only positive and reasonably objective contribution which analytical thought can hope to make to elucidating the justification of modern claims to political authority is to distinguish clearly among the wide variety of grounds that appropriately bear upon these claims and examine the manner in which they are deployed on any particular occasion. (More egocentrically, of course, it can also be exercised in the design and embellishment by individual thinkers of a moral theory which they happen to find personally inviting.[15] But, as Hobbes himself explained very adequately, strongly felt and confidently imagined individual intuitions about political value, whatever other merits they may have, are in themselves more a constituent of the problem of political obligation than a contribution to its resolution.)

[14] Cf. Dunn (1989) especially the epigraph from Guicciardini, p. xiv.
[15] The most elegant and imaginative contemporary political philosopher who sees the relation between ethics and politics essentially in these terms is Ronald Dworkin. See especially Dworkin (1986). But the viewpoint itself is now relatively commonplace: cf., for example, most of the contributors to Waldron (1984).

Perhaps, however, more can be learnt by considering the validity, not of
Hobbes's own general theory of good reasons for human action but of his
more specific theory of just what it is about a state that enables it to offer
to individual human beings a more dependable degree of protection than
their own natural powers can readily afford. Political obligation is self-
incurred by individual choice and personal commitment. The reasons for
making the commitment and incurring the obligations are, *ex hypothesi*,
good reasons. But what stabilizes them and guarantees them in practice,
in Hobbes's contention (what makes them a plainly rational choice,
rather than a reckless speculation), is the character of the alien entity to
which the individual contractors subordinate themselves. What makes
this authority an effective custodian of its desperately vulnerable subjects
is its combination of independence (impartiality), unity of will and judgement, and effective capacity for coercion: for enforcing its own will and
judgement upon the potentially recalcitrant.

Each of these characteristics is obviously open to question. Is the political sovereignty ever aptly seen as independent of (casually unaffected or
unconstrained by) all elements of the society over which it rules? States
may perhaps in general be relatively autonomous of even the most powerful social forces within a society. But does it even make sense to conceive
of the agency of a state (still less an individual monarch) as wholly independent of the specific purposes of all constituents of its subject population? Yet, once its axiomatic independence of that society is doubted, its
impartiality between these different constituents of the subject population becomes far harder to credit.[16] Perhaps no capitalist state could ever
afford to reduce itself to the executive committee of its own local bour-
geoisie. But it is hard to see how any capitalist state could be genuinely
impartial at any particular time between the interests of capital and
labour. And even a state which was in effect wholly independent of its
subject population (as Hobbes's conception of sovereignty was deliberately designed to make it) would not necessarily offer the least guarantee
of impartiality. Real rulers do not merely will and judge for themselves;
they also – and in all cases – possess their own tastes. The political
problem of favourites is not an archaic idiosyncrasy of mercifully super-
annuated courts. It is a permanent hazard of the exercise of political
power. Modern favourites are more likely to be social or ethnic or ideological groupings than they are to be individual persons of special erotic
allure. But the fact that they are generally drabber and more numerous
than their historical forerunners does not render them any less offensive

---

[16] Compare the suspicion within the civic republican tradition of the independence of political authority itself. See Skinner (1989, esp. p. 104); Green (1988, p. 59).

to the majority over whom they are preferred. (And, of course, it could in principle be the case that the favourites in question actually were the majority themselves, though this is scarcely a very frequent historical hazard.) Besides the recipients of favour, moreover, there are also usually the objects of special malignity, the scapegoats, and those whose interests are comprehensively ignored. Every society has its favourites and its scapegoats, the more democratic just as much as the less. It is never reasonable to expect full impartiality in a ruler (and quite hard to see even how the idea itself can be rendered entirely clear). Rulers, then, are never wholly independent and seldom, if ever, wholly impartial. Some of the peril of the state of nature lingers within even the sharpest and most edifying structure of human authority. This is a point which John Locke saw appreciably more clearly than Hobbes did (Dunn 1969, 1988b). It is of immense political importance.

A more interesting and obscure limitation of Hobbes's sovereign is the implausibility of its claim to possess a unitary will and judgement. Certainly, on Hobbes's analysis, the sovereign is entitled to take the final choice on any matter of practical dispute. But entitlement to final choice does not ensure either the disposition or the causal power to make such choices in any but the idlest of circumstances. Something very like akrasia (the incapacity in practice to do what very palpably should or must be done) is a rather blatant feature of most contemporary states at most times; perhaps of all modern states at all times. Uncontested entitlement to act is no aid to the indecisive, the painfully cross-pressured, or the congenitally muddled. Real sovereigns, moreover, are never aptly seen as single biological individuals, with a single will and judgement indisputably their own. The Leviathan is an artificial, not a natural, person (Aylmer 1961, 1973). Since the days of Hobbes the practical reality of the modern state has moved steadily further away from the model of a unified will, intelligence and judgement and towards that of a vast and inchoate bureaucratic shambles. Not even the most shapely theory of good reasons for action can transform the latter into an evidently dependable guarantee of the interests of anyone. Hobbes himself feared disunity of will at the centre of a state because he saw this as apt to foment political strife and even civil war. But modern students of his theory of political obligation have more reason to doubt the realism of his construction of the state's unitary will and judgement because they fear the latter's sheer ineffectuality in the face of so many of the existing threats to human security. (Consider the streets of Washington, DC – to say nothing of the subways of New York City.)

The incapacity to arrive at a definite decision may perhaps be best understood as a real failure of will on the part of at least some human agents, and the absence of any unitary centre of will and judgement in a modern state, as less a failure in agency than an indication that the metaphor of agency is severely overstretched when applied to the modern state. But there is a third weakness in Hobbes's model of sovereignty, when the latter is considered as a potential solution for the problem of political obligation as this stands today. In the state of nature, all human beings can and will judge the requirements for their own preservation firmly for themselves. The consequences of these judgements is a condition of war. The principal service which the Leviathan performs for them is to guarantee that under the vast majority of circumstances they no longer need to judge these requirements for themselves; and the means by which it supplies this service is by withdrawing from them the right to assess such requirements for themselves, except in the face of imminent and unmistakable peril. Since Hobbes's day the range of knowable potential hazards to human life has become far wider, the problems of appraising them immeasurably more intricate, and the range of strategies for meeting them dramatically harder to assess. There was every reason in Hobbes's day to doubt the judgemental skill of holders of sovereign power in issues of international war and peace.[17] But the range of damage which lay within their causal reach still fell appreciably short of the chaos of the state of nature. Today, however, this is less evidently the case. If the principal threats to protracted human survival now come less from atavistic confessional or ethnic hatreds, or even immediate clashes of class interest, than from uncontrolled ecological degradation and imperfectly controllable structures of instrumental menace,[18] it is plain that the holders of state power do not necessarily enjoy the cognitive skills to judge how best to assure human security, and quite plausible that their judgement is often (or even usually) worse than that of particular unofficial groups among their own subjects. Where this last condition does obtain, the problem of political obligation, as Hobbes conceived it, can scarcely have any solution at all. What is required is precisely a contest for state power[19] which leaves this in the hands of other agents who are cognitively better equipped to exercise it well.

States, then, may well prove unable to supply the security from which Hobbes derives the duties of their subjects, simply because they lack the independence and unity of will and judgement, or the potential sagacity, to make them reliable instruments of the end for which they are entrusted 'with the sovereign power, namely the procuration of the safety of the

---

[17] Consider the human impact of the Thirty Years War.
[18] Bracken (1983) and compare, on the whole more encouragingly, Allison *et al.* (1985).
[19] Not, of course, necessarily (or indeed desirably) a violent contest for it.

people' (Hobbes [1642–51] 1946, p. 219). They may lack the disposition or the skill required to furnish this security. But they may also fail simply because they lack the effective power to provide it, either in relation to external threats from other and more powerful states, or indeed from some of their own personnel. The authority of Leviathan lies in its capacity to intimidate. He 'hath the use of so much power and strength conferred on him, that by terror thereof, he is enabled to form the wills of them all to peace at home and mutual aid against their enemies abroad' (Hobbes [1642–51] 1946, p. 112). Provided that its practical judgement is sound, it is no defect in the right of a state that the mutual aid of its subjects may in the end prove insufficient to protect them against a powerful external enemy. (Sufficient unto the day is the evil thereof.) But it is more perturbing if the degree of terror achieved proves inadequate to protect the subjects against one another. A failure in domestic protection is not merely a deficiency in coercive power; it is also a definite encroachment on the structure of good reasons on which Hobbes hopes to ground the duties of subjects. Most contemporary commentators would agree that manifest failure to secure the safety of their own subjects has by now virtually eliminated the claims to political authority of the government of Afghanistan, as it did for many years those of the government of Lebanon, and eliminated with these the putative political obligations of their subjects. But it is worth considering how far the rights of any state that lacks the effective coercive power to protect the lives of its subjects really can extend. (What implications, for example, does the acute physical insecurity of many inhabitants of great American cities have for the scope of their political obligations? In the face of the international drug traffic of the late twentieth century, can it really be coherent to combine a civic republican theory of the right of every citizen to bear arms with a Hobbesian understanding of the nature and scope of the rights of the American state and the duties of American subjects?)

In these ways the structure of Hobbes's theory can serve to bring out the crude disparities between the services which modern states need to be able to supply, if they are to vindicate rationally the scope of their claims to authority, and the distinctly less impressive services which they are in fact in a position to provide. Where this ineffectuality is essentially domestic, the theory does little to clarify the nature of possible remedies. Few participants in modern politics frankly commend acute physical insecurity as such. But the extent of disagreement, in good and bad faith, about the best techniques for minimizing it is virtually limitless and follows no sharply demarcated contours. In the case of external threats to physical security, however, the theory may still prove a little more illuminating. Thermonuclear weapons concretize and intensify the problem of security, augmenting the threats of personal mortality and the destruction of family or community with the perfectly real possibility of universal human extinction. Less hectically, but perhaps in the end more intract-ably, the prospective destruction of the human habitat through the slowly cumulative unintended consequences of human agency underlines the point that purely biological security for a modern population over time cannot be guaranteed within the confines of a given territory or by means of even the most extravagant accumulation of coercive power.

To remedy each of these sources of danger requires either a dramatic further concentration of effective control over human agency or a com-prehensive transformation in the moral quality and in the intelligent coordination of that agency. Neither change is to be anticipated soon (if ever). But, on Hobbes's analysis of the problem of political obligation, only the former could even make coherent sense, since even a complete replacement of human beings by a population of angels would leave the problem of coordinating their actions intelligently wholly untouched. A Hobbesian remedy for the menace posed by nuclear weapons, like the process of compacting in the state of nature, would move from the good reasons of insecure individuals (in this instance, states) to fashion an effective guarantee of security, to the construction of a single centre of will, judgement and effective coercive power which alone could furnish this guarantee. The existence of a multiplicity of states with nuclear or thermonuclear armaments violently generalizes the problem of security, forcing upon these states an endlessly hectic causal analysis of a complex and necessarily largely inscrutable field, whether their active responses at any given time exacerbate or mollify its dangers. The Hobbesian (and putatively rational) solution to this predicament is the creation of a single world government (or universal empire), furnishing security for all by removing the capacity for harm from any: except, of course, itself. This solution has both the strengths and the weaknesses of the state as remedy for the state of nature. (It is a state; and what it is designed to remedy is a state of nature.) Even as a purely abstract idea, however, it is scarcely a very plausible remedy, being open to all the doubts about independence, impartiality,[20] unity of will and judgement,[21] and capacity for effective enforcement to which Hobbes's Leviathan itself is subject. But there seems little reason to doubt that it is the most plausible remedy we have. Its crucial defect is not the strain which it imposes on our credulity but the simple fact that it *is* only an abstract idea, whereas Hobbes's state,

---

[20] What would it decide, for example, about the allocation and enforcement of property rights within the territory which it controls? Cf. Waldron (1989) and Barry (1989).

[21] In what language would it communicate with itself?

however mythically rendered in the pages of *Leviathan*, is an interpretation of what was, and has remained, a historical actuality. Moreover, even if nuclear weapons have made the construction of a universal empire rational for human beings, they have also set formidable obstacles in at least one of the potential paths towards its construction. In a world with at least two great nuclear powers, universal empire can scarcely, any longer, be a commonwealth by acquisition.

The world in which we live is clamorous with proclamations of the rights of states. But it is not a world in which we can hope to distinguish justified claimants to political obligation from unjustified pretenders with the crispness and decisiveness which Hobbes promised. (It is fair to say that the simplicity of the criterion which he recommended earned little applause at the time.) To have rational force, modern conceptions of political obligation have to be more limited, more tentative, and altogether less peremptory. They have, that is to say, to be consciously weaker claims; and in addition they have to abandon any hope of monopoly. There is no ideal manner in which to set out this enfeebled plurality, and little reason for confidence that examining it must prove politically instructive. But there are perhaps two relatively promising approaches to further analysis. One is to distinguish among the various types of duty which thinkers have seen as yielding political obligation. A second approach, more diffuse but more exacting, is to consider the distinctive obstructions to political understanding imposed by the trajectory of modern philosophy. We may consider these in turn.

Political obligation may be seen, for example, as an obligation of prudence. Its source then lies in the needs and purposes of human beings. If it is to be genuinely obligatory for all, there must be real advantage for each and every subject in his own political subjection.[22] As an obligation of prudence political obligation is necessarily directed principally towards the future, the sole setting which we have the power to affect by our actions. But political obligation may also be seen as an obligation of gratitude. To obligate in this case, political subjection must already have yielded real benefits. Obligations of gratitude are intrinsically directed towards the past. They stem from favours received, even if they can and would be overridden by future consequences that are unequivocally harmful and of greater practical importance. There are also, of course, many other candidates for the particular variety of obligation which best models the nature of political obligation: notably obligations of fidelity and obligations of fairness. (The duty of fidelity requires that a promise

---

[22] See Barry (1989) for a powerful demonstration of the strength of this criterion and of its very dubious compatibility in many instances with the requirements for justice.

has been given; the obligation of fairness that the practice in question be genuinely fair.) But the contrast between obligations of prudence and obligations of gratitude already serves to pick out the principal polarity in understandings of the nature of obligation; the polarity between teleology and deontology. Obligations of prudence are rational, modern and, at least incipiently, utilitarian. They are fixated upon the future. Obligations of gratitude, by contrast, are decidedly more traditional. They focus obsessively upon the past; and their rationality is today very actively in dispute.[23] The conflict between these two perspectives is irresolvable. If the balance of consequences will be clearly negative, how can it make sense (or be justifiable) to bring those consequences about? What is the point of lashing a stone? But 'if the past is not to bind us, where can duty lie?' (George Eliot 1860).

It is, however, eminently questionable whether this is a conflict which we should even wish to resolve. Both perspectives are rather evidently relevant to living a human life and neither has the least claim to a monopoly of valid understanding. The teleological option is best expressed today in utilitarianism, a theory of value which locates it within individual human experience, uniting a highly subjective conception of the nature of value with a very high degree of objectification in its overall perspective. In its most sophisticated modern forms[24] it conceives of value fairly firmly in terms of individual reasons but yields rather weak grounds for individual agents to act in accordance with the demands of the good (but cf. Parfit (1984)). An individualist and instrumental consequentialism certainly gives no cogent justification for political authority, for accepting a duty to act however the sovereign commands and to do so precisely because this is what the latter does command (Green 1988, esp. p. 156; Dunn 1980, esp. pp. 269–70, 276, 285–6, 296). Its very form precludes it from yielding any such result. But there is no reason whatever to see such a conception as yielding an adequate understanding of either the nature of human value itself or the significance of social membership. Nor is there any reason to suppose either that the conception itself can be applied to practical decisions, except in the haziest and most blatantly metaphorical fashion, or that the theoretical perspective required to lend it a determinate content can even be specified in a wholly coherent fashion. If human beings are social and historical creatures both by nature and by moral destiny, human value cannot be specified solely out of the contingencies of individual consciousness at a given point in time; and the idea of a

---

[23] It has been so fairly continuously since at least the publication of William Godwin's *Enquiry concerning Political Justice* in 1793.
[24] For a careful recent account see Griffin (1986).

method guaranteed to specify such value accurately is intensely unappealing. The conception of a unified scientific perspective upon human existence and human value which can be occupied by particular human beings at a particular time is not a coherent idea. In relation to the field of politics, its incoherence is both peculiarly obvious and exceptionally unattractive (Dunn 1985, chapter 7).

In the bureaucratized and rationalized world of modern politics (and economics) (Dunn 1990b), utilitarian arguments will always remain of urgent practical importance. In such a world utilitarianism's conceptual impetus towards comprehensiveness and the demystification of imaginative habit are likely to retain a permanent capacity for moral edification. But there can no more be an adequate evaluative interpretation in purely utilitarian terms in the case of modern politics than there could have been in that of any earlier epoch of human history (or in that of Vico's giants). In relation to politics, moreover, the perspectival evasiveness of utilitarianism is peculiarly important. Considered as a theory proffering normative guidance to an individual agent contributing consequences at a historical margin, utilitarianism is frustrated by the sheer political debility of most individual agents for almost all the time (Dunn 1980, pp. 285–6). But at least its political impotence is offset by some degree of epistemic determinacy. Human history, and all other human agents, being taken exactly as these are, none of us may be able to do much. But at least there is a determinate context for our actions, and one about which we can hope to deliberate in a controlled fashion.

But no human agent can apprehend the cumulative outcome of human history or know how all other human beings now are; and the conception of such understanding is not an appropriate element to include within the perspective of practical reason. What is politically possible – what the consequences of given actions will in fact be – is plainly of central importance in political agency. But what is politically possible itself depends, *inter alia*, on the beliefs of human agents about their own causal powers, about their own social and political responsibilities, and about the causal powers and social and political responsibilities of others. It is possible to objectify this dependence from the viewpoint of a particular agent at a particular time; to treat it as an inventory of external constraints upon and opportunities for acting and envisage it purely strategically. But this viewpoint is a heroic imaginative presumption, not a practical epistemic option. Whatever its practical utility (as 'an idea of reason') within the *raison d'état* of a particular state, it is profoundly unsuitable for capturing the political significance of the predicament of most ordinary denizens of the modern (or any other) world (Dunn 1985, chapter 7). No doubt all human beings do a great deal of strategic calculation. But only impressionable readers of the *Neveu de Rameau* could be led to suppose that most of them never think in any other fashion – let alone that they never have good reason to do so. The provision of public goods is often politically difficult; and dilemmas of collective action can pose a formidable political challenge. But a human world constituted solely out of individual agents who accepted a purely instrumental conception of rationality and applied it relentlessly to the contexts in which they found themselves would (as Hobbes insisted) not merely face difficulties in resolving these dilemmas and securing many public goods; its denizens would find all but insuperable barriers to living with each other at all.[25]

The claims of political duty can have profoundly malign political consequences. Where they do, we need not hesitate to reject them unequivocally. (It was simply bad to do almost anything to sustain the power of Adolf Hitler or Pol Pot; and we may well wonder what posterity is going to make of the contribution of western governments to the prospects for resuscitating the power of the latter.) But it is not morally intelligent to view political authority with settled suspicion whenever it appears uncertain to prove consistently to one's personal advantage. Indeed, in a relatively benign polity, it is not even morally decent to do so. No human agent can be exempt from responsibility for judging when a particular command or act of authority is a great crime. But this responsibility is best seen not as an instance of a general duty to maximize autonomy, but as a particular duty to avoid complicity in profoundly and obviously evil acts. Autonomy is an impressive moral ideal; but it is only as impressive a title to act as the quality of moral understanding which the agent in question is able to bring to bear. Very many human agents, in the more edifying of modern states, have better reason to distrust their own capacity to reach sound political judgements about virtually anything but immediately criminal acts than they do to doubt the benignity or competence of the legislative or executive authority to which they are subject.[26] The world of modern politics is too complicated and opaque for anyone to understand it very clearly (Dunn 1990b). But it is appreciably further beyond the cognitive reach of those who are ill placed to be aware of most aspects of it and who have little, if any, inclination to try to make themselves any better aware. Autonomy can be a grand goal for the moral life; but it cannot be a sound excuse for the lazy or self-satisfied to repudiate the claims of a benign political authority.

What sorts of claims, then, to political authority can have some real

---

[25] For this aspect of Hobbes's problem see especially Hampton (1986).

[26] I do not mean, of course, that they have no reason to distrust the latter; just that they have more reason to distrust the former.

force even today? The most evocative case for political obligation is still the case stated by Plato's teacher Socrates in the *Crito*. Political obligation can be an obligation of gratitude for past benefits received, an obligation as direct and natural as the obligations of a child to its parents.[27] But it can also be an obligation incurred by consent. Since any Athenian citizen could freely emigrate with all their property, anyone who had chosen to remain had 'thereby by his act of staying, agreed with us [viz. the laws of Athens] that he will do what we demand of them' (Plato 1979 edn: 51e; 52a–3). The entire life which Socrates had lived had shown his full commitment to being a citizen of Athens, rather than any other city. It would be ignominious of him now to desert it, 'contrary to the contracts and agreements by which you covenanted with us to conduct yourself as a citizen of Athens' (52d). These commitments were freely entered into and clearly understood. Moreover, in Athens each citizen had a full opportunity, through its free and democratic political institutions, to persuade the city to alter any law which he regarded as wrong (51e–52a). In Athens, on Socrates' reading, even in the face of the personal calamity of his trial and death sentence, each citizen was genuinely bound to the laws by the duties of gratitude and fidelity (prior self-commitment). An Athenian civic life could justly be treated as a promise to obey the city's laws because, in Athens at least, each citizen had practical opportunity to leave freely and without paying a prohibitive instrumental price[28] and each citizen likewise enjoyed a full and just right to participate in determining what the laws in fact required (cf. Pateman 1979; Singer 1973).

All of these arguments have had their descendants. Each retains some contemporary force. But the single most powerful consideration in modern understandings of politics, the sheer practical expediency of settled political authority, makes no direct appearance in Socrates' account. Modern interpreters of the nature and scope of political obligation must choose either to ignore it, as did Socrates, or to attempt to unify the objectifying perspective from which expediency is most effectively assessed with the subjectivity of reasons for individual agency in which it may well be not merely imaginatively occluded but sometimes practically absent. Because it would be inconvenient for any individual, sooner or later, if there were no settled social or economic order, it simply does not follow that most individuals most of the time have good instrumental reason to inhibit their actions on behalf of such an order. Hobbes

---

[27] Plato (1979 edn: 50d; 51a–b). This is itself an obligation the extent of which is much affected by the ways in which the latter have treated the child in question.

[28] For the importance of this argument see, classically, Hume [1748] (1985); also Simmons (1979) and Green (1988).

attempted to derive comprehensive political obligation from nothing but expediency and rationality. But his attempt did not succeed. Subsequent attempts to derive it from the conjunction of expediency and fairness to other members of society (cf. Hart 1984), or expediency and fair political decision processes (Singer 1973), either yield far weaker arguments or have a dismayingly limited field of application (Singer 1973; also Pateman 1979). Duties of gratitude and fairness may be conceptually well shaped to restrain the hastiness and self-righteousness of an ultra-individualistic political culture. But within such a culture they can only appear as moralizing external reasons and of correspondingly questionable rational force (Williams 1981, chapter 8; Williams 1985). Only the eminently individualist criterion of consent retains a comfortable force in the face of this culture (Green 1988). But its political significance is sharply restricted by the severely limited presence of anything that could readily be mistaken for consent in the practical political life of modern societies.

It is easy enough to construct more imperious theories of political obligation, today as in the past. (States construct or refurbish them all the time.) But the linchpin of any such theory must be a vigorously corrective theory of reasons for individual action. States can do their best (or worst) to impose such a theory through the sheer power at their disposal. But individual theorists cannot reasonably hope to make much headway in doing so just by rational persuasion. Where it succeeds, rational persuasion converts an external reason (a piece of moral or prudential nagging) into an internal reason, a genuine reason for a real agent to act (or, to put it more eirenically, discloses that what previously appeared to that agent as a brusquely external reason – or failed to obtrude on their attention at all – was in fact an internal reason all along).

In a reasonably sedate and prosperous modern polity we can savour its plurality of perception and sentiment with some complacency, rejoicing in the social progress of enlightenment and in our own unsuperstitious understanding of the character of the societies to which we belong. In sedate and prosperous modern polities the problem of political obligation retains little urgency.

But we should not assume that it is the demystified plurality of these societies (the degree to which they embody the progress of modern thought) which renders them both sedate and prosperous. Where their calm rhythms are disturbed and their prosperity is actively threatened, their plurality soon shows a less bland face. If a society subjectively amounts to no more than a conjunction of the theories of its individual members, it can be a war of each theory against every other theory at least as readily as it can a preordained harmony in any dimension whatever.

Hobbes's construction of the problem of political obligation does not offer a valid proof that we are all politically obliged (or even that any particular human being has ever been politically obliged). But it still serves as a tart reminder that human social life has always been potentially hazardous and that it is likely always to remain so. Whenever that life is at its least inviting, the only effective recourse open to human beings is still the fashioning of more benign and more effective states. As the Lebanon and Sri Lanka,[29] those erstwhile showcases of social pluralism, daily emphasize, mere plurality is not itself the solution to the riddle of modern history. For it to aid and not impede such a solution, we need and will always need peace. And to have peace, it is always perfectly possible that we may well need Leviathan, and need it very urgently.

REFERENCES

Allison, G. T., A. Carnesale and J. S. Nye 1985. *Hawks, Doves and Owls: Agenda for Avoiding Nuclear War.* New York: Norton
Anderson, P. 1980. *Arguments within English Marxism.* London: Verso
Aylmer, G. E. 1961. *The King's Servants: The Civil Service of Charles I, 1625–42.* London: Routledge and Kegan Paul
   1973. *The State's Servants: The Civil Service of the English Republic, 1649–1660.* London: Routledge and Kegan Paul
Barry, B. 1989. *Theories of Justice.* Hemel Hempstead: Harvester-Wheatsheaf
Baumgold, D. 1988. *Hobbes's Political Theory.* Cambridge: Cambridge University Press
Bracken, P. 1983. *The Command and Control of Nuclear Forces.* New Haven: Yale University Press
Dunn, J. 1969. *The Political Thought of John Locke.* Cambridge: Cambridge University Press
   1980 (ed.). *Political Obligation in its Historical Context.* Cambridge: Cambridge University Press
   1985. *Rethinking Modern Political Theory.* Cambridge: Cambridge University Press
   1988a. 'Rights and political conflict'. In *Civil Liberties in Conflict,* ed. L. Gostin. London: Routledge
   1988b. 'Trust and political agency'. In *Trust: The Making and Breaking of Cooperative Relations,* ed. D. Gambetta, pp. 73–93. Oxford: Blackwell
   1989. *Modern Revolutions,* 2nd edn. Cambridge: Cambridge University Press
   1990a (ed.). 'Elusive community; or the political theory of Charles Taylor'. In *Interpreting Political Responsibility.* Cambridge: Polity Press
   1990b (ed.). *The Economic Limits to Modern Politics.* Cambridge: Cambridge University Press
   1993. *Western Political Theory in the Face of the Future,* 2nd edn. Cambridge: Cambridge University Press
Dworkin, R. 1986. *Law's Empire.* Cambridge, Mass.: Belknap Press

[29] For an earlier perspective see Dunn (1980, pp. 157–205).

Eliot, G. [1860] n.d. *The Mill on the Floss.* Garden City, New York: Doubleday

Gauthier, D. 1969. *The Logic of Leviathan.* Oxford: Clarendon Press

Green, L. 1988. *The Authority of the State.* Oxford: Clarendon Press

Griffin, J. 1986. *Well-being: Its Meaning, Measurement and Moral Importance.* Oxford: Clarendon Press

Hampton, J. 1986. *Hobbes and the Social Contract Tradition.* Cambridge: Cambridge University Press

Hare, R. M. 1967. 'The lawful government'. In *Philosophy, Politics and Society: Third Series,* ed. P. Laslett and W. G. Runciman. Oxford: Blackwell

1976. 'Political obligation'. In *Social Ends and Political Means,* ed. T. Honderich. London: Routledge and Kegan Paul

Hart, H. L. A. 1984. 'Are there any natural rights?' In *Theories of Rights,* ed. J. Waldron, pp. 77–90. Oxford: Oxford University Press

Hobbes, T. [1642] 1983. *De Cive: The English Version,* ed. H. Warrender. Oxford: Clarendon Press

[1642–51] 1946. *De Cive; Leviathan, or the Matter, Forme and Power of a Commonwealth Ecclesiasticall and Civil,* ed. M. Oakeshott. Oxford: Blackwell

Hume, D. [1748] 1985. 'Of the original contract'. In *Essays Moral, Political and Literary,* ed. E. F. Miller, pp. 465–87. Indianapolis: Liberty Classics

Locke, J. [1689] 1960. *Two Treatises of Government,* ed. P. Laslett. Cambridge: Cambridge University Press

Lukes, S. 1985. *Marxism and Morality.* Oxford: Clarendon Press

McNeilly, F. S. 1968. *The Anatomy of Leviathan.* London: Macmillan

Miliband, R. 1977. *Marxism and Politics.* Oxford: Oxford University Press

Parfit, D. 1984. *Reasons and Persons.* Oxford: Clarendon Press

Pateman, C. 1979. *The Problems of Political Obligation.* Chichester: Wiley

Plato, *The Crito.* In *Law and Obedience,* ed. and trans. A. D. Woozley (1979). London: Duckworth

Rorty, R. 1980. *Philosophy and the Mirror of Nature.* Oxford: Blackwell

1982. *Consequences of Pragmatism.* Minneapolis: University of Minnesota Press

Simmons, A. J. 1979. *Moral Principles and Political Obligations.* Princeton: Princeton University Press

Singer, P. 1973. *Democracy and Disobedience.* Oxford: Clarendon Press

Skinner, Q. 1966. 'The ideological context of Hobbes's political thought'. *Historical Journal* 9, 3, 286–317

1984. 'The idea of negative liberty'. In *Philosophy in History,* ed. R. Rorty, J. B. Schneewind and Q. Skinner. Cambridge: Cambridge University Press

1989. 'The state'. In *Political Innovation and Conceptual Change,* ed. T. Ball, J. Farr and R. Hanson, pp. 90–131. Cambridge: Cambridge University Press

Taylor, C. 1985. *Philosophy and the Human Sciences* (Philosophical Papers, II). Cambridge: Cambridge University Press

Thompson, E. P. 1978. *The Poverty of Theory.* London: Merlin

Tuck, R. 1979. *Natural Rights Theories: Their Origin and Development.* Cambridge: Cambridge University Press

1987. 'The "modern" theory of natural law'. In *The Languages of Political Theory in Early Modern Europe,* ed. A. Pagden, pp. 99–119. Cambridge: Cambridge University Press

1988. 'Optics and sceptics: the philosophical foundations of Hobbes's political thought'. In *Conscience and Casuistry in Early Modern Europe*, ed. E. Leites, pp. 235–63. Cambridge: Cambridge University Press

1989. *Hobbes*. Oxford: Oxford University Press

Unger, R. M. 1987. *Politics*, 3 vols. Cambridge: Cambridge University Press

Waldron, J. 1984 (ed.). *Theories of Rights*. Oxford: Oxford University Press

1989. *The Right to Private Property*. Oxford: Clarendon Press

Walzer, M. 1983. *Spheres of Justice: A Defence of Pluralism and Equality*. Oxford: Martin Robertson

Warrender, H. 1957. *The Political Philosophy of Hobbes*. Oxford: Clarendon Press

Williams, B. 1981 (ed.). 'Internal and external reasons'. In *Moral Luck*, chapter 8. Cambridge: Cambridge University Press

1985. *Ethics and the Limits of Philosophy*. London: Fontana

Wolff, R. P. 1976. *In Defence of Anarchism*, 2nd edn. New York: Harper and Rowe

5   Trust

Few modern philosophers are convinced that the nature and availability of trust between human beings really is a central issue in the theoretical understanding of politics. This is in some ways surprising, since the most prominent recent movement in political philosophy, the largely North American dialogue about the content of social justice inaugurated by John Rawls (1972), has been strongly committed to the theoretical centrality of the idea of a contract: a free, but binding, agreement. The normative force of the standard of uncoerced choice by free and rational agents unites the great seventeenth- and eighteenth-century philosophical exponents of natural law and natural rights with modern contractarian critics of the claims of utility to serve as a uniform criterion for political and social decisions. But the two groups of thinkers differ drastically in their estimate of the practical significance of that normative force.

For early modern theorists of natural law (Locke, Rousseau, even Hobbes), there were the closest of ties between voluntary self-commitment, the obligatory force of a contract or promise, and the psychological and social foundations of human collective life. *Fides*, the duty to keep faith and the practical virtue of discharging that duty in the dependable fashion, was the foundation for social life in its entirety (Dunn 1985, chapter 2), the key practical capacity which made it possible for human beings to live with one another on tolerable terms at all. Modern contractarians agree with their seventeenth-century predecessors on what gives the standard its normative force: the irreducible separateness of human persons – the fact that each human being experiences, values, judges and chooses in the last instance for themselves. It is, above all, this feature of the human condition to which utilitarianism, rightly or wrongly, is held to give insufficient recognition. But unlike their seventeenth-century predecessors, modern contractarians see no apparent connection between the normative force of the idea of free choice and the practical issue of how far and why human beings conceive themselves as bound by their own choices. Which of the two groups is right?

It is easy to lose sight of the importance of this question. The two groups of contractarians plainly differ extensively within their own ranks over a wide range of issues. There is a large measure of unreality in presuming all the members of either group to be discussing essentially the same question; and there are still more obvious and drastic differences between the intellectual and historical assumptions of the two groups taken together and between the very diverse topics with which their members have been severally concerned. But it is not strategically intelligent, either for philosophers or for political theorists, to rest content with noting the historical heterogeneity of assumptions and preoccupations across these rather distant and somewhat arbitrarily composed and juxtaposed groups. From the evident fact that they were discussing widely discrepant issues on the basis of readily distinguishable systems of belief, it does not follow that their views do not imply on some points sharply contradictory judgements. More importantly, if political philosophy is conceived not simply in terms of the lucid analysis of an array of politically current conceptions but also as an understanding of what politics is and what it means, it does not follow that one of these two bodies of human reflection may not and does not offer a far more penetrating and less parochial account of politics than the other (compare Dunn 1990a, chapters 2–4). No one today would be surprised by the claim that some aspects of recent political philosophy mark a clear cognitive advance on the intellectual products of the seventeenth century. (It would be discouraging if none did.) But in so far as that judgement makes coherent sense, it must leave open the real possibility that some aspects of recent political philosophy may represent something of a cognitive retreat on the same level of achievement. In the case of the significance of trust for an understanding of what politics is and what it means, there are grounds for supposing that this is indeed the case. (Compare Bernard Williams's arguments for the superior strategic insight furnished by Greek ethics for a post-Christian era (Williams 1985).)

What are these grounds? The first and most important is the very difficult relation between morality and politics in the two bodies of thinking: the narrowing of scope and the sharp constriction in the scale of cognitive responsibility assumed in the modern recensions of contractarianism. There has been some apparent shift in Rawls's understanding of the nature of his own theory (Rawls 1972, 1980, 1985, 1993; cf. Barry 1989): and there is considerable disagreement among subsequent American contributions to the analysis of social justice about the relation between reflective equilibrium within the mind of an individual moral theorist and political argument between such theorists. But despite these real variations in theoretical strategy and intellectual ambition, it is broadly correct to say that no modern political philosophers of any stature attempt to understand both morality and politics through essentially the same set of concepts, while all major political philosophers of the seventeenth century (and many of the eighteenth) attempted precisely that. This was not because all seventeenth-century political philosophers were religiously, morally or culturally credulous, while all late twentieth-century political philosophers are religiously, morally and culturally sceptical. (Compare Hobbes with Rawls, Dworkin, Walzer or Taylor.) But it is a natural consequence of the greater overall pressure of scepticism in the intellectual atmosphere of the late twentieth century than in seventeenth-century Europe.

For seventeenth-century contractarians, to understand political obligation through the idea of a contract had powerful attractions. It could explain why individual subjects of a legitimate government should be obliged to obey its laws by invoking their own acts and the determinations of their own wills (Riley 1982). The strongest answer that could be given to a political sceptic for why he should regard himself as politically obliged was that he had bound himself by his own acts. (Female sceptics were not yet thought to need an answer: a consideration still tacitly important in late-twentieth-century theories of social justice (cf. Kymlicka 1991).) The clearest example of a free choice binding the future acts of a human agent (or indeed a supra-human agent: Locke [1689] (1988, II, 195, p. 396): '*Grants, Promises* and *Oaths* are Bonds that hold the *Almighty*') was a promise or compact. To keep a promise, to observe covenants made, was both in itself a rational practice and a moral duty. It was above all the capacity to see the rationality of this duty which enabled human beings to live dependably with one another. It constituted the bond (*vinculum*) of human society. This view was common to thinkers who disagreed as sharply as Hobbes and Locke, both about the circumstances in which human beings could be validly inferred to have chosen to accept the authority of their government, about the degree of political subjection which it was rational for them to accept, and about the measure of mutual security afforded in practice by purely verbal undertakings. ('And Covenants, without the Sword, are but Words, and of no strength to secure a man at all' (Hobbes [1651] 1991, XVII, p. 1117).) Hence the overwhelming importance of the question why in the last instance human beings had good reason to keep their word: Locke's estimate of the menace of atheism ('The taking away of God, tho but even in thought dissolves all' (Locke [1689] 1983, p. 51)) and the practical foundations of Hobbes's bleakly minimalist 'laws of nature'. For seventeenth-century contractarians the issue of what human beings had good reason to do (the normative theory of rationality) was in the end inseparable from the question of how they should in practice be expected to behave.

It is the rejection of this connection, the modern epistemic presumption of a categorical disjunction between fact and value, drawn from Locke, Hume and Kant, which has thrust the issue of trust to the margins of modern political philosophy. The question of how human beings can be expected to behave is a matter of fact, consigned to social science. The question of how they should behave is a matter of value, to be decided by free and rational agents, perhaps in the light of the findings of the social sciences (whatever these might be), but in the end in terms of the reflective self-consciousness of an individual moral theorist. Whether human beings should keep their promises is a question of moral theory, with a range of possible answers: usually, sometimes yes, sometimes no. But whether they will do so is a quite separate question of fact, with no intrinsic implications for moral theory. This point of view has deep imaginative and theoretical roots; and it need carry no particular dismaying implications for morality seen as the assessment by individual human beings of how they have good reason to live their own lives. (The question of how dismaying its implications in fact are is simply a matter for future social scientists.) But it is appreciably more destructive to the attempt to understand the nature and significance of politics.

As it happens, the modern social sciences have not been at their most impressive when it comes to analysing either the conditions in which human beings do or do not trust one another or the consequences of their success or failure in doing so (Gambetta 1988). Until very recently, indeed, they have been remarkably unsuccessful even in grasping the practical importance virtually throughout human collective life of the extent to which human beings do trust one another on a small or large scale or of the degree to which their mutual confidence or distrust is well founded (but cf. Luhmann 1979, 1988). A focus on the significance of trust in human relations has been replaced by an image of the more or less rational pursuit of interest; and any attempt to restore that focus has come to suggest sentimentality or a residually feudal social imagination (Hawthorn 1988). This is not an unequivocal instance of intellectual progress. The model of rational pursuit of interest is illuminating enough as far as it goes. But it severely underemphasizes the epistemic difficulties which human beings face in identifying their interests in the first place, their modest capacity to pursue them effectively even in their own immediate environment, and the massive further obstacles which confront them in concerting together to pursue such interests in the refractory medium of political and economic competition. For creatures with the properties of human beings the problem of mutual trust today is no closer to the margins of practical life (no more narrowly domestic and personal) than it was in the high Middle Ages. It lies at the centre of all political processes; and it cannot be adequately modelled in terms of rational egoists pursuing clearly conceived individual interests.

Trust is both a passion (an affective condition, linked to expectations of others' future actions) and a policy (a method of dealing with the fact that most important human interests depend profoundly on the future free actions of other human beings). These are probably better seen over time as two ways of conceiving essentially the same reality, not as descriptions of two comprehensively distinguishable phenomena. (You are credulous; but I trust rationally.) The passion, plainly enough, can be disabling as well as enabling. (So too can its antithesis: a more or less acute or compulsive mistrust.) The question of whom to trust and how far is as central a question of political life as it is of personal life. Modern philosophy has essentially given up on this question (not just a concrete question of existential or political judgement, where seventeenth-century philosophers, no doubt, overestimated the epistemic resources available to them, but as a domain which requires philosophical comprehension precisely because no understanding of politics which did not do justice to it could in principle be coherent and well founded; but cf. now Baier (1994)). If it is right in committing itself to this by now rather deeply motivated imaginative option, we can be confident that the political contribution of academic philosophy (as opposed, for example to that of academic economics) will remain severely marginal (Dunn 1985, chapter 10; cf. Dunn 1990b). But can the option really be right?

There are several strong reasons for supposing that it is in fact right. In the first place, if human values are essentially human inventions, then even the most elegant and imaginatively attractive theory of human values could at best be only an especially impressive human invention, and one which would be impressive only in so far as other human beings happened to find it so. One reason why some seventeenth-century philosophers saw fidelity as a morally and epistemically decisive foundation for human relations was their confidence in the existence of an effective sanction for that virtue independently of the wills or mental processes of any human beings whatever. The Law of Nature was not merely a set of humanly beneficial precepts. It was also an authoritative, and in the last instance an effectively enforced command of nature's omniscient and omnipotent Creator. With the effective disappearance of the assumption that Nature was created for a purpose, and with the associated awareness of the variability in human values and social arrangements over time and space, it is hard today to believe that Nature has any Law, and quite hard to believe that human beings, in any politically illuminating sense, share a common nature. The Law of Nature specified a supra-political context for human politics and one within which that politics must, *ex hypothesi*, be understood (Dunn 1969). But few contemporary thinkers presume that there is in this sense any supra-political context for human politics, over and above the naturally given universe within which human beings still have to live: a setting to be understood, as best it can be, through the sciences of nature.

In the second place, in so far as trust must be conceived as a passion, its causal incidence must surely be understood (if at all) through the resources of the human sciences, the sciences of man envisaged as a natural creature living in society over time. What causes people to be able (or unable) to trust others is a no doubt complicated matter of fact. We may not yet have learnt much about it. But it can only be the human sciences (individual and social psychology, political science, sociology, anthropology, economics, the theory of games) that could teach us how to understand it.

In the third place, even if trust is viewed firmly as policy, a more or less consciously adopted strategy for dealing with the freedom of other human beings over time, any assessment of how far it is well or ill founded would have to distinguish given purposes and preoccupations sharply from available means. It would have, in effect, to endorse the values of particular human agents or groups (family, village, tribe, city, class, firm, nation, ideological movement) and ask how these values could be most effectively implemented in a heavily objectified social, economic and political setting, seen as a set of constraints upon and opportunities for the agents in question. Within this framework, values are taken as given (causal products of socialization of varying effectiveness) or as freely chosen: and policies of giving or withholding trust are monitored solely in terms of their strategic or tactical effectiveness. Contemporary philosophers aspire to ask clear and manageable questions and to answer them frankly and with some intellectual economy, passing firmly on to other clearly prescribed intellectual specialists responsibility for answering the parts which their own professional competence cannot reach. It would be silly to deny the cumulative intellectual advantages which have come from determined adoption of this policy. But in relation to politics the trade-off between these palpable cumulative benefits and the equally apparent cumulative costs of its adoption has been peculiarly unfavourable.

Why should this have proved so? Why, to take a somewhat tendentious example, should central elements in the political arguments of Hobbes and Locke three centuries later not merely have come to serve as leading themes in modern conceptions of political authority across the world but even been firmly incorporated into the practical structures of a large range of modern states (Skinner 1989; Dunn 1991, 1992; Fontana 1994)?

Why, by contrast, should the sophisticated modern theorization of social justice, the grounds for allocating the costs and benefits of social membership in a rationally defensible manner (which certainly addresses a central question in contemporary democratic politics), have been so readily brushed aside by the electorates of western democracies over the last fifteen years when they came to take their sovereign decisions?

There is no reason to suppose that either Hobbes or Locke (or, for that matter, Rousseau or Hegel) succeeded in providing a convincing theory of political obligation: or how far and why individual subjects of particular governments should see themselves as bound by (and not merely menaced by) the laws issued by those governments (Dunn 1980, 1991). It may well be the case that the leading western political philosophers of the last twenty years have asked clearer and more manageable questions than their great contractarian predecessors, and even that in some cases they have given neater and more convincing answers to these questions. But in contrast with the vividly political and often intuitively compelling efforts of these predecessors, they have been notably ineffectual in the suggestions they contrived to offer their readers for how the latter had good reason to act (Dunn 1980, chapter 10; Nagel 1991).

Unsympathetically considered, contemporary theorists of social justice have advanced moral theories about a distinctively political subject matter, and done so within an at least formally democratic space in which their own moral consciousness is, *ex hypothesi*, on a par with that of any of their readers. (It may be far better thought through; but it cannot carry any greater intrinsic authority.) They have advanced their theories, moreover, without attempting to develop an accompanying conception of the place of morality in human life (a modern analogue of the Law of Nature) that might give them some capacity to penetrate and re-order the moral consciousness of their readers (cf. Nagel 1991). But, more importantly, they have done so, too, without making any real effort to reconceive the nature of the political space within which that offer will be either accepted or rejected. In tacitly (or in some cases explicitly) presupposing a massively objectified and alienated vision of the nature of that space they have offered an apolitical answer to an intensely political question (cf. Unger 1987; Dunn 1990a).

If they are right in endorsing this massively objectified and alienated vision, their offer is pre-condemned to political futility. If they are wrong, they have been directing their moral and political imaginations on far too narrow a target to give their moral vision any real political chance. Whether they are in fact wrong may seem simply a question for others: in particular, the practitioners of the social sciences. It is clearly under active dispute amongst the latter. But it may well be a question which requires a more philosophical answer: not in the discredited sense of appeals to grandiose metaphysical structures but in the simpler sense of an answer that captures and relates clearly together the key elements in the subject under consideration. If a less alienated and objectified understanding of what politics is is epistemically appropriate, this will in the end be because what politics consists in (at least from a human point of view) is a huge array of free agents coping with each others' freedom over time. In politics so understood the rationality of trust will always be the most fundamental question.

REFERENCES

Baier, A. 1994. *Moral Prejudices*. Cambridge, Mass.: Harvard University Press
Ball, T., J. Farr, and R. Hanson 1989 (eds.). *Political Innovation and Conceptual Change*. Cambridge: Cambridge University Press
Barry, B. 1989. *Theories of Justice*. Hemel Hempstead: Harvester-Wheatsheaf
Dunn, J. 1969. *The Political Thought of John Locke*. Cambridge: Cambridge University Press
   1980. *Political Obligation in its Historical Context*. Cambridge: Cambridge University Press
   1985. *Rethinking Modern Political Theory*. Cambridge: Cambridge University Press
   1990a. *Interpreting Political Responsibility*. Cambridge: Polity Press
   1990b (ed.). *The Economic Limits to Modern Politics*. Cambridge: Cambridge University Press
   1991. 'Political obligation'. In *Political Theory Today*, ed. D. Held. Cambridge: Polity Press (Chapter 4 above)
1992 (ed.). *Democracy: The Unfinished Journey*. Oxford: Oxford University Press
Dworkin, R. 1977. *Taking Rights Seriously*. London: Duckworth
Fontana, B. (ed.) 1994. *The Invention of the Modern Republic*. Cambridge: Cambridge University Press
Gambetta, D. 1988. *Trust: Making and Breaking Cooperative Relations*. Oxford: Blackwell
Hawthorn, G. 1988. 'Three ironies in trust'. In *Trust: Making and Breaking Cooperative Relations*, ed. D. Gambetta, pp. 111–26. Oxford: Blackwell
Held, D. 1991. *Political Theory Today*. Cambridge: Polity Press
Hobbes, T. [1651] 1991. *Leviathan*, ed. R. Tuck. Cambridge: Cambridge University Press
Kymlicka, W. 1991. 'Rethinking the family'. *Philosophy and Public Affairs* 20, 77–97
Locke, J. [1689] 1983. *A Letter concerning Toleration*, ed. J. Tully. Indianapolis: Hackett
Locke, J. [1689] 1988. *Two Treatises of Government*, ed. P. Laslett. Cambridge: Cambridge University Press
Luhmann, N. 1979. *Trust and Power*, trans. H. David, J. Raffan and K. Rooney. Chichester: Wiley
   1988. 'Familiarity, confidence and trust'. In *Trust: Making and Breaking Cooperative Relations*, ed. D. Gambetta. Oxford: Blackwell

Nagel, T. 1991. *Equality and Partiality*. New York: Oxford University Press

Rawls, J. 1972. *A Theory of Justice*. Oxford: Oxford University Press

    1980. 'Kantian constructivism in moral theory'. *Journal of Philosophy* 77, 515–72

    1985. 'Justice as fairness: political not metaphysical'. *Philosophy and Public Affairs* 14, 223–51

    1993. *Political Liberalism*. New York: Columbia University Press

Riley, P. 1982. *Will and Political Legitimacy*. Cambridge, Mass.: Harvard University Press

Skinner, Q. 1989. 'The state'. In *Political Innovation and Conceptual Change*, ed. T. Ball, J. Farr and R. Hanson, pp. 90–131. Cambridge: Cambridge University Press

Taylor, C. 1989. *Sources of the Self*. Cambridge, Mass.: Harvard University Press

Tuck, R. 1979. *Natural Rights Theories: Their Origin and Development*. Cambridge: Cambridge University Press

Unger, R. M. 1987. *False Necessity*. Cambridge: Cambridge University Press

Williams, B. 1985. *Ethics and the Limits of Philosophy*. London: Fontana

6 The claim to freedom of conscience: freedom of speech, freedom of thought, freedom of worship?[1]

It is certainly easier to see the religious outcome of William of Orange's accession to the throne of England as an abatement in the practice of persecution than as a firm espousal of the principle of tolerance.[2] There remains ample disagreement about the implications of this aspect of the Revolution settlement; but there is relatively little dispute at present about its causes. Jonathan Clark, for example, has recently insisted at some length that the Revolution of 1688 left England as still very much an *ancien régime*, its national society firmly framed by a state founded upon the political privileges of its first two estates: the clergy of its state church and a landed aristocracy (Clark 1985, 1986). How much real light is shed by this comparison, either on the nature of English society itself or on the societies of Europe's absolutist monarchies, is eminently contestable (cf. esp. Innes 1987). But there is at least a measure of demythologizing astringency to the claim that post-Revolution England was every bit as much a confessional state as France had been during the protracted interval between the issuing and Revocation of the Edict of Nantes. In contrast with these residual ideological provocations, however, recent historians seem relatively united in their interpretations of the pressures that determined the form of the Revolution's religious settlement: a series of unelevated and provisional political solutions to what were plainly seen as delicate and highly immediate political problems.

There is nothing surprising about this. Nor, indeed, is there in the last instance anything necessarily inappropriate about it either. Toleration may often be claimed by human groups and individuals as a matter of right – of intrinsic entitlement. But it is only ever conceded by incumbent political authorities as a matter of practical political judgement. The *politique* advocacy of toleration was a highly self-conscious practical lesson drawn from the grim experience of sixteenth- and seventeenth-century

---

[1] I am very grateful for the advice and help, in connection with this chapter, of David Wootton and Quentin Skinner.
[2] Watts (1978, esp. pp. 222, 254); Speck (1988, pp. 40, 155, 172–4, but cf. p. 142); Miller (1973); Cragg (1957). For a more elegiac note, see Bennett (1975).

wars of religion. It was seen by its exponents as a discretionary concession on the part of the custodians of the state's absolute power; and both its scope and its limits were to be decided consistently on the basis of their own best judgement of the requirements for the effective discharge of their governmental responsibilities. Modern post-Kantian theories of entitlement to freedom of thought, judgement or speech tend to confine the perspective of governmental responsibility as narrowly as possible. But no coherent political theory of toleration can simply elide the perspective of governmental responsibility without committing itself, frankly or inadvertently, to anarchism – with all the fecklessness and aberration of political judgement which that commitment implies (cf. Dunn 1988a). In practice, also, there is no clear behavioural difference between the absence of persecution and the presence of toleration, or between the cessation of persecution and the commencement of toleration.

It is plainly of great moment for the understanding of England's social, religious and political history (and of even greater moment for an understanding of the history of the United Kingdom) to grasp just what the post-Revolution religious settlement meant in the lives of its inhabitants. Because of the European (and even the global) economic and political context of that settlement, it is also of great importance to understand its implications for the power, integration and vulnerability of the English state. But it is of some interest also to consider the settlement from a rather different angle. For the challenge which faced the English state in the aftermath of William's landing was also a particularly dramatic moment in the protracted shaping of modern conceptions of the legitimate scope of political authority. To consider it in this perspective we must concentrate our attention on the boldest and most trenchant attempts to formulate coherent principles for defining the limits of political authority over religious practice in the great crisis of European Protestantism that followed the Revocation of the Edict of Nantes (Prestwich 1985, Introduction and chapters 10–12; Labrousse 1985a; Dunn 1989). We must do so, of course, not because it was these sharply demarcated principles that directly determined the institutional forms of state regulation of religious activity, either then or later, in the history of England or anywhere else; but simply because the clarity with which these principles were articulated brings out the structure of a severely limited range of fundamental options in a way that the shiftier but more immediately consequential accommodations of professional politicians cannot hope to do.

To establish this structure of fundamental options we may consider two late-seventeenth-century texts, one composed before and one composed after the Revocation, and contrast their handling of the issues of freedom of conscience, worship, belief and speech with the shape that these assume in modern post-Kantian discussions of human entitlements to liberty. The principal focus will be upon a text composed in the immediate aftermath of the Revocation and first published after William of Orange had firmly occupied the English throne – John Locke's *Epistola de tolerantia* or, as it is better known in William Popple's bold, if sometimes inaccurate, translation, *A Letter concerning Toleration*.[3] But I shall contrast this deservedly famous text in one central respect with the viewpoint sustained in an earlier work by Locke's great Huguenot contemporary, Pierre Bayle, the *Pensées diverses sur la comète* (Bayle [1683] 1911).

The single most important feature of Locke's understanding of the principles and practice of toleration was the far greater trenchancy and determinacy of his conception of freedom of conscience as freedom of worship than as either freedom of speech or freedom of thought. In one crucial respect Locke always continued to see toleration in the last instance, as he had done in his earliest extended writings (Locke 1967), from an essentially *politique* point of view: as a practical issue of statecraft which no holder of state power could be freed from the responsibility of judging for himself. But by the time he wrote the *Epistola* he had come to combine this consistently (and very perceptively) political perspective with an unyielding conviction of the priority of individual religious duty over terrestrial public right. Because individual religious duty, in his view, must always dominate over any purely human exigencies, the responsibility of individual human agents to assess for themselves and to enact the forms of worship that God required of them always has rational priority over any possible coercive interventions by other human beings.[4] At least from the Christian revelation onwards, the political space of collective public life in any society at any time was a space of potential confrontation between two ineluctably present *loci* of judgement, the individual believer, interpreting the requirements for saving his own soul, and the political ruler, interpreting the demands of the public good.[5] Neither could escape the responsibility for making this judgement: and each, of course, might very easily prove to be wrong in the judgements at which he arrived. What there could not be in the last instance, in Locke's view, was

[3] Locke [1689] (1968). Locke [1689] (1983) reprints the Popple translation.
[4] For a practical instance, see Locke [1689] (1975, II, xxi, 57: p. 272): 'A neighbour Country has been of late a Tragical Theatre, from which we might fetch instances, if there needed any, and the World did not in all Countries and Ages furnish examples enough to confirm that received observation, *Necessitas cogit ad Turpia*.'
[5] Locke [1705–7] (1987, II, 524 n.13): 'it was by the positive law of God only that men knew that death was certainly annexed to sin as its certain and unavoidable punishment'. For the importance of this, see Locke [1689] (1975, esp. I, iii, 6: p. 69).

any coherent human mediation between the authority of these two judgements, if and where they came into serious conflict.

What, Locke asks, if the magistrate believes that what he commands
lies within the scope of his power and is useful to the commonwealth, but
his subjects believe the contrary? Who shall be judge between them?
'Respondeo: Solus Deus, quia inter legislatorem et populum nullus in
terris est judex' (Locke [1689] 1968, p. 128).

Of the two criteria in question, it is the issue of whether the magistrate's
commands do genuinely fall within the scope of his legitimate power that
is of primary importance in relation to toleration. Locke himself was consistently relaxed and pragmatic in his approach to the exercise of governmental responsibilities over purely terrestrial matters, fully recognizing
that interpretations of legitimate individual interest and of the public
good are bound to clash regularly amongst human beings, and amply
acknowledging the need for governments to judge the content of the
public good and defend their conception of that content in practice. The
chapter on prerogative in his *Second Treatise of Government* expresses this
recognition in an especially clear form.[6] But by the 1680s he was far from
supposing that the ruler's need to assess for himself the content of the
public good also gave him authority to decide for himself the scope of his
own legitimate power.[7] The central argument of the *Epistola de tolerantia* is
that, whatever the scope of the magistrate's legitimate power may reasonably be thought to be, the regulation of religious worship as such must lie
unequivocally beyond it. As we shall see, it is not obscure why Locke
thought this to be so. But before we consider his reasons for doing so, it is
necessary first to underline the political implications of his acknowledgement of the ruler's duty and entitlement to interpret the content of the
public good. For it is the combination of this apparently sympathetic
recognition of the practical responsibilities of rule with a fierce repudiation of any human being's right to impose his religious judgement upon
the religious judgement of any other human being which explains the
trenchancy of Locke's commitment to freedom of worship and the distinctly more muted support which he felt impelled to give to freedom of
thought, or speech, or private conduct.

Like his great but alarming predecessor Thomas Hobbes, Locke supposed that the central political problems of human societies are best
understood as arising less from men's limited mutual goodwill or the
practical disparities between their several interests (factors of which each

---

[6] Locke [1689] (1960, II, chapter XIV). See Dunn (1969, esp. chapter 11).
[7] For the best discussion of the political experience which led to this conviction, see
Ashcraft (1986).

was eminently aware) than from their persistent partiality and from the ineradicable source of that partiality in the individuality of human judgement. The actions of all men, as Hobbes pointed out in *De Cive*, 'are ruled by the opinions of each'.[8] All 'controversies are bred from hence, that the opinions of men differ concerning Meum & Tuum, just and unjust, profitable and unprofitable, good and evill, honest and dishonest, and the like, which every man esteems according to his own judgement'. It is this factor which necessitates the creation of a supreme power to establish common rules which apply authoritatively to all citizens and provide them with a clear public definition 'by which every man may know what may be called his, what anothers, what just, what unjust, what honest, what dishonest, what good, what evill, this is summarily, what is to be done, what to be avoyded in our common course of life'.[9]

As Hobbes emphasized, the partiality of human judgement is nowhere more evident and its practical importance nowhere more urgent than in the field of religion. 'There is scarce any Principle, neither in the worship of God, not humane sciences, from whence there may not spring dissentions, discords, reproaches, and by degree war it selfe; neither does this happen by reason of the falsehood of the Principle, but of the disposition of men, who seeming wise to themselves, will needs appear such to all others' (Hobbes [1642] 1983, p. 96). (Note the parallel in this respect between divine worship and systematic attempts to extend human knowledge.) In Hobbes's eyes the imperative need to restrain religious doctrines which 'require obedience to be given to others beside them to whom the supreme authority is committed' necessitates the clear supremacy of civil law in the interpretation of religious duty, not merely in the face of Pope or bishop, but also, as he put it, in the face of 'that liberty which the lower sort of Citizens under pretence of Religion doe challenge to themselves; for what civil war was there ever in the Christian world, which did not grow from, or was nourisht by this Root?'

Analytically, there is little, if anything, in this presentation with which Locke at any point in his life would have seriously disagreed. But by the 1680s there was one aspect of Hobbes's conclusion which he was utterly unwilling to accept. Unlike Hobbes, nothing would induce him to accord to the civil magistrate a right to prescribe the content of divine worship.

[8] Hobbes [1642] (1983, p. 95). (I quote throughout for convenience from this translation edited by Warrender despite its being in no sense authorized by Hobbes himself. The text can readily be compared with Hobbes's own Latin original in Warrender's companion volume.)

[9] Hobbes [1642] (1983). There is a helpful presentation of Locke's political theory as a response to the problems posed by the individuality of judgement in Grant (1987), deficient only in its underestimate of the significance of extraterrestrial sanctions in Locke's ethics.

The reason why no human being could ever possess the right to prescribe this content is exceedingly simple. Whether human beings worship individually or in association with one another, the goal of their worship is the attainment of eternal life.[10] This goal, in the familiar terms of Pascal, is of infinitely greater importance to any human being than any other possible object of his concern. This mortal condition, Locke insists, has nothing which can in any way serve to counterbalance that eternal condition (Locke [1689] 1968, p. 124). The case of each man's soul is fully within his own power and must be left to him alone.[11] In matters of the future life no ruler can repair the damage inflicted on a subject through miscalculation of his eternal interests, and no subject can be given the least security for his eternal fate by any other human being (Locke [1689] 1968, p. 94). A ruler who attempts to coerce his subjects in matters of religious practice is not merely displaying personal arrogance; he is also committing injustice by seeking to impose his own coercive authority on those who are in reality *alieni domini servos* – servants of another master (Locke [1689] 1968, p. 82) – or, as Locke put it in the *Second Treatise*, 'All the Servants of one Sovereign Master, sent into the World by his order and about his business': 'Primum debetur Deo obsequium, deinde legibus' (Locke [1689] 1960, II, 6: p. 289; Locke [1689] 1968, p. 126). It is to God that human beings owe their primary obedience, and only secondarily and derivatively to the laws of the political community to which they happen at the time to belong. The right to freedom of conscience in Locke's eyes is fundamentally a right to worship God in the way one judges that God requires: a right which follows from and is barely intelligible without the duty to do just that. Its priority over all other possible demands for a human agent likewise follows rigorously from the priority of the goal of attaining eternal life over all other human goals. It is a grotesque impertinence for any human political authority to intrude its inept and irrelevant pretensions into this overwhelmingly important individual preoccupation.

To clarify the scope of this argument, and to convince his readers that accepting it would not prove intolerably disruptive in practice, Locke develops a variety of subsidiary arguments. At least some of these provide grounds for a more expansive interpretation of the scope of freedom of conscience as freedom of thought or freedom of expression. But it is important to notice that Locke himself clearly repudiates this broader interpretation and that he does so for two quite distinct reasons.

---

[10] Locke [1689] (1968, p. 76; and see pp. 94, 116, 122).
[11] Locke [1689] (1968, p. 90). Note the robustly Arminian formulation. (See too p. 124: 'ad singulos solum salutis suae curam pertinere'.)

His first reason for doing so rests on his interpretation of the duties of the civil magistrate. Toleration is a privilege – an immunity from legal regulation – to which individuals are entitled because of the priority of their religious needs and duties over their secular obligations, and only in so far as their interpretation of these needs and duties in no way imperils the civil interests or rights of any of their fellow citizens. It is private religious practices, and theoretical beliefs about the point and proper conduct of these practices, which are thus entitled to toleration. Wherever even the sincerest of beliefs encroaches upon the interests or rights of others, it ceases to be intrinsically private; and it is the magistrate's responsibility to judge the incidence of such encroachments and to restrain them accordingly. The only sorts of opinions that cannot in principle encroach in this way are purely theoretical opinions. It is both absurd and futile for a magistrate to attempt to regulate purely theoretical opinions. But any opinion which has definite practical implications outside the restricted purlieus of private worship is perfectly capable of encroaching upon the interests and rights of others; and the magistrate must judge which opinions do possess such practical implications and when and where they are likely to encroach upon the public good. Having made this judgement, he must also do his best to prevent such encroachments in practice. He must do so, not because he is gifted with greater natural sagacity than his subjects possess, but because it is his responsibility to protect the rights of all his subjects and to exercise his judgement as best he can to provide this protection.

Locke's second reason for repudiating any general entitlement to freedom of thought (let alone to freedom of expression) is that at least some beliefs are an inherent menace to every other human being. The belief which he especially singles out, notoriously, is the belief that there *is* no God to worship: atheism. This is hardly an exclusion that any western society today would regard as furnishing a very handsome allowance of freedom for thought – even if it might still evoke some applause in Tehran. As an exclusion, moreover, it is certainly incompatible with at least one of the arguments that Locke himself regularly advances in favour of toleration – that human belief is not a voluntary affair: that no one can simply choose his beliefs or promptly alter them at the behest of another human being. It is important to register that this incompatibility does not represent a mere oversight on Locke's part but instead provides a clear index of the extremely restricted scope that he was prepared to allot to the argument that belief is not a discretionary matter.[12]

---

[12] For the importance of this topic for Locke, see Passmore (1978), and, above all, Tully (1988, pp. 12–71). Cf. the careful and illuminating treatment of this issue in Bayle and Arnauld in Kilcullen (1988).

The non-discretionary character of human belief at any particular time was not in itself a justification – indeed it was not even an *excuse* – for the content of that belief. The central purpose of Locke's greatest work, the *Essay concerning Human Understanding*, was to insist on the urgency and intricacy of the duty of each human being to *regulate* his assent to the content of his own beliefs, to make himself fully responsible for that content and to shape it meticulously and strenuously to fit the obdurate contours of external reality.[13] If Locke saw most of his contemporaries (as he would certainly have seen most of us) as living at the mercy of largely confused and disreputable beliefs, carelessly ingested from others, this was not a condition which he felt the least inclination to applaud. In his view atheism was an extreme example (a polar instance) of a belief to which it was inexcusable to succumb. There is no reason to suppose that he would have believed it any more within the power of an atheist to escape from the thrall of his nefarious beliefs by immediate voluntary choice than it would have been for any other human being to alter his beliefs instantaneously and at will. But it is clear (despite his freely expressed commitment to toleration for Jews, Muhammadans, Socinians, and even American Indians)[14] that he felt not a flicker of charity towards the predicament of a sincerely convinced atheist – an attitude all the less enticing given that he supposed such an atheist did not merely stand in danger of all the machinery of persecution levelled at the Huguenots but also faced the imminent prospect of intense pain in the aftermath of this life and of an eventual annihilation which at least the more fortunate of Christians could confidently hope to avoid.[15]

How, you may ask, in a work full of invocations of the Christian duty of charity and denunciations of supposedly religiously motivated atrocities – *ergastulum, carcer, capitis imminutio, bonorum sectio*[16] – did Locke contrive to sustain such a singularly odious attitude? There are two parts to the answer, neither of which quite suffices to elide the unprepossessing character of the attitude itself, but which, taken together, do at least serve to make it readily intelligible. The first is simply that the work in question is a

---

[13] See also, particularly, Locke (1762), first published posthumously but initially intended as an additional chapter for inclusion in the fourth edition of the *Essay*.

[14] See Locke [1689] (1968, pp. 104, 112, 114, 142, 144, 154).

[15] Cf. Pierre Bayle's notably sly use of critics of his thesis of the rights of erroneous conscience (Bayle [1727] 1966, II, p. 394 along with pp. 399–499). It is at least conceivable that Bayle intended these passages as a comment on the argument of the *Epistola*. On waning confidence in the prospect of eternal punishment amongst seventeenth-century thinkers, see, classically Walker (1964). Its political implications are best explored in a series of studies by Wootton (1983a, 1983b, 1986, 1988).

[16] Locke [1689] (1968, p. 138; and cf. p. 60): 'bonis exuant, corpora mutilent, carcere et paedore macerent, vita denique ipsa privent'. See also pp. 88, 90.

defence of religious toleration, of abstracting the coercive power of the
state from the practice of divine worship. Locke's ground for insisting on
the need for this abstraction, as we have already seen, was the clear priority of an individual's duty to worship God as he deemed fit over any possible duty to any terrestrial authority. Since an atheist, *ex hypothesi*,
repudiated the duty to worship God at all, he could have no such prior
responsibility which merited protection against all earthly power. The
right to worship as one chooses is just that. It cannot be interpreted as an
anachronistic cipher for a broader and more general entitlement to think
as one happens to think or to express one's thoughts as one feels inclined.
For all his eminently cogent doubts about the direct contribution that
human political authorities were in a position to make to the identification of the truth,[17] there was no sense whatever in which Locke recognized any such general right to think whatever one happens to think; and
he could only have regarded any such claim of right as hopelessly confused. (It is still perfectly possible, incidentally, that he would have been
entirely correct to do so.)

In any case, he was entirely consistent in supposing that it would have
been absurd for atheists to claim privileged immunity against the civil
power for the content of their beliefs on the grounds of the priority of religious duty over civil concerns:[18] 'Primum enim debetur Deo obsequium,
deinde legibus.'[19] But if these grounds were transparently unavailable, the
scope of civil authority over the expressed beliefs of an atheist was to be
determined exclusively by the magistrate's assessment of the public good.
Here, plainly Locke's own judgement of the practical menace of atheists
is eminently open to challenge; it was in fact challenged *avant la lettre* in
Bayle's markedly original text on the comet. It was also, evidently
enough, a judgement that few sincere atheists were at all likely to accept.
As I have tried to demonstrate elsewhere,[20] the reasons why Locke
himself regarded atheists as such a practical menace lie at the very
foundation of his thinking over almost half a century and rest ultimately
upon his despondent and disabused views about the structure of human
motivation and about the conflicts between the interests of human beings
seen simply as moral creatures within a natural world. It is possible that
these views are excessively pessimistic, though no one has yet given very
cogent reasons for supposing them to be so; and no one, quite certainly
has in any sense subsequently *demonstrated* that they are so. Where Locke

[17] Locke [1689] (1968, pp. 94, 122).
[18] Locke [1689] (1968, p. 134): 'Praeterea, nullum sibi religionis nomine vendicare potest
tolerantiae privilegium, qui omnem funditus tollit per atheismum religionem.'
[19] Locke [1689] (1968, p 126).
[20] Dunn (1969, 1984; 1985, chapters 1 and 2).

does strain the credulity of most readers today, by contrast, is in his remarkable optimism about the rectificatory services offered by the world to come.

His own estimation of the practical menace of atheism is best captured in Popple's ringing translation: 'Promises, Covenants, and Oaths, which are the Bonds of Humane Society, can have no hold upon an Atheist. The taking away of God, tho but even in thought, dissolves all.'[21] Believing this, Locke would certainly have been justified, on his own theoretical premises, had he ever had to exercise political authority in the matter himself, in refusing toleration to those who denied the existence of a God. But it is important to note that his reason for doing so was simply a personal opinion about a matter of fact. Personal opinions about matters of fact obviously cannot be eliminated from the exercise of governmental authority. But they are distressingly fallible; and the only privilege which they enjoy derives from the prudential preconditions for human beings to live with one another in reasonable peace and security.

In a complex, extensive and highly productive society like that of late-seventeenth-century England, Locke was very clear, human beings did not merely need known standing laws to regulate their relations with one another; they also required an impartial political authority to enforce these rules effectively upon the recalcitrant. But there was no guarantee that this need would be satisfied in practice. Most human political authority was far from impartial even in enforcing its own rules; and very many existing states had no true entitlement to the authority which they exerted. For a political authority to be legitimate, it must derive its title to rule from the consent of its subjects, fully acknowledge this consent as the source of its authority, and deploy the practical power which that authority conferred upon it solely to protect the rights of its subjects. As the *Epistola de tolerantia* painstakingly explains, the single most important right of any subject is the right to worship a deity in accordance with the dictates of his own faith. This is why it would be as much a violation of the *rights* of Jews or Muhammadans for a Christian ruler to interfere in their own authentic acts of worship, as it would for a Muhammadan ruler to interfere with Christian religious practice.[22] In matters of religious faith, physical force and coercive power have no legitimate place and

---

[21] Locke [1689] (1983, p. 51). (Tully's edition is the only accurate modern printing of the original text of Popple's translation and Tully's introduction gives a striking presentation of the historical significance of Locke's text.) For a contemporary appraisal of the degree to which Locke may have been right in his assessment see Gambetta (1988). For a sharp critique of the defensibility of the judgement on Locke's own premises, see Wootton (1989).

[22] Locke [1689] (1968, p. 114; and see pp. 104, 144). Cf. Bayle's treatment of the case of Christian missionary access to China in his *Commentaire philosophique sur les paroles de*

their introduction is necessarily a violation of right.²³ In this context the familiar claims to religious orthodoxy are the idlest cognitive self-congratulation: indices of a fatuous human complacency, not resonant vindications of a genuinely supra-human authority.²⁴ Louis XIV's proud goal of 'La France toute Catholique' was a self-indicting profession of worldly pride, not merely the misconceived interpretation of an individual monarch's religious obligations.²⁵ And, since it was linked so directly in practice to a programme of relentless persecution and to the devastation and depopulation of the defenceless Huguenot communities, it corroded irretrievably whatever claims to legitimacy the French monarch had previously enjoyed. There are few, Locke said in a consciously Tacitean echo, who will believe it to be peace where they see a desert made.²⁶

Tolerance towards those of different religious opinions and sentiments, as Locke insisted, is not merely an eminently Christian and rational virtue (p. 64); it is also a clear implication of the very different goals of church and state, and of the due limits of these two types of human association (pp. 64, 84). A commonwealth was simply a human association for the preservation and promotion of civil goods: life, liberty, bodily health and freedom from suffering, and external possessions (p. 66). A church, by contrast, was simply an association of human beings who shared a common opinion of the rules of faith and worship (p. 148). Religious opinion as such, whether true or false, can do nothing to endanger the civil goods of fellow citizens, and thus nothing to injure their rights. The private judgement of the magistrate gives him no new right to coerce his subjects; and, if he happens to believe that his commands fall within the scope of his legitimate authority but his subjects dissent from that judgement, it must be left to God's final judgement to determine which of the two is correct.²⁷ Since the conflict between ruler and subject in these circumstances cannot, *ex hypothesi*, be resolved through the impartial pro-

---

Jésus-Christ: Contrains-les d'entrer, pt I, chapter 5, and, more domestically, pt II, chapter 5. There is no convenient modern edition of Bayle's text, but see the modern American translation by Tannenbaum (1987) which I have cited throughout as the most readily accessible version for most readers. The *Commentaire philosophique* appears in Bayle [1727] (1966). There is an excellent study of the political force and scope of such reciprocity arguments, focused on Bayle's own deployment of them, in Kilcullen (1988).

²³ Locke [1689] (1968, p. 76): 'nulla hic, quaecunque de causa, adhibenda vis, quae omnis ad magistratum civilem pertinet', and see p. 132.

²⁴ Locke [1689] (1968, p. 5): 'sibi quisque orthodoxus est', and see pp. 96, 112.

²⁵ See Bayle [1686] (1973). And see Labrousse (1985b).

²⁶ Locke [1689] (1968, p. 130): 'quanquam pauci sint qui ubi solitudinem factam vident pacem credant'.

²⁷ Locke [1689] (1968, p. 128). Cf. the criteria for legitimate resistance developed in Locke [1689] (1960); Dunn (1969, chapter 13).

cedures of the law, it will, if pressed, be determined by force: that is to say, by civil war or revolution.

Because of the stark realism of this acknowledgement, it is essential to register clearly just what titles to restrict the religiously conceived beliefs and to control the religious associations of their subjects Locke does concede to the civil magistrate. There are two clear restrictions on the individual and collective immunity of subjects from the magistrate's coercive interventions. Both, in Locke's eyes, follow directly from the goal of political society and the responsibilities of a legitimate political authority. One restriction covers the potential intrusion of an alien sovereignty on to the political terrain of the commonwealth. Just as claims to monopolize religion or to deploy the state's coercive power for allegedly religious ends are an implicit threat to the rights to life and property of fellow citizens (Locke [1689] 1968, p. 132), so no church has any claim to tolerance, whose membership itself entails entry into the *clientela* of a foreign prince.[28] Those who defend the right (or even the duty) to break faith with heretics or depose rulers whom they judge unorthodox can scarcely complain if the heretics or rulers in question feel fully entitled to defend themselves. It is only when it does *not* constitute a direct threat to a legitimate political order that the most vivid and sincere of religious convictions has any clear claim to toleration. And since it is the ruler's responsibility to judge where it does constitute such a threat, no politically engaged confessional allegiance enjoys much protection in the face of his anxieties: as Locke says, no church can serve as a sanctuary for faction, sedition and vice.[29] Not only are externally aligned religious confessions in no way entitled to profess or act upon their strictly political convictions; it is also quite unclear whether their purely religious freedoms are at all amply secured. Locke's position on this point is less than clear and not evidently consistent. But it has behind it such an accumulated weight of political anxiety and such a vehement English chauvinism that there is little obscurity as to why he held it. What needs to be noted about it, from the perspective of today, is what a feeble defence it could possibly afford, amid the swirling ideological struggles of the late twentieth century, for many of the most urgent claims to freedom of thought or speech on political questions.

The second restriction that Locke acknowledges on the immunity of subjects' religious convictions from the coercive interventions of the magistrate is, if anything, of even greater contemporary moment. The reason

[28] Locke [1689] (1968, pp. 132, 134). Cf. Dunn (1969, pp. 37–40); and for the English background see Miller (1973) and Ashcraft (1986).
[29] Locke [1689] (1968, p. 142). This echoes a central contention of Locke's earliest writings: see especially Locke (1967, p. 160).

why the purely theoretical doctrines of any church were, in his eyes, fully entitled to toleration was not just because the attempt to modify them by applying coercive power is inherently futile (a point on which Locke was perhaps a trifle overoptimistic and on which his antagonist Jonas Proast pressed him uncomfortably hard). Rather, it was because purely theoretical beliefs cannot, *ex hypothesi*, damage the rights of fellow citizens.[30] But practical beliefs – beliefs which affect how human beings have good reason to act – carry no such guarantee of harmlessness. It is a central responsibility of the magistrate to watch vigilantly over potential future threats to the civil goods of his subjects. When we examine Locke's own conception of where such threats may lie, it is immediately evident that he felt not the slightest hesitation in sanctioning the magistrate's intervention in many areas of belief and expression that are of the keenest concern to modern defenders of individual freedom.

What the commonwealth as such demands of human beings is that they be honest (*probos*), peaceful and industrious (Locke [1689] 1968, p. 144). It is because of its presumed threat to probity, its corrosive effect upon the binding force of mutual human commitments, in Locke's view, that atheism was so plainly incompatible with the requirements for human society. Any other practical opinions taught in a church, however erroneous they may be, ought to be tolerated, unless they aim at domination over others or at civil impunity (p. 134). It is easy enough to see why threats to peace or to the liberty of fellow citizens fall within the coercive responsibilities of the magistrate. But the precise scope of the latter's entitlement to enforce his conception of probity or industry is harder to identify. Avarice, failure to relieve the needs of others, and idleness are all in Locke's view sins. But none of them ought to be punished by the magistrate because none prejudices the rights of others or disturbs the public peace.[31] Earlier in the *Epistola* Locke had taken the example of an individual's fecklessness over health or financial imprudence as instances in which it was plainly inappropriate as well as futile for the civil law to intervene. No man can be compelled to be healthy or rich against his own will: 'Shall the magistrate provide by an express law against a man becoming poor or sick?' (Locke [1689] 1968, p. 90). But it is notorious that in his own later service on the Board of Trade Locke himself was prepared to advocate the most draconic interference with the rights of at least some of his fellow citizens to be poor in their own way (cf. Fox Bourne 1876, II, pp.

---

[30] Locke [1689] (1968, p. 120). This point is not adequately attended to in Waldron (1988, esp. p. 86).

[31] Locke [1689] (1968, p. 114). In the case of failure to relieve the needs of others (neglect of the duty of charity), this judgement is important and not obviously consistent with views which Locke expressed elsewhere.

377–91). The concern of the commonwealth with industry is plainly not to be taken lightly.

It should certainly be set beside the recurrent indications throughout the *Epistola* that there were other forms of conduct, and more particularly sexual conduct, which Locke was quite unprepared to tolerate, even where they were undertaken under supposedly religious inspiration. 'Plunging into promiscuity (*in promiscua stupra ruere*)'[32] is not lawful at home or in civil life, and is therefore no more lawful on religious pretexts or in an ecclesiastical setting. Anything harmful to the commonwealth can and should be forbidden in common life by public laws enacted for the common good by the magistrate (Locke [1689] 1968, p. 110). It is his responsibility to ensure that the commonwealth is protected from harm (p. 120). Purely speculative beliefs cannot entrench on the civil rights or property of others; and they cannot and will not be altered by the threat of force. But to be confident of immunity from the magistrate's attentions the members of Locke's society must be at pains to avoid not merely sedition, murder, theft and slander, but also, for example, adultery (p. 142). Furthermore (since adultery is presumably an example of a civil wrong as well as a sin), they should be at pains to exhibit '*mores casti et inculpati*'. Certainly Locke stood some little distance away from Professor Dworkin's subtle and far from unsympathetic exploration of the view that there may be a *right* to pornography, and that this right may simply follow from the fundamental human claim to equality.[33]

I have tried to show how strong the case which Locke developed for religious toleration in the Europe of the 1680s really was, and how weak, by contrast, the protection which that case would have offered for many eagerly proclaimed contemporary instances of freedom of personal choice, freedom of expression, and in the last instance even freedom of thought.

In this respect at least there is remarkably little gap between Locke and his Huguenot contemporary Pierre Bayle. Bayle is certainly a harder thinker to interpret confidently from the perspective of today than is Locke; and he left a far less illuminating manuscript legacy behind him than Locke was helpful enough to do. His favoured format for developing his views is often highly elusive: notably in the case of the articles of the great *Dictionnaire historique et critique*. His acute scepticism and intensely

---

[32] Locke [1689] (1968, p. 108). But cf. Bayle's own uneasiness on this point in *Commentaire philosophique*, pt II, chapter ix in Bayle [1727] (1966, II, p. 431; Tannenbaum 1987, p. 168).

[33] Cf. Dworkin (1981). Cf. Bayle's treatment of the threat of conscientious sodomy in *Commentaire philosophique*, pt II, chapter ix in Bayle [1727] (1966, II p. 431; Tannenbaum 1987, p. 168).

ambivalent religious sensibility consort very oddly together; and the relation between them baffles most modern readers.[34]

But at least in one respect his views are impressively clear. In the famous discussions of the practical implications of atheism in the *Pensées diverses sur la comète*, published, of course, before the Revocation, and addressed to wider and humanly less pressing issues than those of mass religious persecution, Bayle dissented categorically from the view which Locke was to express on the practical menace of atheism.[35] Not only are some well-known atheists figures of conspicuous virtue (in sad contrast with many well-known Christians). In addition, the entire psychological basis of the view that atheists should be *expected* to act viciously is radically misconceived. The true motive force of a man's actions is very different from his religion (Bayle [1727] 1966, p. 132). Believers all too often fail to act at all as they should. Unbelievers, like Spinoza, 'le plus grand Athée qui ait jamais été' (Bayle [1727] 1966, p. 134), are capable of imposing levels of rectitude. There simply is no coherent relation whatever between religious faith and moral dependability.[36]

In two eloquent works, published in the wake of the Revocation, he set out a bitter indictment of the realities of *Ce que c'est que la France toute Catholique sous le règne de Louis le Grand* and savaged the Christian pretensions of the policy of enforced conversion grounded over a millennium earlier by St Augustine on the notorious gospel text: 'Compel them to come in.' The second of these, the *Commentaire philosophique*, although it was composed after the greater part of Locke's *Epistola*, was published over a year before this. It shares a wide range of arguments with Locke's text, arguments which certainly echoed sentiments and perceptions that were widely shared in Holland in the wake of the Edict of Fontainebleau and the sharp increase in the tempo of the persecutions. The ghastly death of Bayle's own brother, and the horrors that had recently befallen both his

---

[34] There is no commanding analysis of Bayle's thought as a whole. For interpretations of his views on religion and politics see, *inter alia*, Labrousse (1963–4); Labrousse (1982); Rex (1965); Sandberg (1966); Mason (1963); Jossua (1965); Cantelli (1969).

[35] Bayle [1727] (1966, II, pp. 5–6, 8–9, 11, 17, 36–7, 77–8, 102–3, 107–14, 117–19).

[36] Nor is this disjunction between professed religiosity and personal trustworthiness purely a matter of individual disposition. It extended equally to entire systems of religious belief. It was a property of complete religions as much as one of persons. See, for example, *Continuation des pensées diverses* in Bayle [1727] (1966, III, p. 362): for most Christians, so far from their being especially pacific and eager to compete in observing the precepts of the Gospel, 'leur émulation ne va qu'à se surpasser dans l'art militaire, & dans celui de s'enrichir, & dans celui de mieux tendre une piege par les ruses de la politique … Les Infidels sont des novices en comparaison des Chrétiens dans les ruses du commerce, dans celles de la négociation, dans l'art cruel et barbare de l'artillerie, & dans la piraterie.' What really distinguished Christianity from other religious cultures by the late seventeenth century was that it had (as it were) the Maxim gun, whilst the others as yet did not.

family and the community from which he came, gave these works a remarkable emotional charge. But they also naturally focused Bayle's attention away from the relation between minimal human dependability and religious conviction and towards the enormity of applying human cruelty to deform the expression of religious devotion. What Bayle defends in these works is certainly, as he says himself, liberty of conscience. But it is very much liberty of conscience as the right of private worship in accordance with the convictions of the worshipper (a right which he points out was explicitly conceded even in the Edict of Fontainebleau) (Bayle [1686] 1973, p. 56). Whatever may have been true about Bayle's purely private convictions, a matter on which his distinguished biographer's judgement appears to have become more confident over the years,[37] there is no doubt that his attack upon religious persecution was developed in explicitly religious terms, and that it was in no sense a defence of a secular way of life or of individual rights of political agency.[38] Whilst in some ways more consistent than Locke – as in his respect for the sincere (and presumably involuntary) convictions of the atheist – it is of the greatest importance that Bayle was also consistently politically quietist; and that his publicly proclaimed regard for liberty of conscience rested solidly and obtrusively on his expressed faith in the Christian revelation. The authority of even the most erroneous conscience[39] derives from its status as adjudicator for each individual of the demands that God places upon them: not as the psychological locus of a purely human self-righteousness, but as the immediate judge of the content of religious duty. In the *Commentaire philosophique*, accordingly, even Bayle himself affirms clearly (if a trifle ambivalently) that no atheist is in fact entitled to protection from a disapproving civil power, and, more

---

[37] Cf. Bayle [1686] (1973, p. 25) with Labrousse (1983).

[38] See Labrousse's argument in Bayle [1686] (1973, pp. 20–1) and Labrousse (1983, pp. 84–5). Her assessment of Locke's theory in each case is less carefully informed. It is important, however, to be clear that Bayle's adoption of a religious framework for the defence of the most erroneous of consciences against religious persecution does not in itself establish the authenticity of his own faith. There was a very large amount of religious persecution actively going on; and the prospects for arresting this with any rapidity by recommending radical secularization were profoundly unpromising. Cf. Wootton (1988, esp. pp. 710–11, 724), following Skinner (1969, esp. pp. 33–5). See also Cantelli (1969, chapters 7–10).

[39] See *Addition aux pensées diverses sur les comètes* (1694) in Bayle [1727] (1966, III, pp. 179–80) and *Commentaire philosophique*, pt II, chapters 8–11 in Bayle [1727] (1966, II). For conscience as interpreter of God's requirements for human agents, see *Commentaire*, pt I, chapter 2 (Bayle [1727] 1966, II, p. 371; Tannenbaum 1987, p. 35); chapter 5 (Bayle [1727] 1966, II, p. 379; Tannenbaum 1987, pp. 55–6); chapter 6 (Bayle [1727] 1966, II, p. 384–5; Tannenbaum 1987, pp. 66–7); pt II, chapter 4 (Bayle [1727] 1966, II, p. 410; Tannenbaum 1987, p. 123); chapter 7 (Bayle [1727] 1966, II, p. 420; Tannenbaum 1987, p. 146); chapter 8 (Bayle [1727] 1966, II, p. 425; Tannenbaum 1987, pp. 151–6); chapter 9 (Bayle [1727]

trenchantly, that no atheist can claim for his own belief the shelter, decisively available to every Christian conscience, of St Peter's injunction to obey God rather than man.[40]

There are two broad (and very different) foundations for modern secular defences of entitlement to freedom of thought and speech. One is the severely a priori respect for the capacity of every minimally viable human adult to judge for herself what she does in fact believe. Still more precariously (if more inspiringly), it is the ideal of human autonomy itself – the normative goal of judging and choosing fully and consciously for oneself. The great hero of this intellectual tradition is the German Protestant philosopher Immanuel Kant; and it is his modern American followers, particularly John Rawls and Ronald Dworkin, who have done most to make human autonomy the master ideal of modern liberal ethics.[41]

The second, and in many ways less precarious, foundation is the value which Benjamin Constant christened 'modern liberty' – the practical freedom to live as one chooses and act as happens to please one – which is the dominating value of modern commercial societies[42] and which by now has behind it the accumulated political power drawn from their remarkable economic success. The best philosophical expression of this value (though not one which Constant himself fully accepted) is utilitarianism. It remains correct to associate this conception of human value, as John Stuart Mill does, with the more elaborate consequentialist arguments for the practical benefits of liberty of thought and expression.[43] A modern *politique* interpretation of the problem of regulating opinion and assent, as Mr Gorbachev saw at least as clearly as Mrs Thatcher, leans heavily on the cumulative practical costs, within the

1966, II, pp. 429–39; Tannenbaum 1987, p. 165); chapter 10 (Bayle [1727] 1966, II, pp. 436–7, esp p. 437; Tannenbaum 1987, p. 179): on ne peut gueres consulter l'idée de l'ordre, sans comprendre distinctement, que la seule loi que Dieu, selon son infinie sagesse, ait pû imposer à l'homme à l'égard de la verité, est d'aimer tout objet qui lui paroîtroit véritable, après avoir emploié toutes ses lumieres pour le discerner'.

[40] *Commentaire*, pt II, chapter 9 in Bayle [1727] (1966, II, p. 431; Tannenbaum 1987, p. 167): 'Un Athée, destitué qu'il est de cette grande protection, demeure justement exposé à toute la rigueur des loix, & dès aussi-tôt qu'il voudra répandre ses sentiments contre la défense qui lui en sera faite, il pourra être châtié comme un séditieux, qui ne croïant rien au dessus des loix humaines, ose néanmoins les fouler aux piez.'

[41] Rawls (1972); Dworkin (1977, 1986). For an especially powerful and carefully argued interpretation of the political implications of taking autonomy as master value, see Raz (1988) and more fully in Raz (1986, esp. chapters 14 and 15).

[42] Constant (1820, pp. 238–74). There is an excellent presentation of Constant's political works in English in Constant [1819] (1988).

[43] Mill (1910). See Gray (1983). The most impressive recent interpretation of an essentially utilitarian conception of the nature of human value is Parfit (1984) (very thin on the significance of politics).

complex productive systems of the 1980s, of interfering with intellectual inquiry or with the deeply held sentiments of the populace at large.

Where modern societies happen to find themselves peaceful and prosperous, the temptation to impose the ruler's conception of how human beings ought to be happy[44] and of what they should believe upon the remainder of the population becomes progressively less urgent; and the economic and political disadvantages of insisting on doing so become steadily more blatant. But even the most modern of societies will not always find itself both peaceful and prosperous; and the loosely pragmatist ecology within which modern liberty blossoms so abundantly offers a decidedly feebler protection in the face of sharper political conflict (cf. Dunn 1988b). It does so, more especially, where political belief and expression is reasonably judged to pose a direct threat to the incumbent state power. Then, as we have seen in recent years in Chile or Argentina or Iran or Kampuchea or Turkey, the hideous modern technology of persecution, with its torture chambers and electrodes, and its grotesque *mélange* of cruelty and absurdity, can more than match Locke's *ergastulum*, *carcer*, and *capitis imminutio*. At this stage modern secular regard for the dignity of human judgement, with its elusive blend of pragmatism and relativism, seldom retains the authority which Kant claimed for it.

In the face of acute political conflict the charms of modern contractarian conceptions of justice as a moral ideal are largely offset by their debility as strictly political arguments. The holders of state power judge the demands of the public good by their own criteria (as indeed they must).[45] And between them and their suffering victims there is still no judge upon earth. Within a secular world, as Hobbes explained very well, and as both Locke and Bayle implicitly acknowledged, the right of human beings to voice their own thoughts in public can be no higher than the political viability of the society to which they belong and in which they seek to do so.

In this perspective, perhaps, the shabby accommodation of the Revolution's religious settlement is less open to easy condescension than many like to suppose. Certainly it clashes discomfitingly with modern secular conceptions of a good society and falls some distance short of what either Locke or Bayle saw as the requirements for a genuinely Christian society. But in the circumstances prevailing it did in fact abate the practice of persecution;[46] and it proved in retrospect to have done so for rather a long time. Even today, as Queen Elizabeth II pointed out on

---

[44] Cf. Kant [1793] (1970, p. 83).
[45] What other criteria could it make sense for them to judge by?
[46] Watts (1978, chapters 3–5). Cf. not merely the *dragonnades* (Labrousse 1985b, pp. 308–13; Claude 1686) but also the Popish Plot (Kenyon 1974).

a suitably ceremonial occasion three hundred years later,[47] the level of strictly religious tolerance actually provided by the United Kingdom for many of our fellow citizens is still distressingly partial and insecure. With or without the rectificatory services of the Deity, living civilly and tolerantly with beliefs and practices which we find abhorrent remains an extremely demanding practical challenge for all human beings. There is every reason to expect it to remain so for the rest of human time.

REFERENCES

Ashcraft, R. 1986. *Revolutionary Politics and Locke's Two Treatises of Government.* Princeton: Princeton University Press
Bayle, P. [1683] 1911. *Pensées diverses sur la comète,* ed. A. Prat. Paris: E. Cornély
  [1686] 1973. *Ce que c'est que la France toute Catholique sous le règne de Louis le Grand,* ed. E. Labrousse. Paris: J. Vrin
  [1727] 1966. *Continuation des pensées diverses* (*oeuvres diverses,* ed. E. Labrousse and G. Olms, 5 vols. Hildesheim: G. Olms)
Bennett, G. V. 1975. *The Tory Crisis in Church and State, 1688–1730.* Oxford: Clarendon Press
Cantelli, G. 1969. *Teologia e ateismo: Saggio sul pensiero filosofico e religioso di Pierre Bayle.* Florence: La Nuova Italia Editrice
Clark, J. C. D. 1985. *English Society, 1688–1832.* Cambridge: Cambridge University Press
  1986. *Revolution and Rebellion.* Cambridge: Cambridge University Press
Claude, M. 1686. *Les Plaintes des Protestans, cruellement opprimez dans le Royaume de France.* Cologne: Pierre Marteau
Constant, B. [1819] 1988. *Political Writings,* ed. B. Fontana. Cambridge: Cambridge University Press
  1820. 'De la liberté des Anciens comparée à celle des Modernes'. *Cours de politique constitutionelle,* IV, pt 8. Paris: Bechet
Cragg, G. R. 1957. *Puritanism in the Period of the Great Persecution 1660–1688.* Cambridge: Cambridge University Press
Dunn, J. 1969. *The Political Thought of John Locke.* Cambridge: Cambridge University Press
  1984. *Locke.* Oxford: Oxford University Press
  1985. *Rethinking Modern Political Theory.* Cambridge: Cambridge University Press
  1988a. 'Trust and political agency'. In *Trust: Making and Breaking Cooperative Relations,* ed. D. Gambetta, pp. 73–93. Oxford

---

[47] Queen Elizabeth II to Parliament, Wed. 20 July 1988 (*Daily Telegraph,* 21 July 1988, p. 6): 'The Glorious Revolution won its title because it was initially achieved without loss of life, and with wide popular support. It also marked the beginnings of a new era of religious tolerance. No one could claim that that state has been perfected. In multi-cultural Britain, there is still a long way to go.' The key question is in what direction. It is a nice point whether or not Locke's theory would today favour extending the blasphemy laws to cover the Koran.

1988b. 'Rights and political conflict'. In *Civil Liberties in Conflict*, ed. L. Gostin, pp. 21–38. London: Routledge

1989. '"Bright enough for all our purposes": John Locke's conception of a civilized society'. *Notes and Records of the Royal Society* 43, 2, 133–53

Dworkin, R. 1977. *Taking Rights Seriously*. London: Duckworth

1981. 'Is there a right to pornography?' *Oxford Journal of Legal Studies* 1, 177–212

1986. *Law's Empire*. London: Fontana

Fox Bourne, H. R. 1876. *The Life of John Locke*, 2 vols. London: Henry S. King

Gambetta, D. 1988. *Trust: Making and Breaking Cooperative Relations*. Oxford: Blackwell

Grant, R. W. 1987. *John Locke's Liberalism*. Chicago: University of Chicago Press

Gray, J. 1983. *Mill on Liberty: A Defence*. London: Routledge

Hobbes, T. [1642] 1983. *De Cive*, ed. H. Warrender. Oxford: Clarendon Press

Innes, J. 1987. 'Review article: Jonathan Clark, Social History and England's "Ancien Régime"'. *Past and Present* 115, 165–200

Jossua, J.-P. 1965. 'Pierre Bayle, précurseur des théologies modernes de la liberté religieuse'. *Revue des sciences religieuses*, April, 113–57

Kant, I. [1793] 1970. 'On the common saying "This may be true in theory, but it does not apply in practice"'. In *Political Writings*, ed. H. Reiss. Cambridge: Cambridge University Press

Kenyon, J. P. 1974. *The Popish Plot*. Harmondsworth: Penguin

Kilcullen, J. 1988. *Sincerity and Truth: Essays on Arnauld, Bayle, and Toleration*. Oxford: Clarendon Press

Labrousse, E. 1963–4. *Pierre Bayle*. Paris: Martinus Nijhoff

1982. 'The political ideas of the Huguenot diaspora (Bayle and Jurieu)'. In *Church, State and Society under the Bourbon Kings of France*, ed. R. M. Golden, pp. 222–83. Lawrence, Kansas: Colorado Press

1983. *Bayle*, trans. D. Potts. Oxford: Oxford University Press

1985a. *'Une foi, une loi, un roi?': Essai sur la révocation de l'Edit de Nantes*. Paris: Payot

1985b. 'Calvinism in France 1598–1685'. In *International Calvinism 1541–1715*, ed. M. Prestwich, pp. 285–314. Oxford: Clarendon Press

Locke, J. [1689] 1960. *Two Treatises of Government*, ed. P. Laslett. Cambridge: Cambridge University Press

[1689] 1968. *Epistola de tolerantia*, ed. R. Klibansky and J. W. Gough. Oxford: Clarendon Press

[1689] 1975. *An Essay concerning Human Understanding*, ed. P. Nidditch. Oxford: Clarendon Press

[1689] 1983. *A Letter concerning Toleration*, ed. J. H. Tully. Indianapolis: Hackett

[1705–7] 1987. *A Paraphrase and Notes on the Epistles of St Paul*, ed. A. Wainwright. Oxford: Clarendon Press

[1706] 1762. *Some Thoughts on the Conduct of the Understanding in the Search for Truth*. London

Locke, J. 1967. *Two Tracts on Government*, ed. P. Abrams. Cambridge: Cambridge University Press

Mason, H. T. 1963. 'Pierre Bayle's religious views'. *French Studies* 1713, 205–17

Mill, J. S. 1910. *Utilitarianism* and *On Liberty*. London: Dent

Miller, J. 1973. *Popery and Politics, 1660–1688*. Cambridge: Cambridge University Press

Parfit, D. 1984. *Reasons and Persons*. Oxford: Clarendon Press

Passmore, J. 1978. 'Locke and the ethics of belief'. *Proceedings of the British Academy* 64, 185–208

Prestwich, M. 1985 (ed.). *International Calvinism 1541–1715*. Oxford: Clarendon Press

Rawls, J. 1972. *A Theory of Justice*. Oxford: Clarendon Press

Raz, J. 1986. *The Morality of Freedom*. Oxford: Clarendon Press

    1988. 'Autonomy, toleration and the "harm principle"'. In *Justifying Toleration: Conceptual and Historical Perspectives*, ed. S. Mendus. Cambridge: Cambridge University Press

Rex, W. 1965. *Essays on Pierre Bayle and Religious Controversy*. The Hague: Martinus Nijhoff

Sandberg, K. C. 1966. *At the Crossroads of Faith and Reason: An Essay on Pierre Bayle*. Tucson, Arizona: University of Arizona Press

Skinner, Q. 1969. 'Meaning and understanding in the history of ideas'. *History and Theory* 8, 3–53

Speck, W. A. 1988. *Reluctant Revolutionaries: Englishmen and the Revolution of 1688*. Oxford: Oxford University Press

Tannenbaum, A. G. 1987. *Pierre Bayle's Philosophical Commentary: A Modern Translation and Critical Interpretation*. New York: Peter Lang

Tully, J. 1988. 'Governing conduct'. In *Conscience and Casuistry in Early Modern Europe*, ed. E. Leites. Cambridge: Cambridge University Press

Waldron, J. 1988. 'Locke: toleration and the rationality of persecution'. In *Justifying Toleration: Conceptual and Historical Perspectives*, ed. S. Mendus, pp. 61–86. Cambridge: Cambridge University Press

Walker, D. P. 1964. *The Decline of Hell*. London: Routledge and Kegan Paul

Watts, M. R. 1978. *The Dissenters: From the Reformation to the French Revolution*. Oxford: Clarendon Press

Wootton, D. 1983a. *Paolo Sarpi: Between Renaissance and Enlightenment*. Cambridge: Cambridge University Press

    1983b. 'The fear of God in early modern political theory'. *Historical Papers* (Canadian Historical Society), 56–80

    1986. *Divine Right and Democracy*. Harmondsworth: Penguin

    1988. 'Lucien Febvre and the problem of unbelief in the early modern period'. *Journal of Modern History* 60, 695–730

    1989. 'John Locke: Socinian or natural law theorist?' In *Religion, Secularization and Political Thought*, ed. J. E. Crimmins. London: Routledge

7 Property, justice and common good after socialism[1]

In his recent and impressively lucid analysis of *The Right to Private Property* Jeremy Waldron (1988) takes as his central challenge a question which extends back at least to Plato and Aristotle. As Aristotle expressed it in *The Politics*: 'What are the best arrangements to make about property, if a State is to be as well constituted as it is possible to make it? Is property to be held in common or not?' In the present century the contest between defenders of private and common property has frequently appeared as the principal issue in world politics and it has long been a pressing concern in the domestic politics of Great Britain. (It would certainly take more than Mrs Thatcher to eliminate it from the latter arena.) In the course of the presidencies of Ronald Reagan and Mikhail Gorbachev and of the premiership of Mrs Thatcher it has come to be widely assumed that this contest has reached a decisive outcome. Economies organized largely on the basis of common property, it is now all but universally agreed, cannot assure the prosperity of modern populations; and because they cannot assure their prosperity cannot, in the long run, guarantee their security either. Since the overweening claims to authority made by modern states depend directly for their cogency upon these states' capacity to secure the welfare and safety of their citizens (cf. Dunn 1990a, 1990b), the custodians of modern state power have little choice in eschewing common ownership as a dominant principle in the organization of production. They may still choose to acknowledge this practical constraint with better or worse grace. But they flout it at their peril.

Common ownership as the organizing principle of a system of production might in due course be resuscitated by a clear demonstration of its practical efficiency (a demonstration that may or may not lie within the bounds of natural possibility – be compatible with the laws of nature – but which is scarcely imminent).[2] What is decidedly less clear is that common

---

[1] The immediate stimulus for this essay was provided by a talk by Ernest Gellner in King's College, Cambridge in October 1989 on the prospects for *perestroika* in the USSR.
[2] Cf., for example, Hahn (1990).

ownership can be as readily abandoned as the ultimate justifying principle of a system of distribution. Modern liberal theories of social justice, as classically expressed by John Rawls[3] and as powerfully elaborated over the last decade by writers like Ronald Dworkin and Brian Barry (Dworkin 1977, 1985; Barry 1989) cannot be said to have had much practical impact upon the historical process. But the demise of common ownership in the field of production has not appreciably lessened its imaginative appeal in the domain of distributive justice, despite the intensive political exertions of those who deplore it in either guise or who deny that it can coherently operate in the one domain without covertly doing so in the other also. Yet why should it prove any more durable in the one case than it has in the other?

One simple and reasonably cogent answer is that common ownership signifies something entirely different in the two domains. (If this is valid, it casts grave doubt on the argument, shared both by Marxists and by defenders of the market as a comprehensive principle of social organization, that the two domains are tightly coupled causally to one another: with the organization of production dictating unique terms of distribution of its own.) What renders the principle of common ownership of most of the means of production massively unattractive in the late twentieth century is a strictly causal matter: that it appears at present levels of human comprehension and skill (and perhaps at any naturally possible levels of these) to preclude efficient production.[4] But the principle of common ownership in the domain of distribution is not in itself a causal hypothesis. It does not predict definite consequences for given actions, still less assert a guaranteed benefit from particular lines of conduct, or even from the pursuit of particular social goals. Instead, it simply affirms a criterion for publicly avowable and morally defensible social goals: the interests of at least all the human beings concerned. This criterion certainly raises clear problems about the scope of putative ownership, jeopardizing the status of the territorial state as the uniquely appropriate frame of distributive responsibility,[5] and questioning the normative adequacy of an exclusive concern with the needs and purposes of members of the human species. But it also establishes a powerful claim to normative authority, and one with considerable historical depth. The central premiss of Christian natural law understanding of human claims to own and enjoy economic goods was the presumption that God had given the world to human beings in common, and given it for their use. That was what the

---

[3] Rawls (1972) and many subsequent articles, now summarized in Rawls (1993).
[4] For the overwhelming importance of this judgement, see Dunn (1984).
[5] See especially Barry (1989) and cf. Dunn (1985, chapter 6).

world was for. The secular heirs of the tradition of natural jurisprudence are understandably ill at ease with the presumption that the world really is *for* anything: that it has a clear telos independent of the historical vagaries of human purpose. But they still find it difficult to develop any coherent normative viewpoint without tacitly readopting the Christian natural law presumption, despite the apparent absence today of appropriate foundations for that presumption. Even utilitarians, for example, in effect treat as the telos of the world at least the full set of the historical vagaries of human purpose (along perhaps with the balance of pain and pleasure for every other sentient creature).[6] The Christian impetus towards inclusiveness within the human species itself is extended in its secular descendants, apparently under the sole impress of rationality, across the borders of the species, and perhaps eventually even to non-sentient entities.[7]

Modern liberal theorists of justice offer an appreciably more powerful and coherent viewpoint at present than any of their socialist or conservative critics. (They are better, that is to say, at moral theory.) But their lack of impact upon the historical process has not been fortuitous (cf. Dunn 1985, chapter 10). To consider the assignment of natural goods and of the products of historically developed human powers as morally answerable to at least the needs of all living humans[8] is a plausible precondition for any rationally defensible theory of ownership, use or enjoyment. But it is grimly distant, both imaginatively and practically, from the gritty and confused settings in which actual conflicts over ownership, use or enjoyment invariably occur. Robert Nozick's criticism of the ahistorical unreality of modern liberal theories of distributive justice lends no real support to his own whimsical construction of the normative implications of the history of human production.[9] But it does pick out a profound weakness of these theories: their singularly equivocal treatment of economic causality.

Aristotle's question – what are the best arrangements to make about property if a state is to be as well constituted as it is possible to make it? – is still a central question in modern politics. Indeed it is hard to see, short of the termination of all human politics, how it can ever cease to be such (cf. Dunn 1990c). But, as Aristotle himself firmly realized, it is as much a

---

[6] It is extremely difficult to see how this framework of assessment can generate any coherent and cogent practical conclusions. Compare Derek Parfit's 'repugnant conclusion' (Parfit 1984).

[7] Cf. Parfit (1984), Singer (1977), Griffin (1986) and the extremely interesting review of this in Scheffler (1987).

[8] This is plainly an indefensibly parsimonious standard to adopt. Why not the needs of future generations of human beings? Why not other sentient species?

[9] Nozick (1974); cf. the review by Dunn (1977).

question about the probable consequences of human actions as it is about the rational justification of particular evaluative beliefs or aspirations. Right-wing and left-wing critics of modern liberal theories of social justice have both pilloried the unreality of these theories and the distressing range of unintended consequences of attempts to embody even a minimum version of them in the institutions of postwar welfare states. (It should be noted that these two lines of attack are not obviously compatible.) But these critics have had far less success in contesting their standing as moral theories, being reduced for the most part to efforts to break up or dissipate systematic moral thinking about the domains of economics or politics.[10] These are old ideological quarrels (Machiavelli against the residues of medieval Christianity and civic humanist blandness; Burke against Paine; Weber against Marx). But the form which they take today is remarkably stark and has yet to be captured at all commandingly. Is the choice which we now face really a choice between a world of practical causality which simply repudiates the claims of moral rationality (though it continues to take the precaution of professing a desultory array of good intentions) and a practice of reflexive moral rationality which either has no detectable purchase on the practical world at all or (still worse) affects the latter where it does so only in ways manifestly at odds with its own intentions? Can there still be morally informed and grounded political agency? Or must any claim to act politically in a morally informed and grounded manner be ultimately self-deceptive, where it is not offered in conscious bad faith?

The key issue in modern politics is the issue of agency. The great modern traditions of political understanding – the liberal conceptions of constitutionally protected personal liberty and market-generated prosperity, and the socialist conceptions of the effective pursuit of the interests of exploited class majorities – all depend fundamentally on the validity of their assessment of the nature and efficacy of particular forms of agency. They are all theories of how to act with predictably desirable consequences. Each of these traditions has been subjected to the most corrosive criticism, though it is fair to say that the second has for the present worn decidedly worse than the first, and it ought by now to be possible to explain this disparity with some clarity. Much recent thinking, too, has sharpened longstanding demotic suspicions about the prospects for effective collaborative action under any possible normative inspiration. The intellectually baffling problems of collective action – of coordinating interests which are always partly in conflict, on the basis of highly

---

[10] Compare, for example, Dworkin's harsh appraisal of Michael Walzer's sensitive book (Walzer 1983) in Dworkin (1985, chapter 10, pp. 214–20).

imperfect information and for the greater benefit of the majority of those affected – have been explored with great tenacity in recent decades.[11] The better these problems are understood, the less plausible the expectation that they could be resolved even in principle by clearer thought or better devised institutions. The sense of human collective life as an unmasterable but inescapable strategic predicament, at every level from the single individual to the most populous, powerful or wealthy of contemporary states, presses hard upon modern political consciousness. It does so, not because humans today are less generous or psychologically resilient than their forebears, but because they have been taught to see their lives in this way and because the instruction, however partial it may be and however potentially destructive its results, is also essentially valid. It is the purely cognitive weight of the interpreted causal complexity of the world in which we live that numbs our capacity to conceive political agency with any force and clarity, let alone to enact it effectively in the always refractory world of political practice.

It is an important historical question (as yet very poorly answered) how far such constitutionally protected personal liberties, market-generated prosperity and effectively realized interests of previously exploited class majorities as exist today have come to do so as a result of political action premissed on valid causal understanding. The historical sequences from which these human benefits have emerged have always contained many other and distinctly less reassuring elements: spasms of savage and destructive violence, mass murder, unyielding cruelty and obtuseness. The economic mishaps of socialist production may well in the end prove to outweigh every human benefit credibly attributable to the great twentieth-century revolutions. And even if they do not do so, no serious analysis of the trajectory of these dramatic episodes can present even their more encouraging features as the intended consequences of a political agency informed by valid understanding of the context in which it was acting (Dunn 1980, chapter 9; Dunn 1985, chapter 4; Skocpol 1979).

Nor, to take what is for the present a less dispiriting example, can the recent economic triumphs of liberal democrat Japan be realistically understood as the outcome of clearly conceived and steadily implemented collective goals by an integral political agency which knew what it was doing. Despite almost four decades of rule by a single democratically re-elected governing party in intimate symbiosis with a polished and widely admired public bureaucracy, despite a sustained economic dynamism unmatched on such a scale within the last half century, and despite highly intelligent and illuminating celebrations of its prowess as a

---

[11] For a helpful introduction see Hardin (1982) and Axelrod (1984).

developmental actor (see esp. Johnson 1982), the political vicissitudes of the postwar Japanese state defy interpretation in terms of unified and clairvoyant agency.[12] There is undoubtedly some historical realism to the picture of Japan as a state exploring with unique rigour and determination for well over a century the terms on which a non-western population could hope to defend its own national integrity in the face of western wealth and coercive power, and eventually turn the tables decisively upon its alien intruders. (What price Admiral Perry today?) There is some realism, too, to the picture of the pre-war Japanese public bureaucracy as exploring more concretely, if less prudently, a strategy of economic construction which came in the postwar period to centre on the Ministry of International Trade and Industry (MITI). But whatever the real economic contribution of MITI's attentions (a much disputed matter) and however erratic and humanly expensive (both to the Japanese and others) the learning curve in question (a matter surely beyond dispute), the picture of clairvoyant bureaucratic strategy operating in comfort in a skilfully preserved political vacuum is plainly unsustainable. The MITI strategy of coolly Machiavellian industrial aggrandizement did not merely depend for its success on America's protection of a relatively open world market which relentlessly eroded the latter's own economic dominance (Gilpin 1987, especially chapters 8 and 10; Mandelbaum 1988, chapter 6). It also depended on the domestic political agility and *fortuna* of a poorly integrated assemblage of conservative politicians, operating often in turbulent and threatening conditions, under very severe constraints and in ferocious competition with one another. Improvization in the face of *fortuna* is an occupational requirement for any serious politician in any society. But it is only very recently that western scholars have begun to capture at all vividly the singularly hectic tempo and operating conditions of much of postwar Japanese politics (Calder 1989).

There are one or two countries whose recent political development has been reassuring enough for most of their inhabitants and steady enough when seen from abroad to encourage the view that their states at least are relatively rational and integrated agencies operating in pursuit of clearly conceived goals. Sweden is still a much cited example,[13] indispensable for sustaining the hopes of social democrats in less fortunate lands. The Federal Republic of Germany, Holland and perhaps Canada are other and less ideologically emotive cases. A somewhat wider range of instances

---

[12] See especially Kent E. Calder's dogged and cumulatively decisive book (Calder 1989). The point has become less controversial since the time of writing.

[13] Cf. Esping-Anderson (1985). The case for this assessment has perhaps weakened slightly since the time of writing. But it would be wrong to conclude that it has simply been eliminated.

in which the balance of human benefits is reasonably unequivocal are more plausibly seen in terms of historical serendipity: Italy; perhaps Spain after the demise of General Franco; over one period or another a miscellany of East or South-east Asian countries. It is not only employees of the OECD who see the operation of the world economy over the last forty years as a massive extension of the rewards of modern liberty (cf. Constant [1819] 1988, pp. 309–28). Indeed, compared with any earlier phase of its documented history, only a relatively modest proportion of western Europe's population would be likely now to disagree with them. What is dramatically less clear is the precise relation between this comparatively benign outcome and conscious human agency.

The maintenance and expansion of the world economy has been, and remains, a political as much as an economic process. It is caused by (reinforced or imperilled by) the agency of states and supra-national entities as well as by economic actors in quest of personal or corporate profits. There has been sharp dispute over the last decade as to how far the postwar success of the world economy was a product of the unparalleled power of the United States and the relatively coherent purposes (in this respect at least) of its successive national governments, and more urgent disagreement over just how far the world economy can continue to flourish in the absence of a single global hegemony and in conditions where coercive power and wealth become increasingly discontinuous (Keohane 1984; Gilpin 1987). It takes some optimism to discern relatively coherent purposes in the United States government at present (as it does in the government of Russia or Slovakia or indeed Great Britain). Since politics is an inherently competitive activity (at least after the era of absolute monarchy) most holders of governmental power are provisionally united at least against those who aspire to replace them. But that degree of unity of purpose is plainly insufficient to secure much harmony in practical judgement or in choice of either strategy or goals. It is not necessary to study game theory to appreciate that the worst possible outcome for all in a given predicament can sometimes result from actions which make the best possible sense for each. Effective political agency over any length of time is principally an exercise in the reimagining and practical reconstruction of given predicaments: in the identification and maintenance of compelling solidarities premised upon the reinterpretation of these predicaments. It is not necessarily the best way of enhancing political understanding to concentrate on the attractions of effective political agency for keenly desired ends.

To insist on the importance of efficacy in politics is no novelty: more in the nature of a truism. Most serious political thinkers have paid at least lip service to this imperative. The great eighteenth-century Scottish theorists of commercial society (Hont & Ignatieff 1983, esp. Introduction) and their modern heirs shared with later Marxist critics a clear commitment to it. The need to consider the efficacy of action with as much care as the desirability of goals formed the core of Max Weber's understanding of politics and lent a notably acerbic quality to his nationalist reading of the goals of economic policy (Weber 1948; Weber 1980). But except as a device for belabouring political opponents, it is extremely difficult to adopt the premiss and think on at all commandingly on its terms. This does not mean that adopting minimalist[14] (or publicly unavowable)[15] goals in political agency is guaranteed to do more good or less harm than any more ambitious alternative. (Consider the economic consequences of Mrs Thatcher (Coutts and Godley 1989).) But it does highlight a distressing tension between reasonably rich conceptions of social purpose and accurately understood practical expedients. In this sense the recent political travails of Keynesian macroeconomics (whatever the ultimate verdict on their purely cognitive sources) are perhaps better understood primarily in terms of the degree of political exposure and vulnerability intrinsic to any attempt to do something complicated, generous, lasting and worthwhile through the agency of a modern state.

In a prosperous, just and secure society there is everything to be said for minimalist goals in political agency. (Why imperil what is already very good?) But there are at present no societies which are genuinely prosperous, just and secure, and little reason for confidence that there ever will be any: let alone that there is much danger of all human societies eventually becoming such. The international consequences of Mr Gorbachev have already diminished some appalling dangers; but they have also unleashed plenty of novel perils too. The domestic consequences of Mr Gorbachev[16] are not merely for the present utterly imponderable, they also plainly demand, sooner or later, a relatively ambitious political response. In a society that is neither prosperous, just nor secure and which confessedly cannot go on in the old way, the choice of minimalist political goals (staying in power, prolonging the real political monopoly of the ruling party, maintaining urban food supplies) would demonstrate not sober prudence but a truly Neronic irresponsibility. Yet a relatively ambitious political response is always a perilous adventure. (That is why revolutions almost always, sooner or later, end in tears, whether or not their ultimate

---

[14] For example, enhance the dynamism of an economy by retracting the direct exertion of governmental power from the operations of the economy.

[15] For example, sharply increase the proportion of national income accruing to the wealthier members of the population.

[16] This formula is simply a way of referring to what is happening within the detritus left by the fall of the Soviet Union: not a recommended approach to the causal analysis of this.

consequences prove to be on balance benign.) The reconstruction of an entire state, society and economy cannot in principle be an instance principally of a definite set of human beings (let alone one human being) knowing just what they are doing. But such reconstructions sometimes have to occur; and there is good reason to see the existence of every modern state, society and economy as undergoing a more muted version of such transformation virtually all the time. The view that even the less turbulent passages of this transformation can be aptly understood in terms of reassuring homeostatic mechanisms, popular amongst American social scientists in the postwar decades, now looks staggeringly credulous: blankly at odds with such vestiges of causal understanding as the modern social sciences have contrived to accumulate. (In the last instance game theory will face down any version of systems theory whenever the going gets tough.)

It is an open secret that political leaders in the modern world operate in a setting of which they can hope to have only the shadowiest knowledge and comprehension. No doubt political leaders have always done so; and no doubt the more imaginative and analytical of recent political leaders (like Mr Gorbachev) knew and understood markedly more than the less diligent and intellectually gifted (like Mr Reagan). But it requires no undue personal despondency to infer from the political experiences of the last decade that the real (efficient rather than ceremonial) function of political leaders in modern societies is often principally to sedate the political awareness of the subjects of whose destiny they are nominally in charge.

But however far it may be from the fluent implementation of clearly conceived intentions, modern political agency remains eminently consequential. It matters how state power is exerted, and how states deal with one another. The outcome of the Uruguay Round of the GATT negotiations will affect the economic prospects of most of the world's population; and it will affect very many of them very deeply indeed. The economic, coercive and diplomatic practices of the American government in the face of the trade in illegal drugs will reshape the lives (or occasion the deaths) of many millions, both at home and abroad. To understand politics today would be to understand a reality as urgent and alarming as it has ever been in human history. But it might well also be to understand with quite new clarity how devastatingly narrow and practically unhelpful the human understanding of politics must always remain.

This is not a matter about which modern thinkers have yet had the courage to think very hard. But it deserves more serious attention. One major instance which evidently demands this is the recent and remarkably rapid collapse in the political credibility of socialism, even for those who found it credible in the first place. What has collapsed, to be sure, is not (as yet) in all cases a series of entrenched political interests (in organizations, prebends, rallying symbols and turns of phrase). Nor is it a range of decently avowable social intentions. Rather, it is a rationally assessed and reasonably integral structure of social, economic and political institutions and practices linking the organizations, rallying symbols, turns of phrase and avowable social intentions at all plausibly to the predictable consequences of intended actions.[17] Without such links, the socialist residues may in the short run prove more lasting than the feudal residues of the *ancien régime*: but their eventual prospects must be every bit as unpromising. Socialism is especially vulnerable to clear gaps between predictable consequences and agents' intentions because it embodies such a profoundly intentionalist vision of the nature of a good society.[18] (The gloomy history of Marxist politics underlines the fact that this profoundly intentionalist vision of the nature of a good society is far from being the only conceptual element that socialism can embody. But the telos of history for Marxists, as much as for admirers of Benjamin Constant, is still a world of concrete human freedom. What is lethally misguided about Marxism is less its interpretation of the nature of this telos (which has seldom been very specific) than its gratuitously euphoric estimate of the means for approaching it or the prospects for eventual arrival.)

The collapse in the political credibility of socialism is widely seen by its longstanding opponents (and not altogether unjustly) as the collapse of a distinctive a˙ ¹ congenitally imprudent tradition of political action. But however natural and agreeable this perspective may be for those who share it, it does risk not merely eventual historical refutation (probably a pretty slight risk) but also an immediate and ill-advised superficiality. Socialism is far from being the only modern repository of political imprudence. It may be peculiarly ingenuous in its hopes to embody moral perception and sentiment directly in the texture of collective social life and it has certainly often proved remarkably maladroit in its choice of techniques for effecting this embodiment. But the sad contrast between consequence and (at least avowable) intention was as easy to draw for the avenging government of Mrs Thatcher as it was for those of her postwar Labour (or Tory) predecessors. The intentions which it is easy to embody effectively in the consequences of political practice are characteristically negative and destructive: the dismantling, for example, of the fiefs of

---

[17] Cf. Dunn (1984). The prebends, perhaps, were never very plausibly linked in this way.
[18] For the importance of this, see the forthcoming work of Anthony Butler (1995). See also Przeworski (1985).

political opponents. It is worth pressing the question of just which techniques for embodying moral perception and sentiment even indirectly in the texture of collective social life have proved predictably deft in modern history, or indeed even in the last ten years.

Some candidates for this accolade have worn distinctly better than others: the conception of moderate government explored in Montesquieu's *L'esprit des loix* (Manin 1994) and entrenched so durably in the representative system established by the American constitution of 1787, the vision of expanding market exchange and deepening division of labour classically set out in Smith's *Wealth of Nations*. But it is a very nice question how far the undoubted and protracted services of the United States constitution to the promotion of modern liberty have issued from its formal structure and how far they rested essentially on the unique and successive historical advantages of its physical separation from other powerful states, its vast open land frontier and deep internal market for industrial goods. Certainly, both before and after emancipation, the fate of its black and Indian populations has proved beyond reasonable doubt that moderate government as such is no guarantee of the even-handed extension of the blessings of modern liberty. By the same token, the post-colonial history of Africa and Asia has shown decisively that the best designed of constitutions are at the mercy of economic weakness and intense social and political conflict (Dunn 1990b, chapter 9). Even the palpable collective benefits of capitalist production on a world scale, since by definition they are never collectively appropriated, have continued to serve some so much more handsomely than others, that to conceive them as collective benefits can seem wilfully perverse. (The case for so conceiving them was as well understood by Marx as it was by Adam Smith (cf. Warren 1980; Hart 1982; Sender & Smith 1986) and it has not served modern socialists in the Third World or elsewhere (still less their hapless subjects) to have gone so far in forgetting it.) Under the Ricardian theory of comparative advantage, the gains from international trade would on the whole be justly allocated on a genuinely open market. But Ricardian comparative advantage starkly misrepresents the strategic manoeuvring to appropriate rents that dominates international trade today and it is likely to prove more irrelevant than ever to the increasingly manipulated and protectionist markets of the late twentieth century.[19]

There is one very simple answer to offer to Aristotle's question in the late twentieth century. The best arrangements to make about property –

---

[19] Cf. Gilpin (1987 esp. chapters 5 and 10). It will be interesting to see whether the outcome of the Uruguay Round and the operations of the new World Trade Organization do in practice lay this anxiety to rest.

the arrangements that will render a state as well constituted as it is possible for it to be – are those which will maximize aggregate utility (or collective well-being) for the population of the state in question. But there are an endless series of difficulties with this answer, from vexed issues of distributive justice, through doubts about the capacity of any human agencies (governmental or otherwise) to judge the utility or well-being of others with minimal accuracy, to the blunt and obtrusive fact that no holders of state power today happen to know which arrangements will in practice maximize aggregate utility or even avoid diminishing it very drastically. (It is not plausible, even of Mrs Thatcher, that she intended to deflate the British economy as harshly as she did in the opening years of her premiership, merely because of the incidental political conveniences of having done so.) Few, of course, would be fool enough to explain the level and distribution of fiscal extraction in the United States of America at a given time solely by its government's choice of a particular normative criterion for political success. But even the most disabused vision of policy making as acrimonious bureaucratic and interest group feuding will have to recognize sooner or later the impact within it of dramatic miscalculations of economic causality. No doubt the practice of good government in any society at any time has always been more or less at the mercy of effective lobbying. But a pessimistic observer of the American or Russian (or perhaps even Japanese) political process today might easily view its practice of government as virtually dissolved into a practice of effective lobbying. The state as ideological fiction is the principal contemporary mode for articulating conceptions of social and political value.[20] (Its sole serious competitor in the modern world, despite the Babel of dissonant verbiage with which they share the airwaves of modern politics, is the large-scale capitalist corporation as ideological fiction.) But the view that the state in concrete reality might actually correspond to the ideological fiction and serve to implement any clear conception of political and social value is harshly at odds with virtually every aspect of our causal understanding of its concrete reality.

If we reconsider the demise of socialism in this light, its implication must appear very different. Production on the basis of common ownership appears not to work. The presumption that it would work has proved to be a vast and humanly expensive causal miscalculation. But there have never been compelling reasons for regarding common ownership as an unmediated good in itself. The case for applauding it has always rested on comparisons between the putative consequences of establishing some

---

[20] Cf. Dunn (1990b, Introduction). It is not, of course, necessarily the practical instrument most favoured by all for realizing these conceptions.

variety of it with those of establishing a variety of private ownership: on its presumed effects on moral personality, social peace or conflict, productivity, distributive justice. The proven demerits of socialism as a technique for achieving these ends does not in itself establish the delusory or malign character of the ends themselves (though of course it leaves that possibility entirely open). Still less do the proven demerits of socialism establish the desirability of resigning a given community in its entirety to the supposed requirements of a fetishized and grossly misdescribed process of economic causality (a process which may itself prove a very poor technique for achieving most avowable ends).

In this context it is important to recur to the persisting imaginative force of the presumption of the common ownership of the goods of nature and the accumulated productive powers of human beings in the theory of distributive justice. The underlying normative premiss of socialism is simply the intuition that, despite the dominant role of power and exploitation in human history thus far, every human being remains entitled to a just share of the human opportunities which can be made open to her or him and that human society must be refashioned so that they can secure this right. This is a stupendously ambitious causal project; and no one at present has the dimmest idea of how it could be carried out. But the socialist tradition has kept a better imaginative grip on both its extremity and its moral power than even the most impressive liberal theorists of social justice. It is at least in part because they have sensed the scale of it and tried to implement it in practice that socialists have sometimes done such fearsome harm. Where they have not been wrong is in hearing it as a demand for action.

'What are the best arrangements to make about property?' is still the central question of modern politics (cf. Dunn 1990c). (If we are obliterated in thermonuclear war, we should still be so in the last instance because of the epic misadventures of modern answers to it.) A socialist command economy has proved a disastrous technique for implementing the premiss of common ownership as criterion for just distribution. But it has done nothing to show that it is not the correct criterion. A sound criterion for distributive justice unaccompanied by any credible technique for realizing this in practice can be little more than a taunting and brutal mockery of our limited capacities for shame. To see how any such criterion can be brought to bear upon the texture of collective social life requires an accurate judgement of social, economic and political causality. (To see that it cannot be so brought to bear would be to see that we must keep our moral sensibilities firmly out of politics and adopt the most minimal or private goals within it: a more austere conclusion than Professor Hayek appears to appreciate.) The political question is still

'What is to be done?' Socialism, it seems, was the wrong answer. But it was at least an answer to the right question.

REFERENCES

Aristotle. *The Politics*, trans. T. A. Sinclair (1962). Harmondsworth: Penguin
Axelrod, R. 1984. *The Evolution of Cooperation*. New York: Basic Books
Barry, Brian 1989. *Theories of Justice*. Hemel Hempstead: Harvester-Wheatsheaf
Butler, A. 1995. *Transformative Politics*. London: Macmillan
Calder, K. E. 1989. *Crisis and Compensation*. Princeton: Princeton University Press
Constant, B. [1819] 1988. *Political Writings*, ed. B. Fontana. Cambridge: Cambridge University Press
Coutts, K. and W. Godley. 1989. 'The British economy under Mrs Thatcher'. *The Political Quarterly* 60, 2, 137–51
Dunn, J. 1977. Review of Nozick, *Anarchy, State and Utopia, Ratio* 19, 1, 88–95
    1980. *Political Obligation in its Historical Context*. Cambridge: Cambridge University Press
    1984. *The Politics of Socialism*. Cambridge: Cambridge University Press
    1985. *Rethinking Modern Political Theory*. Cambridge: Cambridge University Press
    1990a. 'Political obligation'. In *Political Theory Today*, ed. D. Held. Cambridge: Polity Press (Chapter 4 above)
    1990b (ed.). *Interpreting Political Responsibility: Essays 1981–89*. Princeton: Princeton University Press and Cambridge: Polity Press
    1990c (ed.). *The Economic Limits to Modern Politics*. Cambridge: Cambridge University Press
Dworkin, R. 1977. *Taking Rights Seriously*. London: Duckworth
    1985. *A Matter of Principle*. Cambridge, Mass.: Harvard University Press
Esping-Anderson, G. 1985. *Politics against Markets: The Social Democratic Road to Power*. Princeton: Princeton University Press
Gilpin, R. 1987. *The Political Economy of International Relations*. Princeton: Princeton University Press
Griffin, J. 1986. *Well-being: Its Meaning, Measurement and Moral Importance*. Oxford: Clarendon Press
Hahn, F. 1990. 'On some economic limits to modern politics'. In *The Economic Limits to Modern Politics*, ed. J. Dunn. Cambridge: Cambridge University Press
Hardin, R. 1982. *Collective Action*. Baltimore: Johns Hopkins University Press
Hart, K. 1982. *The Political Economy of West African Agriculture*. Cambridge: Cambridge University Press
Hont, I. and M. Ignatieff 1983 (eds.). *Wealth and Virtue*. Cambridge: Cambridge University Press
Johnson C. 1982. *MITI and the Japanese Economic Miracle: The Growth of Industrial Policy 1925–1975*. Stanford: Stanford University Press
Keohane, R. O. 1984. *After Hegemony*. Princeton: Princeton University Press
Mandelbaum, M. 1988. *The Fate of Nations*. Cambridge: Cambridge University Press

Manin, B. 1994. 'Checks, balances and boundaries: the separation of powers in the constitutional debate of 1787'. In *The Invention of the Modern Republic*, ed. B. Fontana, pp. 27–62. Cambridge: Cambridge University Press

Nozick, R. 1974. *Anarchy, State and Utopia*. Oxford: Blackwell

Parfit, D. 1984. *Reasons and Persons*. Oxford: Clarendon Press

Przeworski, A. 1985. *Capitalism and Social Democracy*. Cambridge: Cambridge University Press

Rawls, J. 1972. *A Theory of Justice*. Oxford: Clarendon Press

  1993. *Political Liberalism*. New York: Columbia University Press

Scheffler, S. 1987. 'Making the best of Utilitarianism'. *Times Literary Supplement*, 7 August, 835–6

Sender, J. and S. Smith 1986. *The Development of Capitalism in Africa*. London: Methuen

Singer, P. 1977. *Animal Liberation*. London: Paladin

Skocpol, T. 1979. *States and Social Revolutions*. Cambridge: Cambridge University Press

Waldron, J. 1988. *The Right to Private Property*. Oxford: Clarendon Press

Walzer, M. 1983. *Spheres of Justice*. Oxford: Martin Robertson

Warren, B. 1980. *Imperialism: Pioneer of Capitalism*. London: Verso Books

Weber, M. 1948. 'Politics as a vocation'. In *From Max Weber*, ed. H. H. Gerth and C. W. Mills, pp. 77–128. London: Routledge and Kegan Paul

  1980. 'The national state and economic policy'. *Economy and Society* 9, 4, 428–49

8   The dilemma of humanitarian intervention: the executive power of the Law of Nature, after God

There are at least three possible types of view about the justifiability of the use of force by states or private individuals on behalf of other private individuals or groups who are the direct victims of brutal and gratuitous coercion by another state. The first type of view is that no human being, and a fortiori no state, can be justified in using force under any circumstances and for any purpose, because (and *only* because) force is an intrinsic evil. This unflinchingly deontological view is generous but practically absurd. The second type of view is that states (or even private individuals) can be, and often are, justified in using force against the brutally coercive actions of another state when, but only when, the latter is acting outside its own territorial jurisdiction. At least in the case of states what grounds that justification is their entitlement to defend themselves against foreign (as against domestic) aggression, and to defend also any other states with whom they have linked themselves either by standing alliances or by solemn common undertakings to secure each other's safety and sovereignty within the bounds of international law. In the case of private individuals, the corresponding justification would lie in their several personal entitlements to defend themselves as best they can against aggression (a descendant of the classic early modern use of the private law argument (Skinner 1979, II, pp. 343–4, 347)). It is this last justification which ultimately lies behind the state's entitlement both to monopolize coercion amongst its own subjects and to defend them obdurately against foreign threats. This second view is far from being absurd; but it is also not overburdened with generosity.

A third view, more generous but also more open to the suspicion of absurdity, is that states (and perhaps even private individuals) can be and often would be justified in intervening within the legal jurisdiction of another state to protect even the latter's own subjects against peculiarly brutal and unjust coercion by agents of their own state authority. The confused and dangerous international environment since the collapse of the Soviet Union has made the merits of this last viewpoint a question of the greatest urgency. I propose to assume here that a war fought to reverse what at the time was certainly under international law an instance of territorial conquest (Bobbio 1991; Freedman & Karsh 1993) was a paradigm case of a just war, however unedifying some of the participants in the victorious coalition may have been. For it to be just to make war, the combat in question does not have to be a war between the good and the evil, or the just and the unjust. It merely has to be the case that the combatant in question has the right to fight and their immediate enemy does not. (For the unique and standing eligibility of the Iraq regime of 1990 as occasion for just war see al-Khalil (1990) and Makiya (1993).)

The question I wish to press is under what conditions (if any) the use of force by states or private individuals within the sovereign jurisdiction of another state to prevent the brutal coercion of groups of the latter's subjects can be coherently justified. The central point I wish to argue is that the principal grounds for doubt on this score do not arise from the manifest absence of any relevant entitlements, or even from the inherent difficulty of rendering such interventions impartially justiciable under international law, but, rather, from the extreme practical difficulty of generating and sustaining the degree of power required to make such interventions durably effective. I argue, in effect, that the principal weakness of justifications for humanitarian intervention within domestic jurisdictions rests not on any a priori anomaly in the conceptions of right presupposed but in the purely prudential difficulty of carrying such intervention through to a successful conclusion. The justifications for such intervention are justifications for a form of temporary empire; and its inherent perils are those of any imperial venture, perils which are made more blatant, if not necessarily more extreme, by the deliberate intention to assume the responsibilities of dominion temporarily and for a relatively brief period of time. (Protracted empire opens up a far wider – and an inherently massively indeterminate – hypothetical space. While the case in its favour is likely in the modern world to be pretty unpersuasive, the case against it, just because of this massive hypothetical indeterminacy, is very hard to render conclusive.)

In most of its historical guises empire has been vindicated, where it has been justified at all, either as the exercise of a supernaturally validated authority or as the discharge of a civilizing mission: a mission to bring the privileges of urban and law-governed existence to populations hitherto supposedly accustomed to less secure and orderly ways of life. The latter claim has sometimes been presented with a high degree of moral and spiritual self-regard. But in some of its most important historical instances the pretence of justification has been strikingly offhand, and the claim itself correspondingly relaxed:

Tu regere imperio populos, Romane, memento,
(Hae tibi erunt artes), pacique imponere morem,
Parcere subjectis, et debellare superbos. Vergil, Aeneid VI, 851–3

The most in terms of justification that can be extracted from a boast of this character is the sentiment that pride deserves a fall; and the Romans themselves were hardly crippled by collective humility. (Compare Thomas Hobbes [1642] (1983, p. 23): 'What a beast of prey is the Roman people'.) What was asserted in the first instance was less a normative right than a causal capability.

To assert such a causal capability, however, is to make an exceedingly strong claim. In the long and ambiguous history of empire that claim has almost invariably been overstated (for an instance of the claim as provincial farce see Dunn & Robertson (1973, chapter 4)). For it to be true that I ought to do something, it must be true that I can. There are very many great goods which, if only I enjoyed the power to realize them at reasonable cost to myself and others, I manifestly should – to prevent gross injustice, to stamp out famines or ghastly diseases (AIDS, malaria, tuberculosis, cancer), to avert great cruelties or grim sufferings. (It is of some importance that so many of the goods in such lists are naturally picked out in negative terms and could naturally be redescribed, if they fall within the scope of human powers at all, in terms of rights of prospective victims not to be victimized unnecessarily.) Our entire theoretical apparatus for interpreting responsibility rests in the end on perceptions of our own causal powers. We have only the haziest and most undependable intuitions as to what it would be true that we ought or ought not to do if our powers of agency were drastically greater or dramatically less than they in fact are (the rights and duties of angels; the rights and duties of God; the rights and duties of dolphins or domestic cats).

Judging the causal powers of human agents and agencies is a perturbing exercise in which frequent *ex post facto* perceptions of palpable failure are never offset by firm a priori guarantees of prospective success. But there is good reason to regard it as the central prerequisite for thinking adequately about politics (Dunn 1990). Some moral theories cannot readily concede it such centrality, whether because they are wholly deontological in foundation, or because they endorse too many rigid side constraints upon permissible action. But the emphasis on the centrality of causal judgement fits perfectly with a utilitarian framework, and on some understandings may be seen as a necessary component of any such framework.

Michael Walzer, in his famous and attractive study *Just and Unjust Wars* (Walzer 1977) questioned the theoretical competence of utilitarianism to analyse how and when human beings are justified in fighting one another to the death principally on the grounds that it systematically rationalizes extreme interpretations of *jus in bello* (of how one is entitled to conduct oneself once firmly embarked upon war) by its insistence that the point of fighting is to win, and that it thereby eroded the rights of human participants and victims in warfare (Walzer 1977). He argued, in effect, where it ascribes a *jus ad bellum* (a right to make war at all) it is very hard for utilitarianism to concede a true *jus in bello*. But Walzer made little real attempt to show that this line of thought could not be reflexively reincorporated into at least a rule-utilitarian theory of *jus in bello* through some version of Nozick's utilitarianism of rights (cf. Nozick 1975, pp. 28–33). Nor did he do anything to show that utilitarianism does not offer the best available normative approach to considering *jus ad bellum*; the circumstances in which it is permissible to fight at all.

The classical Christian theory of the just war confidently assumes that Nature has a Law to govern it (the Law of its Creator), and that reason, which is that Law, and which is at least to some degree accessible to human beings (cf. Dunn 1989), is sufficient to interpret what they may or may not do to one another by threat or exercise of violence. There are many grounds for doubting the applicability of this classical Christian approach to the politics of the world in which we live: ontological, epistemological, theological, historical, perhaps indeed simply political. If Nature *has* no determinate non-anthropocentrically ascribable properties (Rorty 1979; cf. Williams 1978), it can scarcely be deemed to be subject to a Law. If we cannot *know* what we should or should not do, we are unlikely to come by authoritative guidance over such intense and hazardous conflicts of judgement on the matter. If there may *be* no God, or even if we cannot agree on which claimant to divine authority is the rightful claimant, we shall not readily resolve our disagreements over which of us are genuinely observing that claimant's valid commands. (The predicament of Salman Rushdie has made this glaringly apparent. But only the singular implausibility of Saddam Hussein's claims to Islamic legitimacy prevented it from bearing seriously on a vastly more consequential conflict.) There are no compelling grounds today for doubting that disagreements over the right to coerce one another, from single individuals to entire ideological blocs or cultural alliances, are political all the way down (cf. chapter 6 above; Dunn 1990, chapter 4).

But if Nature cannot today be reasonably supposed to have a Law to govern it, the justification of human actions in conditions of intense conflict (as in other conditions) cannot rest ultimately upon interpretations of the requirements of authority. What else might it rest upon instead? One answer – a highly sceptical one (Williams 1981, chapter 8) – would be that it must rest upon brute culture or psychological fact: on what just happens to appear justified to the members of a particular group or to singular individuals (on what Williams calls their 'subjective motivational set'). I doubt if we in any sense know this answer to be wrong. But it is worth pointing out that accepting it involves construing all human conflict simply and without residue as a collision of power, and categories of justification as mere plastic components within this field of power, without inherent power of their own to modify its grim contours. A second answer (moral realism) would be that it might rest upon some variety or other of facts about human value (about rights, about utility, about an appropriate human term – individual, family, group, tribe, state, ideological alliance or bloc – to which human value must uniquely be relativized). The most crippling theoretical weakness of moral relativism is not its reasonable suggestion that human values must be intimately linked with what human beings happen to be like, but its insurmountable indeterminacy over which exact *unit* of human membership is the appropriate locus for the relativization in question. A third answer, descending from Kant, is that it can only and should only rest upon the increasingly clear apprehension and increasingly commanding exertion of the powers of reason, which are within human reach, but also in some sense above human beings. I cannot comment usefully on this third answer since I have never been able to understand it. But I doubt in any case whether it can in the end be effectively segregated from the second answer.

It is a matter in the first place for moral philosophers to demarcate the theoretical space of potential facts about human value. The degree to which they succeed in clarifying both its appropriate demarcation and the internal relations which structure it will bear directly on the question of when and how it is right or just to coerce other human beings. (The dependence of Walzer's book on a wholly unargued theory of rights gives a clear example of how this is likely to feature in practice.) For the present, however, moral philosophers have yet to reach either decisive intellectual results or a high degree of consensus on how the facts of human value are best understood. Until they do so, political theorists, like ordinary human beings in circumstances of political urgency, will have to consider the experience and exercise of coercion on the basis of vivid, immediate and for the present irreconcilable conflicts in the apprehension of human values. Indeed the sustained exercise of coercion will characteristically (though not invariably) include amongst its causal antecedents highly contentious judgements about human values (consider Bosnia, Kampuchea, Tibet, East Timor, the Sudan, Northern Ireland, and cf. Hobbes [1642] (1983) for the domestic political case).

Under the classic early modern (Christian) understanding of the Law of Nature humanitarian intervention by a sovereign power outside its territorial jurisdiction (concepts, of course, themselves in very active formation in the period in question (Franklin 1973; Skinner 1989)) had the status (like many domestic actions by aggrieved subjects) of an Appeal to Heaven (Dunn 1969, chapter 13). How much difference does it make to this structure, if Heaven is no longer presumed to be there?

The Law of Nature has authority because it is God's Law. Its scope extends to all human beings because they share the same first instance relationship to their divine Creator and have no intrinsic superiority, from His point of view, to one another. In the end, where they disagree seriously enough and in ways which they cannot resolve amongst one another, they are rationally bound to appeal to Him: firstly, because, *ex hypothesi*, they have exhausted the human alternatives; secondly, because He alone has ultimate and dependable power to enforce His Law; and thirdly because only He can authoritatively judge whether or not they happen to be right. The first of these grounds carries through all too effortlessly to the wider, more secularized and religiously conflictual world of today. But it may well seem to do so essentially as a counsel of despair. The second wholly fails to carry; and the third can be rescued, if at all, only by the effective construction of a fresh alternative site of effective human jurisdiction with some real powers of enforcement (that is to say, by effectively overriding the first).

The history of the United Nations tells us something about the prospects for such construction, and rather more about the difficulties which it is certain to encounter. The recent array of humanitarian interventions – in Kurdistan, southern Iraq, Bosnia, Somalia, Kampuchea and so on – may well prove a peculiarly consequential episode in this history, as they very evidently represent a sharp change in its operating rhythms, its practical aspirations and the risks which it is prepared, however confusedly, to incur. The boast *debellare superbos* has always depended for its credibility on the Legions: on the willingness and capacity to take and go on taking military casualties; not merely not to flinch from, but in most cases also to *win*, any wars that prove to arise. If one point is uncontentiously apparent about the United Nations today it is that the nations who make it up are *not* united in a commitment to enforce a shared vision of world order anywhere and everywhere that this is actively subverted, still less to do so by pooling their collective coercive power for the purpose. To take a glaring, and in the case of Kampuchea in some instances a somewhat comic example, it is at least a sustainable interpretation of the constitutional law of what were recently still the two most economically dynamic wealthy states in the world that they are precluded from deliberately risking the lives of their own professional forces of coercion except in defence of their own national territories. (Even Hobbes would have been likely to regard this as an ignominiously parsimonious conception of the responsibilities of career soldiers (Baumgold 1988).) To establish a more united commitment and a steadier capacity to enforce it in practice would require drastic, lasting and politically and economically costly decisions. We need not expect these in the near future. But is it even soberly imaginable in a relevant but less near future? Can we reasonably hope to move towards it rather than away from it?

The answer to that question is intimately bound up with the political significance of the history of European natural law thinking. Is that significance irretrievably eurocentric, culturally partial and politically tendentious? Or can it be recuperated, in more cosmopolitan and culturally detached terms which bear upon the predicaments of human beings across the world? While there are noisily fashionable answers to it in either sense, this cannot really at present be said to be a question which is fashionable in itself. But I think it has pressing significance for human communities across the globe, and especially for those of their members who are weakest, most open to victimization, or at present under most active persecution: in Kurdistan or the marches of southern Iraq, in Bosnia or Kosovo, in East Timor or western Kampuchea.

Classical natural law thinking in Europe provided for several centuries a relatively imaginatively relaxed medium in which to consider how it was permissible for human beings to treat one another, and why it was impermissible for them to do so in other ways, and to judge how they should respond to impermissible treatment in their own or others' cases. (The insistence that the imaginative relaxation was only relative is important. Imaginative relaxation over such questions across a society is never more than relative: we should remember Filmer as well as Locke, Charles Leslie as well as Benjamin Hoadley (Dunn 1969; Dunn 1980, chapter 3).) Even this degree of imaginative relaxation was parasitic upon at least two structural facts: firstly that western Europe at the time was effectively united in presuming that there was indeed a single ultimate legal authority, external and incontestably superior to the members of the species (however virulently they might and did disagree on who was equipped to adjudicate on earth on that authority's behalf; and secondly that, in their collective agreement over the standing of this final authority, they were subject over time to an ever less effective external challenge from the devotees of other equally comprehensive claimants to global authority. The contrast here between the thought world of pre-Lepanto western Europe and that of Gibbon or Adam Smith is decisively important, whether this is seen as simply a matter of relative military potency, or whether it is traced back to the economic, or perhaps political and social, preconditions for such comparative military potency. In any case, the two structural facts taken together were sufficient to sustain an imaginative medium in which it was easy for even the bitterest political opponents at least to comprehend the point (and therefore the potential force) of appealing over one another's heads to this site of incontestably common authority: an index in general to one another, however direly suspected in particular cases, of putative good faith, and therefore also under propitious circumstances of minimal mutual identification and openness to the principle of reciprocity. (This logic comes out clearly in the end, in face of the most painfully refractory experience, in the long debate over the right to religious toleration – most clearly, perhaps, in Bayle's ringing endorsement of the claims of errone-ous conscience (chapter 6, above).

It is an obvious setback in the first instance that there is no cosmopoli-tan contemporary analogue to the acceptance of a common religious sub-jection. But what would be more perturbing (and is often now claimed to be true) would be if the imaginative possibility of normative identification (and perhaps even the plausibility of the claim to common religious sub-jection in early modern Europe) had in fact rested on something extrinsic to it: the decisive shift in relative military and economic power over this timespan between western Europe and the remainder of the world. If classical Christian natural law drew its theoretical plausibility essentially from the cumulative practical confidence bred by imperialist triumph, it is hard to believe that even a cautious and modern recuperation of its resources would prove a promising basis for the far broader and vastly culturally more plural process of identification which will be needed to sustain a universal doctrine of human rights as ultimate standard for legitimate political agency today. Here it is of overwhelming importance that even a cursory consideration of historical sequence shows this suspi-cion cannot possibly be well founded. Imperialist triumph may have (indeed must have) distorted the European understanding of the implica-tions of natural law in application and done so repeatedly and over a very long period of time (cf. Tuck 1979, 1993; Tully 1993; Farr 1986). But in no conceivable understanding of the historical sequence of Christian inter-pretation in Europe itself could it possibly be thought to have caused the theoretical matrix of Christian natural law itself.

We may consider the residual intimations of this matrix for a secular, or drastically religiously plural, world conveniently through A. John Simmons's meticulous and scrupulously honest reconstruction of John Locke's theory of rights (Simmons 1993, esp. chapter 3). Simmons's main purpose is to extricate from the historical Locke's own assumptions the internal structure and workings of the theory which he fashioned, showing where and just how far its conclusions depended upon those assumptions and what further guidance can be elicited from the theory where at least the theological component of the assumptions is abandoned. (There are some analogies between what he attempts for Locke's moral and political theory and what Ayers achieves in his magisterial study of Locke's ontology and epistemology (Ayers 1991).) In Simmons's painstaking reconstruction the post-theological residue of Locke's theory comes through as a largely rule-consequentialist version of moral realism. The two key elements which concern us here, the individual human right to punish breaches of the Law of Nature (the executive power of the Law of Nature) and the right (and duty) to preserve all mankind (where our own preservation is not immediately threatened by doing so and they have not already personally deserved to die), come through quite readily and cogently in this analysis. They do so, of course, in a far weaker and politically more sceptical form, devoid of any guarantee of ultimate backing from power or eventual resolution of conflict. Even in this weaker form, moreover, what their presence principally signals is the historical failure thus far to eliminate the State of Nature (and hence at intervals also the State of War) from many relations between human beings. When and if all human beings come to be effectively subject to known standing laws, with impartial judges and dependable agencies of enforcement, and when and if these laws, judges and agencies of enforcement in turn prove themselves to be subject to an equally dependable structure of regulation, control and considered emendation, then and only then will the executive power of the Law of Nature be conclusively transferred from individual human beings to this single comprehensive scheme of legislative political authority: this global Civil Society. Even then, that authority's process of judging and its capacity to enforce will both go back ultimately to the individual executive powers of the Law of Nature of every one of its human subjects (cf. Vincent 1990).

    In the protracted meantime, however, decisions to intervene in the territorial sovereignty of particular nation states to preserve acutely endangered human lives, however they are adjudicated and whatever coercive power is mustered to carry them through, will remain (as they very obviously are today) both intensely and irretrievably contentious and inordinately dangerous. The Appeal to Heaven, even where the appellants were wholly justified in making it, was always a perilous adventure. In this world, it is no more and no less perilous than it always has been, once the presumption that Heaven can be trusted eventually to right the balance elsewhere has been conclusively abandoned.

    Its principal danger remains the blank futility of anarchism (Dunn 1990, chapter 3) and the massive political costs and the intrinsic military and political hazardousness of empire itself, of the attempt to establish and exercise political authority over alien populations: a hazardousness largely independent of the intentions of those who seek to establish it. No reasonable person (not a self-interpreting category (cf. Nozick 1993)) – and still more no responsibly governed state – would face such hazards gratuitously. But what exactly is the alternative? To stand deliberately by while murder or genocide are being done is not to commit them yourself. But it certainly is to make a deeply implicating choice. The fact that the victims are human, and that the capacity to intervene is also a human power, are enough in themselves, in a wide variety of ethical frameworks (utilitarian, natural rights, reciprocity) to show that it may well be appropriate to intervene. Where victims are very numerous, the capacity relatively overwhelming, and the dangers fully commensurate with the risks (as perhaps in Somalia in 1992), the case for doing so is very strong. But the risks will always be there (as they always remain, too, in any attempt to secure the peaceful government of any political society (Dunn 1990, chapter 3)).

We could for the future decide, both individually and collectively, to ignore what we know about the atrocious sufferings visited upon our human fellows in other states. Indeed we could decide both individually and collectively to ensure that in future we precluded ourselves even from *learning* about those sufferings, since there is nothing clear and dependable that such knowledge necessarily enables us to do, and since there are great and hideously apparent dangers for ourselves in even *attempting* to do anything at all effective about them. But I do not think that there is the faintest chance of our consistently doing either: burying our heads permanently in the sand, or hardening our hearts steadily against the pressure of others' blatant misery. The pressures towards publicity and the relentless deluge of information in the midst of which we now live are a structural constant of the global process of economic rationalization in which we are all engulfed. From now on (at least until that process is effectively reversed) human societies are going to have to live on very much more intimate terms with one another. (For a small-scale picture of this process at work over time see Dunn & Robertson (1973).) This may well not generally enhance mutual human generosity (charity as such). But it is very likely indeed, inductively, to make us even more punitive in face of others' perceived crimes; and it will be surprising if it fails to make us more consistently, if minimally, charitable towards human beings in conditions of extreme necessity.

Because of these pressures, there will go on being at least intermittent demands for humanitarian intervention, and there will therefore be further political efforts to align such intervention with a more firmly institutionalized process of adjudication over when it is or is not appropriate, and to establish and deploy a standing coercive capability to enforce the results of that adjudication. We need not expect to see the proud cast down any more consistently than they have been in the past. But we can, I think, expect to see them indicted more frequently and more punctiliously than has been common in the past, and we can expect them therefore also to find themselves facing more persistent and less partial challenges than those they have been accustomed to encounter.

In the long, slow, unsteady human progress from the State of Nature towards Civil Society, a modest degree of additional pressure from now on could fall, and in due course probably will fall, on some of the grosser instances in which state powers initiate a state of war with their own hapless subjects. We are never likely to recover Locke's 'great and natural community (Locke [1689] 1988, II, para. 128), subject to a single and (eventually) effectively enforced Law. But the impetus to *try*, however falteringly, to do so is linked to the most powerful shaping force of modern human history. It may work through sentiment and identification, with all their treacheries and opacities, rather than through reason alone. But it neither comes from nor rests upon anything flimsy or sentimental. What forces it on our attention is the logic of expanding human powers; and what gives it its imperious authority is the most fundamental interpersonal claim of justice between human beings: the duty to preserve the other members of our species (where our own preservation does not conflict too directly with this goal), as far as we readily can.

REFERENCES

al-Khalil, S. (K. Makiya) 1990. *Republic of Fear*. London: Hutchinson Radius
Ayers, M. 1991. *Locke*, 2 vols. London: Routledge
Baumgold, D. 1988. *Hobbes's Political Theory*. Cambridge: Cambridge University Press
Bobbio, N. 1991. *Una guerra giusta? Sul conflitto del golfo*. Venice: Marsiglio
Dunn, J. 1969. *The Political Thought of John Locke*. Cambridge: Cambridge University Press
    1980. *Political Obligation in its Historical Context*. Cambridge: Cambridge University Press
    1989. '"Bright enough for all our purposes": John Locke's conception of a civilized society'. *Notes and Records of the Royal Society* 43, 133–53
    1990. *Interpreting Political Responsibility*. Cambridge: Polity Press
Dunn, J. and A. F. Robertson 1973. *Dependence and Opportunity: Political Change in Ahafo*. Cambridge: Cambridge University Press
Farr, J. 1986. '"So vile and miserable an estate": the problem of slavery in Locke's political thought'. *Political Theory*, 14, 263–89
Franklin, J. 1973. *Jean Bodin and the Rise of Absolutist Theory*. Cambridge: Cambridge University Press

Freedman, L. and E. Karsh 1993. *The Gulf War 1990–91*. London: Faber
Hobbes, T. [1642] 1983. *De Cive: The English Version*, ed. H. Warrender. Oxford: Clarendon Press
Locke, J. [1689] 1988. *Two Treatises of Government*, ed. P. Laslett. Cambridge: Cambridge University Press
Makiya, K. 1993. *Cruelty and Silence*. London: Jonathan Cape
Nozick, R. 1975. *Anarchy, State and Utopia*. Oxford: Blackwell
  1993. *The Nature of Rationality*. Princeton: Princeton University Press
Rorty, R. 1979. *Philosophy and the Mirror of Nature*. Oxford: Blackwell
Simmons, A. J. 1993. *The Lockean Theory of Rights*. Princeton: Princeton University Press
Skinner, Q. 1978. *The Foundations of Modern Political Thought*, 2 vols. Cambridge: Cambridge University Press
  1989. 'The state'. In *Political Innovation and Conceptual Change*, ed. T. Ball, J. Farr and R. Hanson, pp. 90–131. Cambridge: Cambridge University Press
Tuck, R. 1979. *Natural Rights Theories*. Cambridge: Cambridge University Press
  1993. *Philosophy and Government*. Cambridge: Cambridge University Press
Tully, J. 1993. *An Approach to Political Philosophy: Locke in Contexts*. Cambridge: Cambridge University Press
Vergil (P. Vergili Maronis). *Opera*, ed. R. A. B. Mynors (1969). Oxford: Oxford University Press
Vincent, R. J. 1990. 'Grotius, human rights and intervention'. In *Hugo Grotius and the Theory of International Relations*, ed. H. Bell, B. Kingsbury and A. Roberts, pp. 241–56. Oxford: Oxford University Press
Walzer, M. 1977. *Just and Unjust Wars*. London: Allen Lane
Williams, B. 1978. *Descartes: The Project of Pure Enquiry*. Harmondsworth: Penguin
  1981. *Moral Luck*. Cambridge: Cambridge University Press

In its most elaborately articulated form racism is an array of theoretical views about the epistemic clarity and human import of the practice of individuating human populations in terms of their presumed biological descent. In this form the term can refer with some precision, and largely independently of context, to a quite specific body of beliefs. In far more diffuse and far less theoretical forms, however, and in forms which are also far more widely distributed in human history, it can and does refer just as readily to the highlighting of distinctions which are certainly at least as much cultural as they are genetic, and which are inextricably located in a context of more or less intimate and painful confrontation between human groups. In this second form there cannot in principle be anything comparably determinate for the term racism to refer to.

The main claim that I wish to advance is that it is the second and vaguer guise of racism, and not the first and more theoretically precise guise, which has made it a topic of urgent political importance throughout much of human history and which still makes it of such pressing significance today. This may at first hearing seem paradoxical since the most dramatic and ghastly single impact of the category of race upon human history, the Final Solution, certainly involved the adoption of an array of putatively scientific beliefs about human biology and is scarcely intelligible, even in principle, as anything other than an attempt to enact some of the practical implications of these beliefs for those who belonged amongst the genetically approved segment of the German population. (I appreciate that this last view is a highly contentious personal judgement, not a palpable truism. But since it happens to be my own judgement, I want to underline the fact that I fully accept it.) As an epistemically ambitious, if scientifically ludicrous, concept of race was the central practical premiss of the Final Solution, it is obvious enough that quite technical and precise history of human intellection *can* at times be of key importance in racism's chequered history. But if one asked the ingenuous but far from trivial question just what racism is, and what its history really has been, it emphatically does not follow from the intermittent and appalling importance of highly sophisticated thinking within that history that the best means of specifying or understanding racism is to attempt to do so by focusing on the history of more or less sophisticated biological thought.

As an elaborately articulated array of theoretical views, located more or less decisively within the field of biology, the verdict of polite modern thought has been that racism is irremediably epistemically confused or implausible, that it is intensely imaginatively discreditable (that it involves the thinking of intrinsically dirty or corrupt thoughts), and that it foments (or is characteristically deployed in order to excuse) oppressive and malign political conduct. I have no quarrel whatever with any of these conclusions of polite modern thought. I have been taught to see the world in their terms myself. I feel them spontaneously and with the greatest emotional ease (indeed with a relaxed and agreeable smugness). I keenly reprehend any attempt to call them seriously into question. But if what we wish to do is to comprehend racism, rather than to congratulate ourselves on the excellence of our own moral and intellectual taste, I very much doubt whether they offer at all a promising basis for understanding either the history of racism or its insistent and perturbing modern presence. What impedes them from doing so, I think, is not the estimable answer which they offer to the questions which they choose to ask (questions, of course, which the intellectual champions of racism have forced them to try to answer). Rather, it is the questions which they make no attempt whatsoever even to address, and which they might perhaps be thought to discourage others even from electing to ask.

There are at least three distinct dimensions on which it might for some purpose be appropriate to individuate human populations – a dimension of epistemic validity, a dimension of moral justifiability or decency, and a dimension of political relevance or illumination. The history of the natural sciences is constituted, in the latter's fond self-understanding, by the dimension of epistemic validity. What the sciences aspire to be is knowledge-directed trajectories of inquiry, held together not merely by the more or less confident presumption that they represent a clear advance on their own pasts but also that the future is likely to improve even further on their own present efforts. In this notably demanding dimension the category of race has worn outstandingly badly in the present century. Beginning very much as a category of folk or popular genetics, the attempts to sharpen and solidify its epistemic profile have merely served to dissipate its initial and very considerable folk plausibility. In folk genetics, speaking of course very loosely, race is conceived very much as a natural kind, on the model perhaps of an animal species. But its vague but vivid experiential plausibility in direct encounters between human populations – Japanese really are rather different from the Tutsi, and both in turn perhaps from any of the present populations of the Andes – this vague experiential plausibility has been comprehensively deconstructed by the progress of modern scientific genetics (cf. Modiano 1992). Such few determinate differences as reach firmly beyond the hazy experience already embodied in folk genetics suggest that there could scarcely be an issue of broad human importance for which differentiation between races as such could greatly matter. It is not its residual epistemic charm or promise which makes the category of race still an insistent presence in modern history (and perhaps a more serious one today than at any point since the Soviet army reached Berlin). By the same token, a relaxed contempt for those epistemic pretensions does little to illustrate its present salience and urgency.

If the epistemic distinction between races is inherently vague, and its practical implications so weak as to be essentially nugatory, it could hardly itself provide much support for a conception of how it is morally justifiable or decent to treat the members of a particular human population. In the past there have been many spectacular examples of this form – Greek or Iberian theories of natural slavery (Finley 1980; Pagden 1986; Pagden 1992; Prosperi 1992), Platonic or Nazi conceptions of natural rulership. But even in these settings the epistemic pretensions to ground moral justification in natural difference were often challenged by universalist conceptions of moral justification which in essence refused to recognize the *relevance* of natural difference before they set themselves to dispute much of its alleged factual presence. Since modern epistemology (or anti-epistemology) has increasing difficulty in making sense of the idea of natural difference, and since modern secular ethics is highly suspicious of *any* attempt to justify inequality of treatment by any forms of difference between human beings besides those of manifest need (cf. Dworkin 1981), race is an unlikely foundation for the justification of any modern political projects. And yet the presence of quite explicitly racist consciousness – perceptions of members of another ethnic (and putatively racial) group as the objects of rational and justifiable enmity – is still highly obtrusive: in Britain, in France, in the United States, in Japan, in China, in Amazonian Brazil, in many areas of the former Soviet Union, and very obviously today in Italy itself.

Why should this be so? If we are unable to understand the racism in the midst of which we now live (and which probably in some measure also lives within each of us) we are most unlikely to make much headway in understanding its tangled and often drastically occluded past.

My answer, then, to this question is exceedingly simple. It is not, unfortunately, on closer inspection, anything like as clear as it initially sounds. But its initial simplicity has at least the virtue of underlining

certain definite negations. In particular it implies that the way to explain
the presence and character of racist consciousness is not to focus on the
articulated causal beliefs about how the patterned genetic make-up of
human groups characteristically affects the conduct of members of those
groups, nor to focus on usually less articulated ethical beliefs about how
those presumed effects make it justifiable or decent to treat members of
the groups in question. Each of these two forms of belief, of course, can
and often does *exemplify* racism (insofar as it doesn't simply *constitute*
racism). But in the understanding of racism it furnishes the *explicandum*:
what there *is* to explain. It does not and cannot furnish the *explicans*: what
explains the *explicandum*.

What *explains* the historical presence and human force of racist
consciousness (and even of racist theorization) is the pragmatics of political competition, and more specifically the part played in that competition by attempts to interpret the content of group interest. This may
sound an implausible claim; but it does at least in the first instance sound
a relatively clear one. Rescuing its plausibility, however, drastically
impairs its initial clarity; and I see no point in attempting to deny this. But
even in its more plausible and regrettably less clear form, it certainly does
not denude it of real content.

Often enough in the past, and today virtually everywhere in the world,
groups of human beings need with the utmost urgency to decide whom to
fear and whom to trust, whom to identify with and whom to identify
against, with whom and against whom to seek to cooperate or to struggle,
even, *in extremis*, whom to seek to kill (Dunn 1990, chapter 3; Bobbio
1991). In the domestic politics of nation states and in the international
relations between these states, professional politicians and their amateur
coadjutors do their utmost to persuade themselves, each other, and their
respective constituents and clients how to resolve these unnerving questions, how to judge whom to trust and whom to fear, whom to aid and
whom to punish, and so on. The world of politics is a world of steep
formal and informal hierarchies of power, with an extraordinarily elaborate and visually opaque division of labour. It is intensely competitive
through and through; and some aspects of that competition (electoral
systems, party coalitions, factional intrigue, in the eyes of some
(Przeworski 1985) even the conflict between classes) can be powerfully
understood simply in terms of egoistic rationality.

If this was indeed all that there was to politics, the thesis that it is the
pragmatics of political competition that explains the distribution of racist
consciousness and action would have an arresting strength and economy.
Racism would come out as just a manipulative facility for professional
politicians. But in this tough-minded and mildly imbecile version what

would remain wholly unclear would be *why* racism should serve as a manipulative facility of any real potency. And it is, of course, just this which we most urgently need to explain. Professional politicians may sometimes have good reason to foment racist consciousness and to commission, reward or broadcast racist theorizing. But they could never have reason to do any of these unless racist consciousness itself could, under given circumstances, be successfully, readily or even effortlessly elicited. The fact that it *can* be so elicited is a fact about the potentiality of the human mind, about social imagination and emotion (the less moral sentiments), above all about the dynamics of positive and negative identification. An axiom of egoistic rationality is of very little assistance in interpreting that fact.

What is of more assistance, at least potentially, is the continuing part played in the pragmatics of political competition by the attempt to interpret the content of group interest. This is not a prerogative of professional politicians. Indeed it might well be seen as the privilege of every minimally viable human agent. Political labour is certainly divided everywhere in the modern world in almost every attempt to interpret the content of group interests. But it is unclear that any viable human adult can be totally inert in this seething process of interpretation. At the very least, in a democratic political order, any citizen who elects to vote can scarcely avoid committing themselves to some such interpretation; and there are many other modes of political participation, peaceful or violent, in every modern state from Ethiopia to Kampuchea or Switzerland, in which the commitment is just as clear as (and considerably more exacting than) it is apt to be in the casting of votes.

In such interpretation the division of political labour is not one between manipulators and manipulated, still less one between guilty and innocent. Indeed if the demarcatory criterion for guilt is imaginatively uncommitted manipulative will, and the criterion for innocence is compulsive belief, there is no clear reason to suppose in the case of racism that the professional politician is the paradigm of guilt and the feckless voter the model for innocence. In the right place at the right time, it is obviously just as possible to live *off* racist politics as it is to live off a politics of the unstinting service of a cosmopolitan human good. No doubt many cadres of the Third Reich found themselves doing just the former. But it is also just as possible, unfortunately, to live *for* racist politics as it is to live *for* a politics of universal beneficence or class revenge. There is no reason in general to suppose that politicians who dabble in racism are less sincere in their interpretation of the content of group interests than their more edifying competitors. (To take, for example, the most prominent and distinguished postwar British politician who may be said to have done so, Mr

Enoch Powell, it is very much easier to defend the judgement that he should have known better than to say what he said than it is to lend the least credibility to the judgement that he did not believe it true. And the aspect of his performance which it remains of most political importance to understand is precisely why he judged it his *duty* to say exactly what he said. The assessment of whom to fear and whom to trust, whom to cooperate with and whom to struggle against, is seldom a simple matter in politics. Insofar as it is not simply epistemically impossible to tell in principle, it is well nigh always hard to judge in practice (Dunn 1991; Dunn 1980, Conclusion). Because the twin of trust is betrayal (cf. Dunn 1984, chapter 2), the making of such judgements can only be a relaxed and unperturbing exercise where the consequences of being mistaken appear to be pretty trivial. Wherever what is at stake appears to be of any great human importance the assessment of the political content of group interest is virtually certain to evoke anxiety; and where it genuinely is of such moment, that anxiety is simply appropriate: perhaps *non-rational*, but certainly in no sense irrational, misguided, or misplaced, let alone premissed on necessarily false beliefs.

It is most illuminating and most accurate to think of racist consciousness in the majority of cases as a site or consequence of political misjudgement, a site or consequence no more and no less intrinsically psychopathological in structure than the vast bulk of misjudgement of the political implications of the relations between human groups (cf. Dunn 1990, chapter 12). But if one does think of it this way (and here the pieties of polite modern thought *do* come under some strain), it is necessary to acknowledge that, even if racist consciousness is unlikely ever to be an epistemically sound way in which to express the content of a political judgement, it might under some circumstances embody a perfectly sound political judgement in itself. It is unlikely ever to be epistemically sound, because race is a biological category, and although it could in principle be true that racial characteristics were of intrinsic importance in the practical relations between groups of human beings, we do not as yet, as I understand the matter, know of any instances in which they in fact are or have been. But it might nevertheless in some instances be politically sound because racial characteristics, identified in a rough and ready way at the level of appearance, may on occasion be quite strongly correlated historically with other characteristics which are of the most direct significance for the interpretation of group interests: recency of entry into a local labour market, recency of physical migration, degree of commitment to or distance from the culture of those living at the same site several decades earlier, and so on. In conditions of high unemployment, residential squalor and severe social and economic deprivation, these facts do have the sharpest practical relevance for interpreting the content of group interests. What is journalistically referred to as racism is an ugly response to this relevance; but it is not an unintelligible one. To understand it, even to understand it perfectly, is in no sense to forgive it – let alone to excuse it. It can be (and often is) a real form of human harm, directed at real victims. Wherever this is indeed so, it is for the victims to decide how far, if at all, they are prepared to forgive it. But I see no reason to suppose that we can hope to explain its presence without acknowledging its intelligibility, and even less ground for supposing that we can hope to diminish that presence by refusing to acknowledge its intelligibility.

The place of racism in the human world of today is partly an imaginative precipitate of great world–historical confrontations of the past – the black slaves of North America and their post-European masters (and mistresses), the aboriginal population of Australia and the waves of settlers who have engulfed them over the last three centuries, Christian Europe and the Islamic peoples, the Jewish population of Israel and the Palestinians. All of these are at best half-dormant fields of long-remembered suspicion or hatred, which can flare suddenly at any moment into the most appalling life. But the most persistent and practically important aspect of racism in the world today, the aspect which is virtually never dormant, even if its overt presence is less devastating, is the resentful, spiteful but also strikingly insecure encounters between different human populations forced into ever more intimate and intrusive interaction with each other. Here, what is central is seldom or never a more or less mythic history of great past crimes or triumphs, but simply a growing sense of confusion and vulnerability, and a pronounced shortage of trustworthy protectors. Even in the Union of South Africa, now that the Population Registration Act has been formally repealed (*Financial Times*, 17 June 1991, p. 2), racist politicians have evidently proved less than trustworthy protectors of the interests of those groups that they have had at heart. But however unsympathetic we may reasonably be towards those particular groups, it can hardly be denied that they did have interests which it was reasonable for them to try to protect, or that it has always been quite difficult to see what strategies for protecting those interests could reasonably hope to prove durably effective (cf. Adam & Moodley 1986). In effect the repeal of the Population Registration Act by the precariously post-racist politicians who chose to repeal it is just a later, if less malign, hypothesis about how that protection might most effectively be provided.

In a world of unsteadily but rapidly intensifying economic interaction, with a quickening product cycle and dramatic variations between rates of economic growth and population growth between different territories, national governments virtually throughout the world have found it increasingly difficult to protect the prosperity or livelihoods of large sectors of their own populations. The optimistic postwar presumption that the political right of citizenship was now linked dependably to a social right to a constant or steadily rising standard of living (Marshall 1950, pp. 1–85) has proved to rest on the assumed efficiency of Keynesian techniques of macroeconomic management which have come to work less well everywhere and now in many settings appear barely to work at all. In most cases where the Marshallian social right has been successfully provided over the last decade and a half, it has been so through the skil- fully coordinated and ferociously effective penetration of external markets, not by the steady mastery of a purely domestic economic space. However collectively advantageous over the *longue durée* the expansion of a world trading system has been and may still remain, the ferociously effective penetration of external markets, in the short run and at the receiving end, has much of the quality of a zero-sum game.

In terms of a pattern theory of justice like that of John Rawls (1972) (cf. Nozick 1974; Barry 1989), the massive intrusion into western Europe over the last few decades of populations from outside it (the Mahgreb, Turkey, south Asia, the West Indies, eastern Europe) can reasonably be seen as a marginal but welcome contribution to rectifying international economic injustice (the single most obtrusive social fact about the world in which we all live). But it is more than ingenuous to be surprised that that has often not been at all the way in which it has been experienced or interpreted in the towns or cities to which the immigrants have come. It is a grim busi- ness to live on the margins of, and at the mercy of, a deeply alien and often contemptuous society. Those who suffer most in these great movements of population are almost by necessity the immigrants themselves. But it is wrong to suppose that they are the only sufferers. The residential areas to which they find their way, and the communities in which they have to seek to find a new, if sometimes temporary, home, are all too often amongst the most neglected and rationally pessimistic components of a national population. It is ungenerous and frequently foolish for the existing denizens of these areas to *equate* the arrival of obtrusively alien groups with the least enviable aspects of their own situation: to see it in effect as a further and more dramatic token of the neglect and indifference of their own rulers. But they often have every reason to resent that neglect and at least some reason to fear that the new arrivals will in themselves, and simply by dint of being there, represent a further and direct injury to their own interests: further, more vulnerable and even cheaper and less fastidi- ous competitors in an already overcrowded labour market, even poorer and more despondent tenants of a hideous and decaying housing stock, still greater strains on schools which already extensively fail to fit their pupils for full participation in the life of the national society, hospitals and medical services which are increasingly incapable of sustaining the health of local populations (bringing the disease patterns of the late nineteenth century or the Third World back into the East End of London).

There is nowhere in the societies to which we belong in which the need to interpret the content of group interest accurately and imaginatively is as urgent or the factors militating against its accurate identification are as formidable. Judging whom to trust and whom to fear, whom to cooperate with and whom to struggle against in such conditions has to be undertaken by all concerned in the midst of anger and misery and fear. As a set of articulated theoretical beliefs today racism is simply and irretrievably absurd. But as a tracer of the strains of practical political judgement in the contemporary societies of the west, it is very far from being *just* absurd. (For a balanced and appropriately urgent judgement see Pugliese (1992).)

The most obtrusive and extensive site of racist consciousness in the contemporary world can be well delineated in the (no doubt often confused and ill-motivated) demotic answers to a single pressing and moderately clear question: where should human beings for any length of time *be*? Where should they live and work and seek to shape and plan their lives? The classic form for a potentially racist answer to this question (demotic or otherwise) is simply: wherever these people should be, it is certainly not *here*. They (unlike we) have no business being here. They have no *right* to be here. Here belongs (or should belong) to someone else (to us). Here is ours, not theirs.

One important prerequisite for understanding contemporary racism is not (of course) to deny whatever confused or ill-motivated elements may be found in demonic answers to this question, but simply to recognize the unreality of a widespread and unwarrantedly smug (if often tacit) contrast: the clear, well-motivated and putatively authoritative answers to this question offered by polite modern thought and its enlightened professional advisers or mouthpieces, the practitioners of the contemporary social sciences.

There are at least four extant candidates for an intrinsic answer to this blunt and urgent demotic question, all of them still candidates for the verdict of polite modern thought, as well as a fifth and more explicitly contingent one. What it is important to recognize about these answers is that none retains, in the face of the others, any convincing claim to overall moral or analytical authority.

The first answer, a Utopian liberal answer, is that human beings should be at all times wherever they want. They should be distributed spatially by present-tense personal choice.

A second answer, a conservative one, has no comparably canonical formulations (and not by accident). The gist of it is that human beings should be wherever they were six months ago, or five years ago, or wherever their parents or grandparents used to be. They should be distributed by the contingencies of birth, and should accept (indeed embrace) these contingencies (cf. Scruton 1980). The power of this answer comes largely from the palpable existential force for human beings, and the equally palpable historical vulnerability, of cultural difference.

A third answer, the Utopian economic liberal answer, is that they should be wherever they can produce most value with lowest negative externalities: by their honestly and accurately accounted marginal productivity. They should be distributed by a single unobstructed world market in capital and labour.

A fourth answer, the utilitarian, is that they should be wherever they can individually best enjoy being alive or wherever, aggregatively, their being alive (or dying) can lead to there being the largest total sum of human happiness. (Compare the assessment of the 'repugnant conclusion' in Parfit (1984).)

All of these four answers have a degree of real human force. More or less indiscreet efforts have been made throughout the intellectual history of the modern west to conflate each of them with one or more of the others. But it does not take very hard thought to recognize that each can and very often does clash blatantly with every one of the others.

Each, too, clashes frontally, and in a manner that can be avoided at any time solely by a whim of History, with the fifth and more explicitly contingent answer: that people should be distributed within a given territory (most importantly, by being legally and practically admitted to it or excluded from it) as, and only as, the legitimate political authority sovereign over that territory happens to decide. In a modern representative democracy, that is to say, the legitimate immigration (or indeed, to echo Mme Cresson, the legitimate expulsion) policy for a given community would be that policy constitutionally approved through the prevailing representative institutions by the majority of the community's citizens.

What this last answer brings out is the economic and political unreality of all four intrinsic answers: their stark incompatibility with the fundamental causal logic of the world in which we happen to live – a world which combines a very active (if elaborately rigged) world market in capital and labour with an at least equally active system of territorially sovereign state power. The contradictions between these five answers are structural, objective and ineliminable. They are not an artefact of selective intellectual inattention, severely limited altruism amongst the wealthy, or sheer feebleness of analytical will. They may not be here to stay. But they are certainly here for any future which we can imagine with the slightest degree of concreteness (Dunn 1985, chapter 6). There is nothing more concrete for human beings than where they are, where they are permitted to live and work, and where over time they can plan and try to shape their lives.

We can grasp the weight of these contradictions more readily if we ask ourselves a set of simple and pressing questions.

How do the responsibilities which states owe their own citizens differ from those which they owe to other human beings?

Is the familiar distinction between economic and political refugees (a legal and ideological distinction of key importance, for example, to the wretched boat people of Vietnam, shipwrecked, drowned, plundered, raped and murdered by pirates, festering in Hong Kong camps or flown back at Her Majesty's expense to the country from which they had grimly set sail) in the end morally sound? Does it capture a clear and humanly convincing contrast in rights and needs and in the responsibilities of others?

Should there be any frontiers? Is territorial sovereignty (and the political authority of the modern state, exclusive signatory and sole guarantor of the United Nations Declaration of Human Rights), a clear violation of human right in itself? And if, for example, there perhaps should not be any frontiers, how can it be true that there should be any such thing as an array of social rights, a system of social security, a welfare state, let alone a safer, juster and less polluted world (cf. Dunn 1991)?

If and when we can muster a clear and humanly compelling answer to these and other such questions we will know how to confront confused and ill-motivated demotic responses to the question of where human beings should be (anywhere but here) with a clearer and better motivated alternative. But until we find ourselves in this fortunate position, a less distanced and more egalitarian approach will be more in order: distinctly more prudent, potentially somewhat more effective, and far less devastatingly arrogant (cf. Dunn 1990, chapter 12).

Whatever socialism may have been in the days of Durkheim (1962, p. 41, a less than ideal translation), racism today is certainly a cry of pain. Like socialism, of course, it is also very often a cry of anger. But if we wish to understand it, we are not, I think, well advised (and certainly no better advised than in the case of socialism) to treat it just as an expression of anger, and an expression which is particularly contemptible because predicated on epistemically absurd judgements. At some points in the history of racist theorization there have been intimate links between racism and power. The history of modern slavery and of western imperial expansion are especially notable examples. The most unforgettable and appalling link between racism and power remains the Final Solution. But the most pervasive and practically important presence of racism in the world today is linked not to power but to impotence. I doubt if it will prove wise to neglect that fact as we look back and try to take the measure of racism's long and deeply unobvious history.

REFERENCES

Adam, H. and K. Moodley 1986. *South Africa without Apartheid: Dismantling Racial Domination*. Berkeley: University of California Press
Barry, B. 1989. *Theories of Justice*. Hemel Hempstead: Harvester-Wheatsheaf
Bobbio, N. 1991. *Una guerra giusta? Sul conflitto del golfo*. Venice: Marsilio
Dunn, J. 1980. *Political Obligation in its Historical Context*. Cambridge: Cambridge University Press
    1984. *Locke*. Oxford: Oxford University Press
    1985. *Rethinking Modern Political Theory*. Cambridge: Cambridge University Press
    1990. *Interpreting Political Responsibility*. Cambridge: Polity Press
    1991. 'Political obligation'. In *Political Theory Today*, ed. D. Held. Cambridge: Polity Press (Chapter 4 above)
Durkheim, E. 1962. *Socialism*, ed. A. W. Gouldner. New York: Collier Books
Dworkin, R. 1981. 'What is equality?' Parts 1 and 2. *Philosophy and Public Affairs* 10, 3 and 4, 185–246, 283–345
Finley, M. I. 1980. *Ancient Slavery and Modern Ideology*. London: Chatto and Windus
Nozick, R. 1974. *Anarchy, State and Utopia*. Oxford: Blackwell
Marshall, T. H. 1950. *Citizenship and Social Class*. Cambridge: Cambridge University Press
Modiano, G. 1992. 'Coincidenze e divergenze tra le varie possibili definizioni di razza'. In *Il Razzismo e le sue storie*, ed. G. Imbruglia. Naples: Edizioni Scientifiche Italiane
Pagden, A. 1986. *The Fall of Natural Man*, 2nd edn. Cambridge: Cambridge University Press
    1992. 'Razzismo e colonialismo europeo: un'indagine storica'. In *Il Razzismo e le sue storie*, ed. G. Imbruglia. Naples: Edizioni Scientifiche Italiane
Parfit, D. 1984. *Reasons and Persons*. Oxford: Clarendon Press
Prosperi, A. 1992. 'Tra natura e cultura: dall'intolleranza religiosa alla discriminazione per sangue'. In *Il Razzismo e le sue storie*, ed. G. Imbruglia. Naples: Edizioni Scientifiche Italiane
Przeworski, A. 1985. *Capitalism and Social Democracy*. Cambridge: Cambridge University Press
Pugliese, E. 1992. 'Le interpretazioni del razzismo nel dibattito italiano sulla immigrazione'. In *Il Razzismo e le sue storie*, ed. G. Imbruglia, pp. 265–87. Naples: Edizioni Scientifiche Italiane
Rawls, J. 1972. *A Theory of Justice*. Oxford: Clarendon Press
Scruton, R. 1980. *The Meaning of Conservatism*. Harmondsworth: Penguin

10 Political science, political theory and policy making in an interdependent world

For anyone interested in modern politics there could scarcely be a more pressing issue than how best to approach the task of identifying and comprehending the novel political challenges and opportunities which flow from the ever increasing interdependence of the destinies of human populations. At the intersection between challenge and opportunity there lie both fresh processes of policy making and implementation and distinctly older political routines and habits of mind: the attempt at worst to pour very new and volatile wine into disturbingly antiquated bottles, or at best to bring the accumulated resources of centuries of statecraft to bear upon a bewildering array of often unprecedented hazards.

The novel processes of policy making in this increasingly interdependent world can be thought of in two quite distinct ways: to speak briskly, *either* positively, *or* critically. Seen the first way – seen positively – their core is a set of new institutional sites, supra-national, transnational and domestic, official and unofficial, and an extravagantly complicated array of networks of communication and affiliation which link these sites. At these sites, already, a vast volume of business is transacted and, in consonance with the increasingly taut links between human populations, a far more ambitious and permanently expanding agenda is being tentatively explored. Some of these sites are relatively durable (OECD, GATT, the European Commission, the World Bank, the UN High Commission for Refugees, the Ford or Macarthur Foundations, UNESCO). Others are inherently more transitory – major international conferences of states, like the Rio Summit, or innovative scientific meetings aimed at capturing more sharply for the first time the overall shape of some pressing human emergency which is just beginning to come into focus.

What can political science and political theory as yet tell us about the significance of these sites; and how far are either or both likely eventually to enable us to understand this significance? What takes place at these sites is already plainly both a proper and an attractive subject for political science to study, as are the pressures which lead to the establishment of the sites or to the extension or maintenance of the networks. Equally proper in themselves as a subject, clearly, are the consequences of each, and above all the assessment of the efficacy or otherwise of both in dealing with the practical challenges which they encounter. But here the disciplinary resources of political science are more evidently overstretched, since even to identify adequately these pressures requires both a valid assessment not merely of a distinctively political causality but also of economic, social and even ecological causalities of bewildering intricacy. At the same time, in order to judge the felicity or otherwise of their outcomes one needs a far more profound grasp of all of these causalities, along with a power and precision of distinctively political understanding, which may simply be unavailable even in principle. No human being, as we all know, actually possesses such an understanding (though some, of course, are conspicuously further away from it than others). There are important lines of modern thinking, especially in economics (stemming from the Austrian school and the work of Mises and Hayek in particular) and in ecology, which suggest that there is little danger of any single human being ever coming to acquire such understanding.

The challenge to the political scientist

In this perspective the new processes of policy making present a very distinctive challenge to the political scientist. They offer a relatively novel subject matter for inquiry which is of compelling interest and of indisputable practical importance. The novelty, to be sure, is only relative. The new processes are analytically distinguishable from older processes of policy making not by being wholly discontinuous in either their content or their location, but by connected shifts in their subject matter, participants, physical location, intensity, rhythms, and above all scale of potential human significance. (It is an empirical question just how discontinuous the resulting patterns of policy making really are from their historically protracted predecessors,[1] and we necessarily cannot yet know how different they are going to become. But what is plain is that anyone trying to think seriously about modern politics already needs to do his or her best to assess both these contrasts.) The new processes offer a subject matter in relation to which any soundly educated, attentive and clearheaded political scientist could be confident of making some immediate headway simply setting himself or herself to study it by direct (and ideally, perhaps, participant–observational) methods, and with a reasonable degree of patience. But any such approach would inevitably be a shade

---

[1] For a vivid picture of continuity in difference see Crowe (1993). For light on the policy process inside the EC see Mazey & Richardson (1992).

parochial. It opts for the visual convenience of a small pool of intense light, situated within a vast penumbra of deepening obscurity. But it offers no plausible basis (in the sense of no conceivably relevant technique of investigation) for dissipating most of the surrounding darkness and resigns itself, in effect, to taking the darkness as given.

The optimistic response to this cognitive predicament is to register the well-attested modern advantages of the division of cognitive labour; to insist that political science, like other serious modern practices of inquiry, is inherently cooperative, and to leave firmly to, more or less clearly designated, others the responsibility for illuminating the murky remainder of the space. But this remedy falls some way short of dissolving the dilemma. Its principal weakness is not so much its somewhat ingenuous conception (or at least presentation) of the degree to which political scientists in most fields characteristically *attempt* to cooperate with one another, or of the sensitivity with which they contrive to mesh each others' cognitive preoccupations together, as it is its resolute turning of the back on the single most important feature of the subject matter in question. I take that feature to be its unstable and ineliminable union between quite genuine cognitive inquiry and just as genuine practical conflict over perceived interests.

To see the core of these processes as lying in an heuristic struggle is clearly tendentious. It involves an explicit judgement of value and an implicit (if rather vaguer) judgement about practical causality – about what may crucially happen and is, at least as far as we can now tell, likely enough to do so to make it worthwhile to consider the possibility that it actually will. The first of these judgements, *ex hypothesi*, can receive no direct support from a knowledge, however exhaustive, of what has thus far occurred. The second, plainly, must rest, as best it can, on inductive lessons drawn from the past. But it cannot hope to rest at all securely, for familiar reasons inherent in the reflexivity of human social and political understanding and especially weighty in circumstances of intense economic and political competition.[2]

The problems of cognitive labour

The relation between the division of labour and human interests has always been central to the understanding of politics. Far more narrowly and more concretely, it has been obvious that the extent to which human labour in the world at any time is in fact divided in a way which effectively

---

[2] The importance of these reasons has long been stressed by MacIntyre (e.g. 1973). They are of especial significance for the understanding of revolutions – particularly dramatic instances of the disruption of routine politics (Dunn 1985, chapter 4).

serves the interests of all the labourers, or to which instead this is divided in a manner which conspicuously subordinates the interests of some human beings to those of others, has been the central issue in understanding distinctively modern politics, ever since modern politics first hove into sight some time in the later seventeenth century (Hont 1990). It would be inordinately optimistic (quite false) to suppose that this is a question which we have yet learnt how to solve (though, of course, anyone seriously interested in politics will have a fair number of intuitions about it, and one may reasonably hope that the intuitions of some go quite deep). But if we have no clear and dependable general strategy for demarcating cognitively benign division of labour from deliberate or inadvertent service of necessarily partial interest (as I believe to be the case) then the most important questions about this insistent but still inchoate and relatively opaque redivision of cognitive labour and this more tentative but equally important incipient refashioning of effective political authority turn on how exactly the division of cognitive (and other) labour can be superimposed on the structure of current and future human interests. A sensitive ethnography of what is at present taking place at these sites and along these networks[3] would certainly give some clues to the distribution of interests that are effectively pressed within them or even more effectively excluded from them. But unless it was also informed by a confident assessment, drawn from somewhere else, of just how these interests are in fact objectively related in the last instance (how far, for example, they stand in a zero-sum or a partially complementary relation), it would be very hard in principle for the ethnography itself to yield much more than an internal critique of the consciousness of the occupants of the site in question.

Inadequacy of internal critique

It does not take much reflection to grasp that the principal reason for studying these sites, their vast practical importance for human interests, will not be adequately served just by arriving at such an internal critique. In particular, if that reason is expressed with adequate grossness (for example, as the question of what really is going on politically at present in the human world), it is clear that such an internal critique, even if a necessary element in any such answer, could be at best a very small

---

[3] In social analysis the term 'network' was first extensively employed by social anthropologists studying African urbanization. It is significant that non-official and relatively critical participants in the new processes of policy making should place such emphasis on the instrumental value and personal sustenance of networking. For the use of the concept of social network see Mitchell (1969).

proportion of the answer itself. Put grossly, this is a question at which most educated political scientists would be sophisticated enough to blench. But it is scarcely adequate at this point to remain content with a cultivated shudder. For without facing that issue – without descending to this level of grossness – it is impossible in principle to develop any stable basis on which to comprehend modern politics. What is manifestly going on in these novel processes of policy making is that organized human communities are trying to learn how to cope with the historical predicament in which they find themselves. The key judgement is whether they are at present on balance *succeeding* in learning how to do so or whether they are conspicuously failing to learn anything of the kind, whether they are making headway or slipping inexorably ever further behind.[4] The predicament itself is seen (and rightly seen) increasingly as not merely historical (political, economic, social, cultural) but also natural. Not to see the issue this way is to miss the key point about what is, incontestably, going on. But to address this issue frontally requires a mind-wrenching holism of judgement that anyone of minimal modesty could only find mildly appalling. (Modesty is the distinctive – the first – virtue of the modern cognitive division of labour. But personal modesty, for all its charms, does not necessarily preclude severe epistemic costs.)

To see the new processes of policy making as a painful and precarious heuristic struggle in the face of threats of virtually unfathomable scope and urgency is not to sentimentalize them. It in no way occludes the prominent role of purposeful and often cynical and naive pursuit of presumed interest within them. But it does entail the judgement that to see them merely and exhaustively in these terms is disastrously superficial. The relationship between cognitive and libidinal elements is always complex and significant in politics; between on one side the attempts of political agents, successful or unsuccessful, to apprehend what is going on and what is at stake and, on the other, raw desire, will or preference. But this relation becomes far harder to see accurately and much more impor-

---

[4] The urgency of this question comes out very sharply in Williams (1993). To see technical innovation as a single integrated causal field identifies an *explicandum*; but it does not dictate the choice of an explanatory model of the field itself. To balance fatalist against voluntarist elements within such a model is to bring into focus the inherent political plasticity of that process, the degree to which it really is open to modification by human comprehension and political choice. To balance demand-led (contractors' or patrons') contributions to it against supply-led contributions (the pursuit of scientific comprehension from unrestrainable intellectual curiosity or the personal quest for fame and fortune) is to identify the principal source of its impetus. It is remarkable how unclear we still remain over how to discharge either of these tasks. It is also extremely dangerous that we remain so unclear.

tant to look for as the field of economic and political interaction between human beings widens and deepens, and as the economic activities of human beings exert a more and more disruptive impact on their physical habitat (MacNeill *et al.* 1991).

Limitations of cognitive resources

To see the core of these processes of policy making as heuristic struggle also underlines quite fiercely just how limited are the special cognitive resources that political scientists as such can hope to bring to bear upon their understanding. Political scientists are at their most assured in tracing out in practice the consequences of relatively clearly perceived interests in the interactions of those attempting to pursue them. This subject matter is as thick on the ground within the new process of policy making as it was within the old processes. But if it is the novelty of the processes which interests us (as it surely should be), we can have no a priori confidence that the component of purposefully pursued presumed interest within them, however powerfully apprehended or lucidly conveyed, will be what we most wish and need to understand.

Within the modern academic division of labour political scientists, both in their own and in others' eyes, are professional theorists and interpreters of one aspect of collective human existence (Dunn 1985, 1990a). But the special expertise in which their professional status inheres, while indisputably pertinent to understanding these new political processes, is plainly insufficient to capture the most important (and in an illuminating sense, the essential) aspect of what is going on. In the face of what is in fact going on, there simply are as yet no professional theorists at all: no exponents of clearly specified and plausibly adequate cognitive techniques, attested by close mutual professional surveillance, that have any claim whatever to cognitive mastery over the domain (Dunn 1993). In the face of the gross but essential question, we are all of us all too blatantly the most rankly amateur of theorists. This is in no sense a derogation of the craft skills of the political scientist (most of which can be brought usefully to bear on one or other aspect of what is taking place): merely a recognition of what for the present lies some distance beyond them. Political scientists will clearly be needed to ascertain what the human agents and agencies taking part in these processes are attempting to do and why they are attempting to do these things and not others. They may do much to illuminate, through the exercise of their carefully developed sensibilities and analytical skills, just how the processes have come to be developed and have altered as they have. But it will be hard for them to reach further without jeopardizing the genuinely professional skills which they are bringing to bear, without shifting more or less consciously from a mode of inquiry in which they know what they are doing to one in which they too are gropingly trying to find out. (This is, of course, no reason for discouraging them from making that shift. But it is certainly a ground for trying to sharpen their consciousness of just when and where the shift is occurring and what its occurrence means.)

Political science is excellently adapted to study what has already taken place at these sites, and serviceable enough for attempting to identify the pressures that have led to the establishment of the sites and the extension or maintenance of the networks that link them. It has, of course, done an appreciable quantity of studying of them already, with varying degrees of illumination.[5] But it is far less well equipped to capture the effective consequences of the existence of the new sites or their capacity to cope with the array of practical challenges that already face human populations and will face them in an aggravated form in the future. This issues in an important dilemma. The more epistemically modern and austere – the more scientific, or even just the more intellectually honest – the political scientist in question, the more evidently underequipped to take the measure of what is happening in these sites and through these processes. The dilemma can (and must) be alleviated by intellectual cooperation. But, as we have seen, there are grounds for doubting whether it can in principle ever be simply dissolved.

Political theorists, too, of course, like to think of themselves within the modern academic division of labour, as professional theorists and interpreters of an aspect of collective human existence, though it is dispiritingly hard to indicate to even a moderately sceptical listener just what their peculiar expertise in doing so might reasonably be thought to consist in (cf. Chapter 2 above).

Seen positively, in the professional optic of political science, the key feature of the new processes of policy making (what one might call their real meaning) lies tantalizingly and rather obdurately beyond the horizon. To register this is not to sneer at the intellectual standing of political science, still less to issue an indiscreet boast on behalf of political theory (a professional skill, if it be such, which seldom has anything very definite to boast about). It is merely to recognize once again the vastly greater intellectual felicity of political science in handling well institutionalized routine politics than in grasping either slow or rapid processes of more or less incipient but fundamental transformation.

---

[5] See, for example, Winham (1986), Haus (1992), Bayne (1991), Crockett (1992).

Positive and critical perceptions

To see positively is to see as what is knowably there, as what is already fully given within existing experience. Political theorists, of course, cannot (except by pure fluke) see what is not knowably there any more effectively than political scientists can. (Rather the contrary, if anything.) But they are more resigned to the limits of their vision and less inhibited (for better and for worse) by these limits. For them the issue always must be: what *is* the real meaning of what is going on? Where will it eventually lead? What is it doing to the interests of human populations? How insistently is it likely to sustain its present momentum? Political theorists are seldom genuinely under the misapprehension that they know the answers to these questions (though they sometimes have the professionally indiscreet bravado to express themselves as though they believed that they do). What they are confident of is the peremptoriness and the authentically epistemic significance of the questions themselves. They see, both by professional vocation and by personal disposition, not positively but critically: not through the conception of what is knowably going on, but through the conception of what, in the light of reasonable and attentive judgement, importantly may be doing so.

In that light – seen critically – what importantly may be going on is quite simple (however difficult in practice it may prove to assess). Human beings may on balance be succeeding in learning or they may be failing to learn, in one arena after another, how to restabilize the increasingly violent miscellany of instabilities which result from their growing numbers and their intensifying interaction with one another and with their natural environment across the globe as a whole. There are some strong candidates for an *experimentum crucis* over this question at present: notably the Uruguay Round of the GATT, the Maastricht process, the fate of the European Monetary System, and the existing state of the world currency markets. But the idea of a crucial experiment is misplaced in this context for two distinct reasons. It is so first and formally because of the cognitive asymmetry between past and future, which from a human point of view (as opposed to a pseudo-divine viewpoint) precludes the drawing of conclusive inferences from past to future. But it is misplaced also for a second and less ambitious reason: that past success in any very complex process of inquiry in principle furnishes no guarantee of future success. (This is at present a genuine truism of the philosophy of natural science: comfortably available from the full range of theoretical positions entertained within that discipline.) Even if it were demonstrably true (which as yet it certainly is not) that human beings at large had recently been making headway in their quest for physical security, that would be no guarantee whatever that they will continue to do so either in the near or more distant future. There are (thus far, no doubt, fairly unreliable) measurements of whether the surface of the world itself is getting warmer or colder. But there is nothing even conceptually analogous to (let alone practically available as) a measure of whether human beings are on balance becoming, through extraordinarily complicated institutional interaction, collectively more or less prudent.[6]

The GATT example

The recent vicissitudes of the primary institutional framework for the coordination and regulation of international trading practices, the GATT, are a vivid instance of the urgency and inherent obscurity of this question. They show, beyond the possibility of rational doubt, that any presumption of guaranteed progress in such learning is gratuitous. But at the time of writing they have yet to prove definitely that in this respect regress is now inevitable. The huge economic costs of failure in the Uruguay Round (see Dodwell 1992), were signalled clearly to all participants (and were of course clearly anticipated in all except numerical formulation throughout the protracted process of negotiation). The far greater costs which would have followed from the collapse of the round into a deepening vortex of trade wars were at the forefront of the attention of US and EC trade and agriculture officials for some years. Here the cognitive assessment of the scale of potential gains and losses across the actors as a whole is more than counterbalanced in many settings by an equally cognitively plausible assessment of how the costs of securing the coordination might most conveniently be distributed amongst the coordinated, by the robust determination not to be anyone else's sucker and the fond hope that others may be induced to forgo their immediate interest to the advantage of one's own. Narrowness of interest (the electoral implications of the subsidy advantages of a relatively small group of French agricultural exporters) is often more than offset by intensity of preference. Game-theoretical explorations of the rationality of cooperation did not prove that there could not be a successful outcome of the GATT round (a feature of them which became especially felicitous when there proved to be a successful outcome). But they plainly do register suggestively some important causal features of the negotiations themselves, and might in principle have helped to clarify why the round eventually failed, if fail it had. (To express the point in more archaic vocabulary, they might show in the most rigorous manner possible quite what a remarkable political

---

[6] For the centrality of prudence, see Dunn (1990a).

achievement it could be if the round eventually succeeded. And show this even if it is in fact true that the prospective gains from its success and costs of its failure are as huge over time for every sovereign participant in the negotiations as the OECD analysis suggests. What they probably could not in principle show – and what is of the greatest significance – is how much of a contribution to achieving that outcome in the end came not from leading state officials or national political leaders in the negotiating states but from the steady on-going diplomatic pressure and intellectual persuasion emanating from the GATT secretariat or from essentially advisory transnational bodies like OECD.)

But although the continuing struggle to shore up and strengthen, or weaken and dismantle a framework for the regulation of international trade has remained prominent ever since, it is by no means obvious that it is the most important component of the new processes of policy making. The principal convenience of commencing with trade regulation is the range of considerations which it directly raises and the relative determinacy of what is being contended for within it. In the case of the GATT round, it is reasonable to suspect that the key feature of the negotiations was the degree to which the negotiating partners (principally, the individual sovereign nation states and the groupings into which they have chosen to form) have contrived to develop relatively impartial sites to undertake the urgent task of specifying overall collective benefits with sufficient clarity and authority to give them a real chance to counterbalance the frenzied pressure of local interest group lobbying upon the governments of the individual negotiating partners. The charms of riding free on facilities paid for by others are particularly evident within the endless competition between states to foster local comparative advantage and erode foreign competitive advantage through the use of government power, to bend the terms of trade to national benefit. The instruments deployed in this competition – tariffs, local regulatory requirements on imported goods or services, anti-dumping measures – proliferate constantly (see Gilpin 1987; Haus 1992). All have eminently respectable possible uses. All are constantly modified for what (at least from the viewpoint of global economic welfare) constitutes quite deliberate abuse. In the Uruguay Round the EC, largely because of the widely resented external damage which it inflicts on agrarian producers across the world, effectively negotiated for many purposes as a single actor (though it plainly determined its negotiating position as a result of often bitter internal quarrels). But the same issues of immediate tension between overall collective benefit, national governmental convenience and direct interest group losses – of confrontation between concentrated and immediate welfare costs for particular groups and less immediate potential gains for far larger groups, who for the most part see and feel no immediate implications for their own interests – come out just as sharply within the Community itself in the Commission's attempt to extend a single-market competitive policy to the individual member countries.

New and old views of free trade

The fundamental antinomy between the Ricardian image of free world trade as a global public good and the more sceptical vision of trade as a worldwide battleground, on which only the most manipulative and ruthless of statecraft can effectively protect the interests of national populations, goes back to the dawn of modern politics (see Dunn 1990b; Hont 1990). Academic students of international political economy (to say nothing of economic journalists and economic historians) have amassed a vast range of information about the real presence of each within the experience of international trade, particularly over the last century. But we remain no closer today than our ancestors were three centuries ago to seeing exactly how these two images now articulate with one another. Once we recognize clearly that this is so, it is also all too easy to see that the implications of this visual opacity (the shadowy fault line between the two images in their detailed application to current economic and political reality) are just as important and just as hard to pick out within domestic governmental economic policy making or attempts to concert the collective interests of particular domestic interest groups (the CBI, the British Chamber of Commerce, the TUC) as they are in international negotiations within supra-national units like the EC or between the entire membership of the GATT. If one thinks of the new processes of policy making in terms of the realities which they are struggling to apprehend, it is plain that the crude contrast between old and new sites of deliberation and action, policy formation, choice and enforcement, is not sustainable. The new processes do not stop at or start from the more novel institutional sites. They spill over into sites which have been in existence in many cases for centuries.[7] What can be said relatively uncontroversially, however, is that the new sites offer a better focusing device for discerning what is novel in these processes, precisely because so many of these sites were devised and installed by the old sites (individual state governments acting for and by themselves) in recognition of their increasing incapacity

---

[7] In the case of states the continuity can readily be exaggerated. It is often the state as ideological fiction (Skinner 1989; Dunn 1990a, Introduction and chapter 8) which has had a clearly continuous historical identity rather than the state as a reasonably determinate causal entity.

to cope on their own with many aspects of the practical challenges which confronted them.

It is easy enough to see where these challenges have come from – above all from the vast expansion both in the physical volume and the economic value of international trade and in the increasingly direct involvement of the bulk of modern working populations in activities which are immediately affected by that trade. On the Ricardian image, there is no palpable reason why the sheer growth in international trade should accentuate instability in any way at all. But gluts and slumps have been an inevitable concomitant of commercial economies throughout their known history; and their disruptive impact on a world scale was never likely to prove less perturbing than it has always been on a more parochial scale. Over and above the destabilizing potentiality inherent in the sheer scale of mutual commercial dependence across the globe, there are a number of far more specific sources of instability in other features of international economic relations today; most notably the difficulty of developing effective international regulatory arrangements to cover the immense and sometimes bewilderingly rapid financial flows and international currency movements that have followed the expansion in trade itself and been amplified by the dramatic technical acceleration in means of communication. The scale and volatility of international currency markets makes them already plainly beyond the control, under some conditions, of even the Central Banks of the major capitalist states. In the case of securities markets also the weight of derivatives markets is increasingly out of proportion to that of the markets in underlying securities; and the problem of regulation (as the 1987 crash strongly suggested) is already inherently an international rather than a national problem. There appears to be no coherent and reasonably widely supported suggestion as to how a stable monetary basis for international trade can be recreated under present conditions; and the relatively clear relationship in the past between economic hegemony and international trading regimes (Keohane 1984; Gilpin 1987; Lawrence & Schultze 1990) and the circumstances in which the last such framework collapsed (Gowa 1983) make it clear how difficult (and perhaps also how unpromising) would be the political assignment of attempting to reconstruct one.

There is, however, good reason to believe that, within the national economies of the world as these now exist and are likely to develop in the near future, even the bemusing challenges of international economic cooperation are a less drastic and alarming source of instability than the interaction between human beings and the natural habitat within which they live out their lives (MacNeill *et al.* 1991; Hurrell & Kingsbury 1992). The assumption that this framework could take care of itself over time in the face of large groupings of human beings, and still more that it could do so in the face of the human species as a whole has been one of the boundary assumptions of the tradition of western political thinking, reinforced rather than weakened by the modern secularization of that tradition. Now that this assumption is urgently in question, no element in that tradition (even in its most minimalist and politically sceptical core) can be confidently anticipated to hold good (Dunn 1993, Conclusion).

Political scientists versus political theorists

For these reasons at least (and there may be many others) political scientists at present are plainly in no position to instruct us on how to take the measure of these new processes of policy formation and implementation, though some of them, of course, can cast much light upon them (as can diplomats, economists, journalists, natural scientists of many varieties, civil servants, career politicians, cadres of ecological pressure groups and of the managerial hierarchies of major economic enterprises, most of which are now ineluctably transnational in exposure, even if they happen not to trade formally as incorporated entities in more than one sovereign territory).

The claim that political scientists at present cannot show us how to take the measure of these processes is a claim of political theory. But it does not, of course, imply that political theorists somehow can tell us how to understand them.

What political theory can hope to contribute is a small number of relatively simple analytical thoughts that may prove helpful in the (we must hope) unending and necessarily exhausting attempt to comprehend both in theory and practice the task of handling the economics, politics, and social, biological (and even physical and chemical) relations of an increasingly globalized human habitat.[8]

A handful of such thoughts can be divided for convenience into points about values, points about history, and points about the intrinsic difficulties of understanding politics. In their ensemble they can be seen as bearing directly on the issue of how to understand the concept of prudence for a modern population.

The key points about values concern priorities – specifically the priority of biological survival over any proposals for the content of a good life both for individual human beings and for groupings of human beings of any possible scale. This is a truism of natural jurisprudence (Locke [1689] 1960, II, para. 6; Dunn 1984) which should descend intact into any more

---

[8] The scale of this task is very well brought out in Williams (1993).

obdurately naturalistic modern secular viewpoint with the least claim to address the realm of politics. It is reasonable to read it as a criterion for the validity of any such claim. In some ways, plainly, this is quite a weak ordering principle, and irremediably vague as well as contentious in application (as the controversy over Hobbes's political theses long ago showed) (cf. Hampton 1986; Baumgold 1988).

But weak though it is, it may well, as we now know, be strong enough to overrule any claim to justifiability in a huge range of energetically reinforced and amplified contemporary practices – even for most of the existing world economy and a large proportion of prevailing human reproductive habit. The clearest influence from it is the priority of preserving a viable extra-human habitat for human beings over any set of historically inherited or aesthetically improvised human preferences. But for individuals and groups this priority, palpably, does not terminate with the privileging of ecology over human economy, but extends deeply into the causal texture of economic and political interaction themselves.

A subsidiary (and more heartening) point about values is the merit of attempting to specify criteria for success and failure of social, political and economic arrangements not through the illusory clarity of revealed preferences or the arbitrary simplicity of a schedule of alleged rights but through the more naturalistic, empirically open, and evaluatively responsive category of human capabilities.[9]

Historical perspectives

Three major historical points follow directly from these evaluative points: points, in essence, about the history of human ecology, about the history of the state as an institutional form, and about the historical development of modern economies and of the understanding of their causal dynamics. The first and by far the most important is that none of the new sites or practices are very plausible facilities as yet for ensuring the effective service of the first human priority of preserving a viable human habitat in face of nature's cumulative response to human agency. Some hold more heuristic promise. Some have greater immediate capacity to implement their practical judgement. But none yet holds much promise of each of these; and neither contribution will be of much value without the other.

The second point concerns the direct threat to the survival of individual human beings or groups not from the fragility of their natural (non-human) habitat but from the actions of other human beings. The state,

---

[9] This case has been pressed extremely effectively in recent years by Amartya Sen in response to his extensive work on famine and crises of subsistence.

the unit of action which is now manifestly unable to establish effective control over (and therefore unable to take effective responsibility for) the destiny of its own subjects (see Held & McGrew 1993; cf. chapter 4 above), was established in its own self-understanding, principally to safeguard these subjects against the physical threats of other human beings, at home and abroad (Skinner 1989). It has always been clear that it can hope to furnish this guarantee only insofar as it can become and remain an effective and unified coercive power. It would be wholly unreasonable to expect any version of the new processes of policy making to stand in effectively for the failures of states in this respect on any but the most temporary of bases. The proposal that they might take the power to do so more durably is a tacit proposal for the revival of empire. This is the issue over which the American government has been deliberating sporadically ever since the collapse of the Soviet Union. The superficially less perturbing category of international law could not in principle stand in for empire in this role, though very optimistic political thinkers might perhaps hope (and have sometimes hoped in the past) for the eventual construction of an empire not of men (or even of women and men) but of laws.

The third point, already indicated, is the vast importance for understanding modern politics of being able to distinguish both analytically and practically between the degree to which the world economy and the exchange of goods and services within this can reasonably be seen as a single integral public good and the degree to which it can only reasonably be understood as an endlessly differentiated and unfathomably opaque series of zero-sum or positive-sum games. This contrast lies at the very heart of a process like the GATT round and it is striking how little definite collective headway human beings have made in comprehending it since the days of Adam Smith. An optimistic view of this apparent impasse would be that transnational civil servants and their intellectual mentors or clients are now the bearers of relatively sound causal judgement on the topic, and that the only serious problem which it still poses is that of how to bring the more or less corrupt ranks of national career politicians and state officials, and the as yet comprehensively unedified demos to whom they are to some degree accountable, around to the same degree of enlightenment. But the pessimistic elements in this assessment appear all too well founded, while the more optimistic ones may be less well warranted.

Understanding politics

The two points about the intrinsic difficulties of understanding politics follow relatively directly from these three historical points. They bear on the question of how far it is reasonable to suppose that human progress can be achieved not merely in comprehending a collective predicament of this scale but also in cooperating effectively together, despite their palpably widely discrepant interests, in coping with this predicament. No one knows the answer to this question. But there are at least two things which it is reasonable to believe about it: one very abstract and the other relatively concrete. The abstract point is that the question of how far it is reasonable to suppose that human beings could cooperate with one another has both a logical and a causal sense to it. It concerns the logic of rational choice and the modalities of moral agency. But it also concerns the psychological and sociological causation of human action within highly concrete historical contexts.

The results of modern study of rational choice show that it is harder for human beings to cooperate rationally with one another than idle moralizing or urgent spiritual witness have often suggested.[10] These results also suggest, however, that the more dispiriting forms of mutual frustration (prominent items in the experience of every practical politician) can often be eluded, thanks to the iterative character of political interaction, by an adroit switch from one type of game to another. (There are none so terminally hemmed in as those who can barely see.) Psychological and sociological visions which stress personal obstinacy or chauvinist bigotry and malice retain all too much plausibility. But insofar as the dilemmas of collective rationality can in principle be eluded, it is optimistic but not unreasonable to hope that these disagreeably insistent psychological and sociological pressures may in the very long run be effectively overridden by the genuinely Hobbesian rational priority of the claims of self-preservation (at least where the selves in question are credibly social enough to display some temporal depth and lateral extension).

Integration as a principle

But the most concrete point is for the present less optimistic. The new processes of policy making are new in large measure in that they are not essentially state-created or state-bounded. Actual states plainly consist of contending groups of imperfectly mutually comprehending or sympathetic human beings. But they do have at their core a very strong principle of integration. Indeed, understood theoretically and on their own terms, what they ultimately consist in is a very strong principle of integration. What they integrate, as Hobbes carefully explained, is not merely the enforcement of a single judgement on irretrievably contentious matters, but also the content of that judgement itself. That, at least, is their task,

---

[10] For the importance of this see chapter 7 above.

their privilege and their function. It is clear at present that the diffuse sequences of diplomatic negotiation in which the new processes of policy making so largely consist achieve no such integration of judgement, and that they often lack the capacity to enforce such integration of judgement as they do manage to achieve upon the recalcitrant. But the same, of course, has always been true of most actually existing states. What is important is not this present level of failure (which could only reasonably have been anticipated), but the fact that few, if any, of the sites in question appear as yet to be even designed to remedy this decisive deficit in authority. In this sense our complaint (if complaint is what it is) should therefore be precisely the reverse of Lady Thatcher's pronounced antipathy towards those sites.

REFERENCES

Baumgold, D. 1988. *Hobbes's Political Theory*. Cambridge: Cambridge University Press

Bayne, N. 1991. 'In the balance: the Uruguay Round of international trade negotiations'. *Government and Opposition* 26, 3, 302–15

Crockett, A. D. 1992. 'The International Monetary Fund in the 1990s'. *Government and Opposition* 27, 2, 267–82

Crowe, B. 1993. 'Foreign policy making: reflections of a practitioner'. *Government and Opposition* 28, 174–86

Dodwell, D. 1992. 'Trade war: what it means to you'. *Financial Times*, 7 November, p. 10

Dunn, J. 1984. *Locke*. Oxford: Oxford University Press

    1985. *Rethinking Modern Political Theory*. Cambridge: Cambridge University Press

    1990a. *Interpreting Political Responsibility*. Cambridge: Polity Press

    1990b. *The Economic Limits to Modern Politics*. Cambridge: Cambridge University Press

    1993. *Western Political Theory in the Face of the Future*, 2nd edn. Cambridge: Cambridge University Press

Gilpin, R. 1987. *The Political Economy of International Relations*. Princeton: Princeton University Press

Gowa, J. 1983. *Closing the Gold Window: Domestic Politics and the End of Bretton Woods*. Ithaca, NY: Cornell University Press

Hampton, J. 1986. *Hobbes and the Social Contract Tradition*. Cambridge: Cambridge University Press

Haus, L. H. 1992. *Globalizing the GATT*. Washington, DC: Brookings Institution

Held, D. and A. McGrew 1993. 'Globalization and the liberal democratic state'. *Government and Opposition* 28, 261–85

Hont, I. 1990. 'Free trade and the economic limits to national politics: neo-machiavellian political economy reconsidered'. In *The Economic Limits to Modern Politics*, ed. J. Dunn, pp. 41–120. Cambridge: Cambridge University Press

Hurrell, A. and B. Kingsbury 1992 (eds.). *The International Politics of the*

Environment. Oxford: Oxford University Press

Keohane, R. O. 1984. *After Hegemony*. Princeton: Princeton University Press

Lawrence, R. Z. and C. L. Schultze 1990 (eds.). *An American Trade Strategy: Options for the 1990s*. Washington DC: Brookings Institution

Locke, J. [1689] 1960. *Two Treatises of Government*, ed. P. Laslett. Cambridge: Cambridge University Press

MacIntyre, A. 1973. 'Ideology, social science and revolution'. *Comparative Politics* 5, 321–42

MacNeill, J., P. Winsemius and T. Yakushiji 1991. *Beyond Interdependence: The Meshing of the World's Economy and the Earth's Ecology*. Oxford: Oxford University Press

Mazey, S. P. and J. J. Richardson 1992. 'British pressure groups: the challenge of Brussels'. *Parliamentary Affairs* 45, 92–107

Mitchell, J. C. 1969 (ed.). *Social Networks in Urban Situations*. Manchester: Manchester University Press

Skinner, Q. 1989. 'The state'. In *Political Innovation and Conceptual Change*, ed. T. Ball, J. Farr and R. Hanson, pp. 90–131. Cambridge: Cambridge University Press

Williams, R. 1993. 'Technical change: political options and imperatives'. *Government and Opposition* 28, 152–73

Winham, G. R. 1986. *International Trade and the Tokyo Round Negotiation*. Princeton: Princeton University Press

11   Democracy: the politics of making, defending and exemplifying community: Europe 1992

No thoughtful person today could suppose that democracy is a term with a single clear meaning. But in contrast with other prominent items in the lexicon of modern political values – justice, equality, liberty, obligation, right – it has at least had a single and relatively determinate history, and one which is not radically at the mercy of translational discretion across languages or mutual cultural opacity. To write a history of the ideas of justice, equality, liberty or obligation is not merely to undertake a task which would tax the resources of the most imaginative, learned and incisive of possible scholars.[1] It is also to treat as a determinate cognitive assignment a venture which possesses no plausible historical determinacy even in the first instance (Dunn 1968). But with democracy, for all the haziness of reference and the mental indolence or purposeful bad faith with which the term has often been deployed, the position is in the end quite different. Here, we do confront a single historical sequence: one which certainly has a clear beginning, and which, for all its proliferating subsequent variety, ought in principle to be intelligible as a historically natural outcome, across time and space, of that singularly concrete and distinctive commencement (Dunn 1992).

There are two different respects in which democracy stands out in this way from the swirling and irritable confusion of modern political discourse. The first is by the crisp idiosyncrasy of its origin; the second by its recent (and for the present remarkably comprehensive) triumph in a single relatively definite institutional format – the modern constitutional representative democratic republic (Fontana 1994). The second of these is still very much an experience of the hour, and nowhere in the world has its impact been deeper than on the continent of Europe (Harding 1992). But this second respect is far less clear in its ultimate significance than has yet been acknowledged. Its clarity is overwhelmingly negative, and

---

[1] Even to do so over a relatively short time period and within the terms of European political experience is a savagely demanding assignment. For the most successful recent venture of this kind see Tuck (1979).

correspondingly vulnerable in face of the fresh challenges which history will certainly continue to pose to human societies, for as long as the latter exist (Dunn 1994).

The determinacy of origin, in contrast, is memorably and stably clear. In the city state of Athens, in the two and a half centuries and more which separated the reforms of Solon from the Macedonian conquest, democracy began not as a theoretical conception of how human beings can best live together (a matter over which Athenian residents in due course set quite new standards of imaginative ambition), but as a hastily improvised political expedient in the face of intense and highly unstable local conflict. Democracy was a regime before it was in any sense a political value. Indeed, for all that we know, it may well have been a regime before it became a word. (We have no evidence that Kleisthenes himself, when he established democracy in Athens by taking the people into his own temporarily defeated aristocratic faction in 508/7 BC, in fact used the word *demokratia* to describe the regime which he was establishing, or that anyone else employed the term for that purpose for two decades or so subsequently (Hansen 1991, pp. 69–70).[2] But we also know that the Athenian democracy, as it took shape from the days of Kleisthenes, through those of Ephialtes and Pericles, up to the era of Demosthenes, was a singularly literal and unobscure description of an entire system of rule. The modern constitutional representative democratic republic has a fair degree of shared institutional definition. But it is in many ways a markedly inexplicit system of rule, one in which most of the weight falls somewhere very different from the locus suggested in its official public self-description (see especially Przeworski 1985, 1991). But in the case of Athenian democracy, as a result of obsessive and highly ingenious political design,[3] democracy itself was in fact made, in due course and by extensive trial and error, into a remarkably simple and accurate description of a large proportion of the real political life of a whole society.

As Aristotle's careful reflections in *The Politics* make evident, a wide range of institutional arrangements, with sharply varying degrees of popular participation, were considered to be democratic by fourth-century Greeks. Critics of the democracy naturally disliked the less institutionally inhibited and buffered examples far more than the others (Ober 1991; Finley 1983; Hansen 1991), seeing in the obstructions to immediate exercise of popular will greater security for the property of the wealthy, and ampler aristocratic opportunity to edify the erratic taste and

---

[2] Note, however, Hansen's own scepticism about the significance of this point (Hansen 1991).

[3] Of which Hansen (1991) gives a wonderfully vivid and illuminating account.

judgement of the *demos*. But, at least in Athens itself, the prudential force of these criticisms seems by the fourth century to have been largely taken by the political leaders of the *demos* itself, with the political centre of gravity of the regime shifting in some degree from the assembly to the courts in a more self-conscious affirmation of the merits of the rule of law over that of particular human beings (Hansen 1991). But even in this fourth-century form there was little trace of ambivalence in Athenian public commitment to democracy as a system of collective self-rule. In retrospect, what remains most astonishing about this unique regime was not its relatively marginal concessions to the practical need for expertise or to the social pressures exerted by status authority or drastic inequality of wealth, but its steady dedication to a pervasive political and administrative amateurism throughout the great bulk of Athenian political life, and the degree of institutional inventiveness and the formidable endurance which it devoted to acting out that dedication in daily political practice. A striking example of this commitment, still genuinely shocking to most modern admirers of democracy, was its sharp recognition of the deeply undemocratic significance of elections as a mode of choosing governors[4] (because of their evident user-friendliness to the rich, the well-born and the conspicuously successful, in contrast with the painstakingly randomized average Athenian, who filled the great majority of public offices, and even, for one day in a lifetime, acted as the personal representative authority of the state of Athens itself).

The modern constitutional representative democratic republic, which now virtually monopolizes credible claims to political legitimacy, is extravagantly unlike the democratic regime of ancient Athens. In the first place, the very conception of a modern state has remarkably little in common with the classical *polis*, being created largely for the purpose of repudiating popular claims to rule which had survived, within the literary legacy of the ancient world, exposure to many centuries of brusque military and economic domination by a heavily armed landed nobility (Skinner 1989). To be sure, the modern state might choose, as readily as the Roman empire, to ground its claims to rule ultimately in the will of the people. But its central motif was a firm appropriation of the capacity for subsequent political agency from the people. In no modern state do the people in fact rule, and despite the spirited efforts of Jean-Jacques Rousseau, the resolute modern constitutional fiction of popular sovereignty, and the idler reveries of Marx or Lenin (Harding 1992; Przeworski 1991), there is little reason to see in the history of any modern state over

---

[4] I owe my recognition of the categorical character of this contrast to an extremely powerful text by Bernard Manin (1995).

any period of time a reasonably straightforward intention to permit them to do anything of the kind.

In the second place, no modern economy can operate for any length of time in essential independence of the political decisions of its ruling political authority, as Athens effectively did, with only the most marginal interruptions, from the days of Solon to those of Demosthenes. One of the main keys to Athenian democratic stability was the effective depoliticization of ordinary property rights, especially in land – the legal outlawing of the popular war cry of the democratic faction in innumerable other *poleis*, for the abolition of debts and the redistribution of lands. Sustaining this firm principle of political non-intervention was, of course, a continuing political achievement of the democracy itself: not a passive enjoyment of a whimsical historical privilege. But despite the collapse of socialism (and even where socialism, as in the United States, has never had much of an imaginative presence in national politics) the prospect of durably depoliticizing property rights in a state today is overwhelmingly forlorn. Modern political philosophers in the west focus predominantly on the question of social justice, seeking to steady their own intuitive sense of what sorts of social and economic arrangements really are just, and to lend the resulting conceptions a fresh and more decisive authority from this enhanced clarity.[5] But the diversity of the conceptions on which they settle, and the consequent flimsiness of the claims to authority which can be levelled on behalf of each of these, bring out with ever greater clarity the overwhelmingly forlorn character of the quest in which they are engaged.

It is tempting, therefore, to view the political record of ancient democracy as an irrelevant distraction from the sober task of assessing the meaning and viability of modern democracies: a wrecker's lantern beckoning otherwise serviceable political regimes insistently on to the rocks, or a futile reverie about an irretrievably lost world. But this does less than justice to the practical significance of the formidable opacity of the modern representative democracy: to its tenacious, and surely in some measure deliberate, withholding of the secrets of its own operation from the formally sovereign *demos* over which it so palpably rules.[6] To those who hope and expect to rule themselves in person, as the *demos* of Athens genuinely did, the political roles provided by the elaborately professionalized party politics of representative democracies can only be thin and unenticing. But very few adults in any modern democracy really have the

---

[5] For the limitations inherent in this approach see Dunn (1985, chapters 9 and 10).
[6] As Przeworski (1991) incisively demonstrates, it is essential, too, that it should contrive to withhold the same secrets with equal tenacity from several potential enemies of the *demos* also.

slightest expectation of doing anything of the sort – and, in the light of modern political history, very reasonably so.

Those who do hope (or even expect) to take part in ruling do so essentially by offering themselves as candidates for palpably professional roles, in career bureaucracies or political parties. If the essence of ancient democracy was ruling and being ruled by turns for any random citizen, the essence of modern democracy is distinctly less amateur: grounded, as Sieyes long ago insisted, on a blunt and often remarkably rigid division of labour, in which most citizens most of the time were far too busy working to give up any appreciable proportion of their lives to the discharge of public responsibilities, and only those who devoted the great bulk of their energies to mastering the range of knowledge and skills required could hope to carry such responsibilities in a competent and informed manner. Put like this, to be sure, modern democracy can readily appear lamentably unopaque: all too frankly authoritarian and exclusionary. But to see it this way is to neglect the large and formidably appealing services which it has proved well able to provide, whenever it has been politically sustained – in some settings now for a full two centuries. It is these political services for which modern populations for the most part hope, and which they would understandably prefer to be able to expect: a set of constitutionally protected civil rights of personal and legal security, a regular (if necessarily modest) degree of accountability of governors to governed through the electoral process, and a measure of assurance about the practical protection of a predominantly market economy, fostering growing popular prosperity across the generations.

In Europe, with the memory of the Second World War and the communist regimes of the east as stark and still recent contrasts, virtually no one today has difficulty in seeing the force and centrality of these three services. It is the clarity and (at least for the present) the stability of that contrast that unites the populations of western and eastern Europe in a firm rejection of an alternative (and now utterly discredited) model of political authority, and in the more diffuse hope of forging and maintaining institutions of political and economic cooperation which will ensure the provision of such services across the continent, and do so for as much of a future as anyone can yet foresee. It was largely the clarity of that contrast, too, which prompted the speed and confidence of popular mobilization across eastern Europe in 1989 as the Soviet empire withdrew its military guarantee from the incumbent regimes: the confrontation, as Timothy Garton Ash memorably put it, between 'a set of ideas whose time had come' and 'a set of ideas whose time had gone' (Garton Ash 1990).

In the Europe of 1992 – from the Atlantic to the river Bug, if not perhaps to the Urals (see Robinson and Wolf 1991) – there is no credible

alternative to modern constitutional representative democracy: not because there could not be, and may not well be in fact, other and more makeshift and openly authoritarian regimes, in one setting or another from time to time, but simply because there is no real surviving competitor for political legitimacy. The challenge to democracy in 1992 looks very different at the heart of the European Community in Brussels than it does in Sofia or Tirana or Budapest (or even Warsaw): harsher in the latter cases, but perhaps in some respects more elusive in the former. In both cases the collapse of its hated enemy – the end of the Bolshevik menace – has deprived constitutional representative democracy of any durably plausible rival. But in neither case are there at present grounds for confidence that the conception of constitutional representative democracy in itself intrinsically contains the political resources to meet these challenges. As seen today, it is a uniquely undiscredited framework for the taking of political choices. But there is no reason whatever to presume it in any way a guarantee that these choices will be made prudently or implemented effectively.

The choices in question, plainly, are of very different kinds. In the east, they centre on the formidable task of disentangling societies from the ruins of four and a half decades of massive economic malformation. Constitutional representative democracy, insofar as it can be reliably secured, is a sound enough guarantee against the revival of the authoritarian subjugation to which each of these societies was long exposed. Its limitation, from this point of view, lies principally in the difficulties it is likely to face in sustaining itself against political challenge in conditions of drastic economic disruption and hardship (declines of a third or more in national product), and of far-reaching political confusion. The experience of Poland, whose initial democratic government at least enjoyed the backing of a huge and provenly committed movement of popular resistance in what in some respects is still a remarkably solidary national population, already makes it very evident how hard it will be for debt-ridden and disorganized societies to hold themselves together, as they settle down to reconstruct their entire economies and political systems, even under clear-sighted and courageous political leadership. It is scarcely surprising that the beleaguered political leaderships of eastern Europe should look so insistently towards the west, for the credit lines required to sustain their precarious trade balances and to husband their scarce foreign exchange, and for the open markets, and imports of capital and technology, needed to revive their flagging productive capacities (see Dullforce 1991). What they receive is always far less than they hope (or ask) for. But in the face of the formidable obstacles to reorganization of a socialist economy (obstacles explored more clearly and with greater honesty by some eastern European thinkers in the last two decades than anywhere else in the world (Brus & Laski 1988; cf. Kornai 1990) it is hard to think what else of a more robust character they can reasonably hope to rely on.

From the vantage point of western Europe there is for the present little agreement on how to see the significance of these transactions: as acts of immediate, if relatively parsimonious charity, as long-term investments in building a larger pan-European domestic market or a more powerful pan-European political bloc, as well-considered individual decisions to exploit local comparative advantage (cheap and relatively highly educated labour), or as hasty insurance policies against the prospect of a flood of refugees from the ruined lands of the east to the fat lands of the west. (The issue of immigration is a particularly perturbing one, not simply for would-be political protectors of existing popular living standards in representative democracies which already have large bodies of unemployed citizens, but also for anyone who sees the political power of representative democracy as lying largely in its unique capacity to relate the reality of contemporary political authority to a coherent universal standard of political right (see chapter 9 above). The fact that modern understandings of political right have no coherent basis on which to answer the blunt question of where human beings ought to be is going to cut painfully into cosmopolitan political complacencies in the next few decades.) What is especially burdensome for the new representative democracies of eastern Europe is the fact that they must use their novel institutions of political choice quite openly, not merely to destroy the immediate economic security of great masses of their citizens (in the hope of improving their longer-term economic prospects), but also that they must allocate economic opportunities and privileges quite openly in the first instance to some rather than others of their citizens (Kornai 1990). This combination of direct and (from a personal point of view) sharply punitive intervention with apparently capricious (or all too transparently personal) favouritism amongst the ranks of the *demos* is just what Athens contrived to avoid for over two centuries. Even within the relatively opaque structures of modern representative democracy, it is hardly the sort of experience which can be confidently anticipated to cement the loyalties of a whole citizen body. No one knows how grim the fate of post-communist eastern Europe is going to prove, though already in parts of the erstwhile Soviet Union, in Yugoslavia, and in Albania, ample occasion for dismay is on full view.

The challenges to democracy in western Europe in 1992 seem as yet comparatively unintimidating (except perhaps to one recent British prime minister). But they are in some ways every bit as bemusing. No reasonable person could regard representative democracy as a guarantee of success in reconstructing an entire economy (cf. Dunn 1990). But it is a more interesting question at present how far the political institutions of the European Community are, or are likely soon to become, well able to sustain what is still an extremely prosperous population. Even those who are relatively sanguine about that question often place a large proportion of their confidence in institutional features of the Community that have little, if anything, to do with either democracy or representation.

To think clearly about these questions it is first necessary to come to a conclusion about two crude but extremely challenging issues. Neither is in any sense novel as a question. But the human world to which they are now addressed is very different from that in which the central terms of European political understanding were initially formulated; it is still changing with great (and perhaps constantly accelerating) rapidity; and it is painfully apparent (by even the most preliminary historical induction) that no one within it at any particular time can hope to form a very clear and steady understanding of even the main axes along which these changes are occurring. So, however familiar in form the questions them-selves may at first appear, there is no reason whatever to assume that valid answers to them will necessarily be anything like as familiar, still less that these answers, in a concrete and informative form, must already be part of (dependably inscribed within) an inherited stock of intellectual or cul-tural capital. The first of these questions is exceedingly simple. Just what are modern governments really *for*? What major human purposes can they, and only they, at present hope to serve with any genuine efficacy? The second is appreciably less simple, but it is also obviously in some sense prior to the first. What exactly should we think of modern govern-ments (or states) as consisting in? What forms and sites of real agency, what structures or institutional formats, carry a genuine power to govern in the astonishingly complicated societies in which we all now live?

Both of these are old questions in Japan, as they are in Europe. It is unlikely that anyone in Europe or North America is at present convinced of the existence of a distinctive potency latent within the cognitive resources which Japanese intellectual traditions can bring to bear upon the first question. But you must all be well aware by now that the principal focus of American social scientific attempts to understand Japan for at least the last fifteen years has been on the increasingly uneasy suspicion that the Japanese state itself, through some more or less ingenious (and perhaps imitable) array of devices, is now a more effective and serviceable resource for realizing the purposes for which modern populations are compelled to rely on their governments – should they be fortunate enough to be able to rely on anything at all (see, for example, Johnson

1982, Calder 1988, Okimoto 1989). The implicit contrast case, unsurprisingly, is always the American state. The histories of Japan, from the founding of the Tokugawa *bakufu*, and of the United States, from the drawing up of the federal constitution, offer a sufficiently drastic contrast to make it far from puzzling that there should be some human purposes that are more reliably served in the one than in the other. In particular, the remarkably continuous imaginative commitment in Japan to the idea of devoted and effective bureaucratic authority as key instrument for ensuring the material needs of an unusually homogeneous national population (Najita 1974), and the profound (and still thoroughly institutionalized) American commitment to the systematic inhibition of the executive power of the federal government (Skowronek 1982) provide as starkly antithetical approaches to the problems of collective political agency as can readily be found within what is now an increasingly homogeneously capitalist world.

In Europe itself there are, naturally, quite sharp variations in national tradition on these very points: between France and the reunited Federal Republic of Germany, between Britain and Belgium, between Sweden and Portugal. But the history of the European Community, since its inception, has shown that these sharp variations in national political experience and cultural formation, once incorporated into its gravitational field, have come to be subordinated to a relatively steady and unobtrusive logic of common accommodation to the practicalities of dealing together with a wider and often fiercely competitive world. In public politics what has stood out in this sequence has often been the more conspicuous deviations from it: the flighty French insistence on keeping its own nuclear forces outside the framework of NATO military command, the stunningly elaborate assemblage of palliative side-payments and interest group placation which makes up the Common Agricultural Policy. But in the history of the Community, especially in retrospect, what has been both far more important and far more potent has been the steady, surreptitious, relentless process of institutional and legal assimilation: the consolidation of a shared social, economic and political habitat.

That process could not have proceeded without the sustained, if often ill-tempered, assent of the national governments of the constituent countries, and that assent itself was seldom, of course, in any way passive. What it represented is best seen as an immense series of equilibrium points in often fiercely contested bargaining games between a huge and constantly shifting range of participants. But the process itself has had an integrity and unity of its own, as even its present outcome already makes electrifyingly clear. It also has a definite momentum, and one which has insistently altered the location of equilibrium points within these bargaining games, subtracting final control over one element after another from the national legislative authority, executive discretion or appellate jurisdiction of the constituent states.

What aspects of this process are of greater importance is not something which can be determined independently of the concerns of a particular inquirer. It has been as much a cultural process as it has economic or political: and, for all the constitutional formalities, as much a military or police adjustment as a reorientation of production, distribution and exchange. If the initial prize was largely the consolidation of an already desperately expensive peace, in the face of a new, and apparently chillingly menacing enemy,[7] its present outcome is perhaps principally a political and economic framework orientated to face (if not necessarily well equipped to deal with) the challenges of international economic competition in an epoch in which the institutional framework of that competition is no longer secured by the hegemonic power of a single effortlessly dominant economic and political actor, and in which, accordingly, no one can at present assess with real authority just how that framework itself will be sustained, reshaped or disrupted, as the decades go by (Keohane 1984; Gilpin 1987).

Whether this insistent movement, the central movement of postwar history in western Europe, is a ground for confidence or an occasion for panic is still very much at issue. But it is probably, on balance, more illuminating for the present to refuse to consider the question in this grossly impacted form. What is more immediately pressing is the intellectually more manageable (if also more overtly extensive) question of just what promises it offers and just what threats it carries for each of the full variety of political, economic and social actors who make up modern populations across the territories of the Community's existing members. The evanescence of an especially imperious and historically protracted executive authority is likely to be viewed with keener regret by those (like Mrs Thatcher) who have recently had the opportunity to deploy it with such memorable vigour than it is by those (like the British Union of Mineworkers) who have (also recently) been its all too immediate targets. The vicissitudes of the British government before the European Court of Justice in the face of long drawn out IRA insurgency, or in embattled defence of the tattered privacy of its security services, bring out the implications of the seepage of sovereignty in the most vivid fashion. If the *arcana imperii* are justiciable ultimately by a court superior to any British national court, where can *imperium* now reasonably be thought to lie?

---

[7] No one need doubt today that the Soviet Union at the time was an excellent candidate for an enemy, quite irrespective of sober judgements of the probability of its at any point mounting a full-scale military assault on a well-armed, well-organized and notably unsubmissive population.

It is important to be clear that what is in question here is in the end less the comparative trustworthiness of national as opposed to supra-national institutions (a matter of the predictable dispositions of distinct agencies) than a matter of the comparative efficacy of different types of institution (public bureaucracy, political party, career judiciary, central bank, professional corps of academic analysts, economic, social or ideological interest group), whether national or supra-national. If it were only the former, the answer to the question could hardly be elusive. Those who feel fully at home with 'their own' nation will naturally, within a representative democracy, find it easier over time to trust its political and judicial institutions, while those who persistently do not find it so are likely for the most part to belong to groups who have some real grounds for hostility towards the state itself. Good citizens will wish to be ruled, broadly, through their own national representatives; and those who emphatically would not are apt to be at least incipiently subversive in their allegiance – dubious as to whether the nation in question is in any sense authentically their own, or whether it offers them an unfraudulent opportunity to secure their own effective representation. The national question is a real, if not necessarily an especially active, question in every modern society, even if it is far more pressing in some sites than in others. Supra-national institutions can mollify it by blurring the immediacy of subjection. But they cannot simply abolish it, any more than creating a world government by constitutional fiat would automatically do so.

But it is not the special intimacy of citizen rights and obligations, or governmental authority and responsibility, which the formation of the European Community has called disturbingly into question. Rather, it is the less refined and emotionally implicating issue of what forms of institution really work effectively in the world in which we now live. Human beings, the evidence goes, choose their political representatives in large measure by a relatively primitive process of identification; but what they choose them *for*, at least in fond hope, is the service of their own interests. Representative democracy, as Schumpeter indicated (Schumpeter 1950), is essentially a system of rule by competing teams of professional politicians. The sharpest challenge which the experience of the European Community poses to the idea of democracy is the degree to which it has involved a drainage of effective power of political and economic choice from temporarily elected teams of professional politicians to a relatively continuous, if in part politically recruited, supra-national professional bureaucracy. Political scientists sometimes argue that democratic career politicians are appreciably better as responding to new political, economic or social challenges than professional bureaucrats. (It would be very easy, you might think, to exaggerate the prowess of either group at recognizing and responding to novel elements in their environment; but electoral politicians are certainly relatively prompt to react to new foci of discontent amongst large groups of their own constituents.) But societies (perhaps like Japan) in which it is at least as easy to see the public bureaucracy as an effective (if virtual) representative of the interests of the *demos* as it is to see the elected professional politicians as dependable representatives of anything of the kind palpably need a less literal-minded account of the nature of modern representation than even Schumpeter proposes.

The case against the main dynamic of the European Community's history can be presented as the case for national democracy. The battle cries of this case in recent years have been the 'loss of sovereignty' and the 'democratic deficit'. Building the Community has meant the construction of a very real polity, in which the *demos* of any individual country has seen successively withdrawn from it a range of pressing issues on which it no longer enjoys the power to decide for itself (through its own trusty agents, the governing political parties in its national legislature). Not only has control over these issues palpably slipped from its grasp, it has also, even more palpably, not fallen instead into the grasp of another, larger and politically more effective *demos*, the people of the Community at large. The only serious modification to this picture, the creation of the European parliament, has been sufficiently marginal (and thus far sufficiently questionable in sincerity) to exacerbate rather than assuage the sense of injury. There is no doubt that this picture serves as an effective vector for xenophobic sentiment, not least in the United Kingdom. But it is analytically accurate enough, as far as it goes.

The case *for* the main dynamic of the Community's history, accordingly, is largely a case against national democracy: a case for the view that a sophisticated and continuous public bureaucracy, permanently engaged with the exigent demands of a much wider world and well buffered against the momentary enthusiasms and panics of the populace at large, is a far more trustworthy custodian of the latter's long-term interests than the career politicians who are permanently at the mercy of these movements of sentiment and judgement, and thus compelled to respond to them with dangerous alacrity. (This is not a very novel line of thought in relation to democracy.) The case for the main dynamic of the Community's history, in this understanding, rests essentially on its putative superiority at addressing the problem of sustaining continuity in political decision making: the problem, in essence, of rendering sequential rationality compatible with any democratic system of governmental accountability (Hirschman 1991; cf. Dunn 1991). It is controversial[8] how far even Japan

---

[8] Less so now than in 1991.

contrives to solve this problem in practice, and equally controversial just which features of its institutional order or policy choices (let alone its pre-modern history) have enabled it to solve the problem to even this degree. But it is easy to see that a strong and highly sophisticated public bureaucracy and over three and a half decades of consecutive electoral dominance by a single party of government (however faction-ridden) have given it better opportunity to do so than, for example, Greece or Argentina enjoyed over the same period. This is not, of course, the only possible recipe for sustaining coherence and continuity in a government's impact upon the economic life of a society; nor is it very readily imitable in most other societies. But it is plausibly a more feasible recipe, where it can in fact be imitated, than the only prominent cosmopolitan competitor to it: the relatively archaic (though still vehemently current) proposal to solve the problem of political continuity not by rendering the government stronger or more coherent, but essentially by eliminating it from the political process for any purpose other than the direct protection of property rights. What is misguided about this proposal is not merely the moral scandal which it deservedly occasions, but its utter disregard, as Adam Przeworski (1991) shows with great power and concision, for what has made representative democracy a viable political order in the first place.

The importance of recognizing the problem of continuity in disciplining the responses of both professional politicians and electorates within the Community has come out most clearly in the formidable and wholly unscripted role in constraining the real economic policies of its member countries which has been played by the German Bundesbank. It is not an exaggeration to say that the prospects for current agreement on the speed of, and the scope for intensifying, European integration amongst the Community members turn predominantly on the question of whether or not it can itself hope to create a European central bank with an equally imperturbable commitment to monetary rectitude, or whether the political process of creating such an institution will deconstruct this capability in the Bundesbank itself in relation to the German economy, rather than extend its scope triumphantly throughout the Community's members.[9] What lies behind this (in some ways bewilderingly hypnotic) preoccupation is in essence the collapse for the present of the political credibility of Keynesian macroeconomic demand management. What now replaces this is a vision of governmental economic policy which, under circumstances which not infrequently prevail, deprives governments of any instruments whatever with which to act benignly upon the economy for which they are notionally responsible: a reversion to the very conditions

---

[9] Compare the trepidations of its present governor (Norman 1991).

which Keynes set himself to transform (Clarke 1988; Hall 1989). This degree of paralysis is unlikely to last for ever. But escaping it for the better is going to require fairly decisive advances (or perhaps rather clearer recuperations) in the analytic understanding of real economic processes.

In this setting, the most optimistic concrete vision of the Community's future marginalizes the causal role of democracy within it. It sees the locus of hope in an increasingly serene (because increasingly efficacious) supra-national bureaucratic orchestration of collective interests, coercively secured in detail by the residual political authority, and the measure of continuing democratic accountability, of national representative governments. Put as bluntly as this, this is quite a setback for democracy as a theory of political value, grounded in what Edmund Burke mercilessly described as 'the philosophy of vanity' (*Letter to a Member of the National Assembly* [1791] 1989, p. 313). But except in its dislocation of key political sites from national to supra-national levels, it is not so different from the most optimistic view of the future of representative democracy within individual national states – or even, in the end, for all the latter's institutional vagueness, from the most optimistic view of the overall calming effects on international as well as domestic relations of the spread of *doux commerce*. (As early as Aristotle, it was perfectly apparent that if human groupings prescinded from the pursuit of a good life in common, then even international trade would in one sense bind men into a single political community (Aristotle, *The Politics*, 1280a; 1977 edn, p. 214), while a combination of economic exchange, spatial continuity and military alliance would suffice to do so (1280b, p. 216). For Aristotle, of course, what this contrast underlines was precisely the constitutive role of a common pursuit of the good life in forming a political community. But in an economic setting which has brutally eroded the imaginative power of that conception, and in a political culture which has abandoned it, as anything but the most desultory of official pieties, it is the antithesis of his argument which in fact applies.

Where does this leave democracy in the face of Europe's two great current challenges? A short answer would be: in pretty marked disarray. But it is helpful to draw some further distinctions. If democracy is thought of, not as a diffuse and less than convincing idiom of contemporary political cant (cf. Dunn 1979, chapter 1), but as a term which incontestably applies to central aspects of at least one great political experience, we can reconsider the political sense of Europe's future through the very distant prism of ancient Athens. In Athens, for nearly two centuries, the *demos* ruled. It was not, by modern standards, a very large *demos*. But it really did *rule*. The *demos* of Europe, west or east, will never again be able to rule. But perhaps, if it is cunning enough and lucky enough (Przeworski 1991, p. xii), it may eventually prove able to act together predominantly for the better. To do so, it will have to design institutions that make this conception reasonably convincing in practice, and not merely insolently provocative.

Here, however, the experience of Athens is genuinely encouraging. For the *demos* which ruled in the aftermath of Kleisthenes' reforms was not an entity with the slightest prior capacity to act collectively by itself (Manville 1990). To be given the power of agency, to be shaped into an agent, it had to be reorganized extensively for the purpose by Kleisthenes himself. To be made able to act for itself, it needed the decisive intervention of an authoritative external agent, just as abjectly as the smallholding peasantry of mid-nineteenth-century France, in Marx's allegation, required the brusque services of Louis Napoleon to get their interests represented (Marx [1852] 1979, p. 187–93). Democracy does not in itself make a *demos*, a body of human beings capable of collective agency over time, though it certainly reshapes whatever presumed *demos* it finds, and does so continuously over time.

No *demos*, moreover, can simply make itself out of whole cloth, though any *demos*, given the slightest historical cooperation, can readily unmake itself by a sufficient degree of profligacy or pusillanimity. The making of a *demos* requires protracted prior contributions from history, and an ultimate, and sharply focused, passage of pure historical good luck. But it also requires the seizing of the resulting historical occasion by the duly constituted *demos*: its purposeful assumption of the proffered role. We do not know if any such role will ever be on offer to the people of Europe as a whole, or how long even the semblance of it will stay on offer to the several 'peoples' of eastern Europe. Still less do we know that the offers will be accepted and realized in action for any length of time in either setting. But nor do we know that they will not. Kleisthenes was simply a defeated aristocratic faction leader. Why, in the longer run, may not even defeated bureaucratic faction leaders, with equal political flair, do just as well?

A second key lesson of the Athenian experience is the peculiar dependence of democracy on the capacity to protect itself. (What is peculiar about this, of course, is not its need to do so – which it shares with any other political order – but its apparent unsuitability in many respects for so doing.) Here, the Athenian experience is more ambiguous. Its larger and less encouraging implication is the clear disparity between the capacity of a citizenry in arms to protect its own power of sovereign action against domestic and even international enemies, and the capacity of any modern *demos* under real pressure to ensure that it can in the last instance rely for either of these purposes on the loyalty and prowess of its professional armed forces (cf. Przeworski 1991; Cruise O'Brien *et al.* 1989,

Conclusion). But a subordinate and more encouraging implication, strongly lodged in the postwar history of western Europe, is that a felicitous sequence of external enemies and internal economic flourishing can relieve modern populations in this respect from pressures of any great severity, and render the last instance for lengthy periods of time a boundary condition of purely theoretical interest. An Athenian perspective on the future of contemporary Europe, accordingly, is drastically more encouraging in relation to the west than it is to the east.

The democracy of Athens began with the creation of a community capable of political agency. It was sustained for nearly two centuries by the effective defence of that community. But what gave it its enduring power over the political imaginations of human populations across the world well over two millennia later was not these two clear preconditions, but the political experience which they rendered possible. There is no way of epitomizing that experience in an uncontentious formula. But contentious though it necessarily is, I would want to argue that the core of that experience and the source of the remarkable imaginative energy which has radiated from it across time and space was the literalness, and the astounding assiduity, with which the Athenians exemplified the reality of their community in the public political life which they lived out together (Hansen 1991; Finley 1983; Dunn 1992). This is not a matter about which it is possible to speak convincingly in a hurry. But if the judgement itself is essentially correct, its implications remain of burning importance even in a world so overwhelmingly reshaped to extinguish the possibility of realizing Aristotle's conception of what a political community really is. For the Athenian *demos*, the point and substance of Athenian democracy was precisely to live in freedom together. The literal realism of that vision never extended beyond the ranks of the male citizens, and was always challenged even in its application to them. But the power of the idea itself, freedom as a critical standard for human institutions, has no elective affinity with privileged male minorities. It certainly besets the most sophisticated of modern bureaucrats just as peremptorily as it does career politicians in quest of re-election or professional judiciaries; and it challenges structures as pervasive and opaque as the entire relation between males and females across human populations.

In this respect at least, the legacy of ancient Greece to modern political life is not a series of crisp recipes for coping with global and local realities utterly unlike those of which any ancient Greek ever dreamed. Rather, it is a single searing image of what human beings have no intrinsic reason to accept: an image which still calls into question virtually every feature of human collective life, and which we can confidently expect to continue to do so for as long as human beings live together on earth on any scale at all.

These are not questions which we can hope to still by redesigning political institutions. But they are certainly part of what democracy now means; and they follow peremptorily from what it meant for its Greek originators. If the Greek answers to them now strike us as shabby and degrading, we can be very sure that the same will be true in due course for how our own answers strike our more distant descendants.

REFERENCES

Aristotle. *The Politics*, trans. H. Rackham (1977). London: Heinemann
Brus, W. and K. Laski 1988. *From Marx to the Market*. Oxford: Clarendon Press
Burke, E. [1790–4] 1989. *Writings and Speeches* VIII: *The French Revolution 1790–1794*, ed. L. G. Mitchell. Oxford: Clarendon Press
Calder, K. 1988. *Crisis and Compensation*. Princeton: Princeton University Press
Clarke, P. 1988. *The Keynesian Revolution in the Making 1924–1936*. Oxford: Clarendon Press
Cruise O'Brien, D., J. Dunn and R. Rathbone 1989 (eds.). *Contemporary West African States*. Cambridge: Cambridge University Press
Dullforce, W. 1991. 'E. Europe seen as heading for thirties-type depression'. *Financial Times*, 2 December, p. 2
Dunn, J. 1968. 'The identity of the history of ideas'. *Philosophy*, April, 85–104
      1979. *Western Political Theory in the Face of the Future*. Cambridge: Cambridge University Press
      1985. *Rethinking Modern Political Theory*. Cambridge: Cambridge University Press
      1990 (ed.). *The Economic Limits to Modern Politics*. Cambridge: Cambridge University Press
      1991. 'A new book by Albert Hirschman'. *Government and Opposition*, 26, Autumn, 520–5
      1992 (ed.). *Democracy: The Unfinished Journey*. Oxford: Oxford University Press
      1994. 'The identity of the bourgeois liberal republic'. In *The Invention of the Modern Republic*, ed. B. Fontana. Cambridge: Cambridge University Press
Finley, M. I. 1983. *Politics in the Ancient World*. Cambridge: Cambridge University Press
Fontana, B. 1994 (ed.). *The Invention of the Modern Republic*. Cambridge: Cambridge University Press
Garton Ash, T. 1990. *We the People*. Harmondsworth: Penguin
Gilpin, R. 1990. *The Political Economy of International Relations*. Princeton: Princeton University Press
Hall, P. A. 1989 (ed.). *The Political Power of Economic Ideas*. Princeton: Princeton University Press
Hansen, M. H. 1991. *The Athenian Democracy in the Age of Demosthenes*. Oxford: Blackwell
Harding, N. 1992. 'The Marxist–Leninist detour'. In *Democracy: The Unfinished Journey*, ed. J. Dunn. Oxford: Oxford University Press
Hirschman, A. 1991. *The Rhetoric of Reaction*. Cambridge, Mass.: Harvard University Press

Imbruglia, G. 1992 (ed.). *Il Razzismo e le sue storie*. Naples: Edizioni Scientifiche Italiane

Johnson, C. 1982. *MITI and the Japanese Miracle*. Stanford: Stanford University Press

Keohane, R. O. 1984. *After Hegemony*. Princeton: Princeton University Press

Kornai, J. 1990. *The Road to a Free Economy*. New York: Norton

Manin, B. 1995. *Principes du gouvernement représentatif*. Paris: Calmann-Lévy (English translation Cambridge University Press 1996)

Manville, P. B. 1990. *The Origins of Citizenship in Ancient Athens*. Princeton: Princeton University Press

Marx, K. [1852] 1979. *The Eighteenth Brumaire of Louis Napoleon*. In K. Marx and F. Engels, *Collected Works* XI, pp. 99–197. London: Lawrence and Wishart

Najita, T. 1974. *Japan: The Intellectual Foundations of Modern Japanese Politics*. Chicago: University of Chicago Press

Norman, P. 1991. 'Bundesbank opposes control of reserves'. *Financial Times*, 2 December, p. 3

Ober, J. 1991. 'Aristotle's political sociology'. In *Essays on Aristotle's Politics*, ed. Carnes Lord. Berkeley: University of California Press

Okimoto, D. I. 1989. *Between MITI and the Market*. Stanford: Stanford University Press

Przeworski, A. 1985. *Capitalism and Social Democracy*. Cambridge: Cambridge University Press

1991. *Democracy and the Market*. Cambridge: Cambridge University Press

Robinson, A. and M. Wolf 1991. 'Europe's reluctant empire-builders'. *Financial Times*, 2 December, p. 2

Schumpeter, J. 1950. *Capitalism, Socialism and Democracy*. London: Allen and Unwin

Skinner, Q. 1989. 'The state'. In *Political Innovation and Conceptual Change*, ed. T. Ball, J. Farr and R. Hanson, pp. 90–131. Cambridge: Cambridge University Press

Skowronek, S. 1982. *Building a New American State*. Cambridge: Cambridge University Press

Tuck, R. 1979. *Natural Rights Theories*. Cambridge: Cambridge University Press

12 Is there a contemporary crisis of the nation state?

Formulating the question

Nations consist of those who belong together by birth (genetically, lineally, through familially inherited language and culture). States consist of those who are fully subject to their own sovereign legal authority. A true nation state, therefore, would consist only of those who belonged to it by birth and of those who were fully subject to its sovereign legal authority. By this (for practical purposes, no doubt absurdly stipulative) criterion it is unlikely that there is a single nation state in the world at present, and moderately unlikely that any such state has ever existed. But, as with most political ideas, the force of the idea of the nation state has never come principally from its descriptive precision. What it offers is a precarious fusion of two very different modes of thinking: one explicitly subjective, urgent and identificatory, and the other presumptively objective, detached and independent of the vagaries of popular consciousness. (It is hard to exaggerate the shaping impact of this second mode in forming the category of state (Skinner 1989).) Common birth is both a ground for, and a source of, allegiance. External authority is a device for furnishing protection. Taken together, they furnish a basis for rulers and subjects to live together with greater imaginative ease than either party would be likely to draw from the other taken separately: a contemporary version of the *pactum subjectionis* (chapter 3 above).

It is unsurprising that this unsteady mixture has proved unsuitable for clear analytical thought. But its analytical debility has been no bar to ideological or practical potency. The ideas that every nation should have its own state and that every state should be a single nation (Gellner 1983; Anderson 1983) may not have much solid merit either as normative or as practical proposals. But between them they have made a great deal of the political history of the twentieth century.[1] Each of the three great geopolitical shifts of this century – the First World War and its aftermath, the

---

[1] For a helpful and balanced resumé see Hobsbawm (1990) and compare Greenfeld (1992).

Second World War and the unravelling of European empire which succeeded it, and the collapse of communism in eastern Europe and decomposition of the Soviet Union – has drastically extended the nation state as a political format and strongly reinforced it as an ideological option.

Why, then, has it come to be a commonplace of contemporary political journalism that the nation state is today somehow in crisis: palpably unable to master problems which it once handled with aplomb, incapable of ensuring an order of its own (ecological, economic, civil, even spiritual) on its subjects' behalf, baffled by the novel challenges of a turbulent global economy and a decaying global habitat?

The first question to press in this context is whether the journalistic commonplace is in fact valid. Has there been, for some specifiable set of reasons, a clear deterioration in the capacity of the nation state format to master the hazards to the security and prosperity of its subjects, in comparison with some distinct and earlier phase in modern history? Has there been some definite change in the sources or intensity of such hazards, sufficient to render a long-serviceable formula, normative or practical, palpably inadequate to control dangers which it once met with relative serenity? The first view locates the crisis in a diminution of the power of the nation state as such – a clear lessening in either its normative appeal or its practical capacity (or, of course, in both). The second locates the crisis in a sharp rise in the acuity or scale of the hazards which now confront its subjects.

The least plausible of these hypotheses is the claim that the practical capabilities of states today in any general fashion fall short of those of their predecessors. Such a claim is not simply absurd. There have been forceful arguments that modern political and economic organization has a strong internal impetus towards immobilism, an impetus which can be reversed only by massive disruption (war, conquest, perhaps large-scale natural disaster) (Olson 1982). At a more ideological level, also, the right-wing economistic critique of rent-seeking and of the allegedly inherent economic inefficiency of state as opposed to market distribution[2] has achieved considerable impact in many settings over the last two decades. But it is hard to see firm grounds in any of these lines of thought for judging that the intrinsic practical efficacy of modern state forms has deteriorated over the last half century.

Far more plausible is the judgement that the present sense of crisis in the efficacy of the nation state comes from a resonance between two very

[2] Buchanan (1986); or, at a more refined level, Friedrich von Hayek (Gray 1984; Hayek 1978, 1973–9).

different types of shift: a fading in all but the most extreme settings (typically those of armed conflict) in the normative appeals of the idea of the nation state, and a brusque rise in awareness of a series of new and formidable challenges (economic, ecological, military, political, even cultural) the scope of which plainly extends far beyond national boundaries and effectively ensures that they cannot be successfully met within such boundaries. Seen this way, the sense of crisis, whether well judged or otherwise, is at least easy to understand. It is a sense, above all, of political crisis: crisis in the efficacy of political action (cf. Dunn 1990a, chapter 8).

It is in the nature of politics that new political challenges should arise all the time. But some such challenges are manifestly far more formidable than others. It is most unlikely that the causal capabilities of the nation state as an organizational format should have declined significantly and persistently in conditions of peace and appreciable long-term economic growth. But even in these conditions the combination of drastic new challenges and inherently limited inherited powers of action might easily have lessened the normative appeal of the repository of those powers and should rationally have impaired the practical self-confidence of national governing elites. Even if this emergent sense of political inadequacy did not in itself impair the normative appeal of the state form in question, it might readily expose the intrinsic limitations of that appeal in the face of the far harsher demands which are now placed upon it. Whatever else might be needed to meet them effectively, the drastic new challenges of global interdependence plainly require vigorous political action: a preparedness on the part of immense numbers of human beings to alter substantially and rapidly major aspects of how they choose to behave. Such changes place formidable strains on the political capacities of any human population. There may be a reason (perhaps inherent in global economic rationalization or in the dawning awareness of environmental peril) why the normative appeal of the idea of the nation state as such is already weakening. But even if it were not (indeed, even if it *is* not), it might still be true that the novel challenges of rapid global transformation would pose strains on the nation state, as an arena in which to concert political action, far greater (and perhaps unmanageably more severe) than those which have previously faced it.

The immediate appeal of the idea of nation has nothing in particular to do with efficacy. We may not like, or choose to espouse, the social relations into which we are born. But we are born into them, whether we like it or not; and their claims are there, to embrace or to reject, quite independently of any practical impact on our own life chances. But the immediate appeal of the idea of the state is virtually confined to the latter's presumed efficacy (Skinner 1989). States which are in fact effective in promoting the security of their subjects undoubtedly win (and deserve)[3] – a higher degree of loyalty than those that fail lamentably to furnish anything of the kind. But even states that notably fail to furnish security (even Iraq (Makiya 1993), or Myanmar or the Republic of Somalia) are compelled today to pretend not merely to wish to do so, but to be within realistic reach of at least becoming able to do so. Because this is so, the normative appeal of the idea of the state is inherently vulnerable to a sense of political crisis, and the practical dissipation of such a sense through effective political action is greatly impeded by any prolonged weakening in the normative appeal of the state as a system of agency.

It may be difficult to judge whether or not particular states (or even all states considered together) are or are not for the present gaining or losing in the practical ability to handle the collective predicaments of their own subjects (see chapter 10 above). But it is extremely easy to judge that there is widespread and disagreeable suspicion across the even minimally politically concerned populations of most countries in the world at present, from career politicians and high-ranking state officials to the most reluctant and despondent of voters, that their own states (and perhaps most other states also) are at present palpably weakening in their capacity to cope with these predicaments. At the limit, a sense of political crisis converges with the objective dynamics of state collapse – with revolution (cf. Dunn 1989; Dunn 1990a, chapter 6) or descent into the state of nature (Liberia, Somalia, much of Afghanistan). It is clear for the present that all the OECD states (for example) are very far indeed from collapse, and even further from revolution. But it is perhaps equally clear not merely that their practical adequacy for many purposes is genuinely subjectively in doubt in the eyes of their own subjects, but also that this adequacy may in addition be quite objectively in doubt.

A prevailing sense of political crisis is volatile and potentially misleading, an unreliable tracer of real changes in economic, social and even political circumstances. But it is also a political factor in itself, and capable under some conditions of exerting its own causal force in reshaping or dismantling political arenas: consider the recent decomposition of Italy's postwar political system and the emergent challenge to Japan's for long remarkably successful postwar conservative hegemony.[4] At this level, accordingly, the journalistic commonplace that there exists a contemporary crisis of the nation state might well prove virtually self-validating. By being reiterated, and through coming to be believed, it could make itself

---

[3] See chapter 4 above; Dunn (1980, Conclusion).

[4] The importance of crisis as a mechanism of adjustment in postwar Japanese politics has been illuminatingly emphasized by Calder (1988). Compare Johnson (1982) and Okimoto (1989).

true: consider, for example, the backwash from the Maastricht agreement. Because a sense of political crisis is itself an important political phenomenon, it is certainly pertinent to study its sources and its potential consequences. But, if we wish to understand what is going on in contemporary politics, it is likely in the long run to prove more rewarding to concentrate principally on the more external and objective features of the contemporary situation of nation states.

Locating crisis

Every actual nation state is both a somewhat hazy amalgam of at least two constitutive ideas and a disorderly, complex and profoundly opaque fact (Dunn 1990a, Introduction; Dunn 1985, Introduction). If we are to determine how far, and in what sense, the nation state is today in crisis, we first need to consider whether the prevailing sense of its being in crisis (if and where this does prevail) comes principally from the ideas or principally from the facts. Whether at the level of ideas or at the level of facts, it is inherently unlikely that all nation states should ever be equally in crisis at the same time. (A world in which they were so would already have become one in which the hazards to the human species were palpably beyond the reach of human powers to meet: a condition of uncontrollable biological or physical catastrophe, a planet which now precluded life, the heat death of the universe.) In the world of today, incontrovertibly, some states (Liberia, Somalia, Angola, Afghanistan) are far more in crisis than others (Switzerland, Singapore). As far as we know, this has always been true in the past; and we still have dismayingly little reason to expect that it will ever cease to be true in the future.

The judgement that the nation state is today in crisis is not founded on the experience of the feeblest of contemporary states (cf. Cruise O'Brien *et al.* 1989, Introduction and Conclusion). There is nothing either in the idea of a nation or in that of a state to ensure that Liberia or Chad will ever be firmly viable again (even though Liberia, for example, had in some respects a longer continuous political history than any other single sub-Saharan state in Africa before it first slipped into anomic military tyranny and then dissolved into competitive banditry).[5] We should not be surprised that ideas alone prove insufficient to ensure peace and prosperity for any human population, even though the idea of the state, both at the level of ideological pretension and at the level of international law

---

[5] See the chapters by Christopher Clapham in Dunn (1978) and in Cruise O'Brien *et al.* (1989), and contrast Clapham's treatment of the fate of the other longest lived of sub-Saharan Africa's extant polities (Clapham 1969, 1988).

(Vincent 1990), inhibits the acknowledgement of such insufficiency with some obduracy. But in a world in which human populations are technically compelled to live on terms of ever greater intimacy with one another, the inability to guarantee minimal security to particular populations may prove over time an important threat to the appeals of ideas through which their interests are supposedly protected.

In this respect there is an important asymmetry between the ideas of nation and state. In conditions of adversity, nation might become a purely passive category, a pure community of suffering. But even in conditions of adversity, the category of state retains in itself both a claim to be an agent and a corresponding burden of responsibility. Settings in which the idea of the state carries no factual structure of effective agency along with it (Cruise O'Brien *et al.* 1989, Conclusion; Hawthorn 1994) threaten the chances of their inhabitants to act together strategically and effectively in the face of their predicament. But they also threaten the prospects for the normalizing political instruments of the world economy (the IMF, the World Bank) to prevent concomitant disruption in the latter's trade and credit flows. The ending of the Cold War has left a world of less imminent eschatological horror (cf. Bracken 1982), but also one of even more discomfiting tension between social intimacy, gross disparities in human misery, and limited political and military capability and will to alleviate the misery or even suspend the intimacy (see chapter 8 above).

In itself the fact that some parts of the world are at present in no condition to instantiate convincingly the category of the state is conspicuously worse news for those parts of the world than it is for the category of the state. But if we consider the role of that category in articulating relations between states – horizontally and globally, rather than vertically and locally – local inefficacy may in the end prove a major impediment to the capacity of states in happier settings to furnish the services which they too purport to supply. (It is an important question about the realist strand in the understanding of international relations whether (or how far) its trenchantly zero-sum conception of the nature of these relations makes it obtuse to this possibility.) Where it plainly is unviable in practice, therefore, there is more than one way in which the failure of the nation state may react back on its appeal as an idea in less beleaguered settings. But even if these negative reactions do more on balance to impair its appeal than they do to reinforce it (which is far from evident), we can be confident that a sense of political crisis in the core countries of the OECD has not arisen from the travails of Liberia or Somalia (or indeed even from the uncomfortable experience of post-communism from Saxony to Bosnia and Vladivostok).

Nationhood

In this ampler, and for the moment altogether more comfortable, setting is it reasonable to see a sense of political crisis as emanating in any degree from the properties of the idea of the nation state? To answer this question, we need to consider its two core constitutive ideas in turn. The idea of a nation is that of a community of birth (in more liberal interpretation, perhaps, a community of birth and mutual choice). But actually existing nation states (as with actually existing socialism (Dunn 1984)) are altogether scruffier than this: medleys of birth, mutual choice, provisional instrumental exploitation approximately within the law, and vigorous manipulative penetration from well outside it. In idea, membership of a nation should be wholly uncontentious; a brute matter of fact, and prior to (a premiss of) any conceptualization of interest. In fact, however, few things are more contentious (already) in the more prosperous of modern nation states than who exactly at any particular time is entitled to full membership of the nation; and conflicts of interest over this question (while hard to demarcate either stably or accurately) are acute and intensely inflammatory (see chapter 9 above). (Consider the prospective impact of the NAFTA free trade agreement, especially upon relations between Mexico and the USA.) These conflicts have increased; they are increasing; and there is no reason whatever to expect them to diminish for the foreseeable future.

As a fact, the nation state is a rough and ready mechanism for furnishing a set of real services (Gellner 1983). But the relation between fact and idea is increasingly slack; and there are no imaginative or analytical resources within the idea to alleviate the increasingly prominent strains within the fact. It may in the end prove important that the idea of nation should be so conspicuously exposed from two very different angles. From a realist viewpoint it is too vague and too sentimental to serve convincingly as a device for assessing interests (but cf. Weber 1980). From a liberal viewpoint it is too particularist in taste and too recklessly submissive to contingency to serve as a device for interpreting value for human beings.[6] But these threats, if threats they are, are as yet scarcely imminent. While it is reasonable to suppose that the idea of nationhood should be under somewhat greater practical strain as a framework for organizing collective action in conditions of massive and (at the receiving end) largely involuntary external penetration of citizenship as well as with

---

[6] Note, however, the increasingly strenuous and protracted struggle of John Rawls to surmount these impediments; and compare the more realist assessment in Dunn (1993, chapter 3).

unpleasantly slack national labour markets, the strictly civic aspect of such conditions is still in most OECD countries more a fear about the future than a fact about the present.

Statehood

Insofar as a sense of crisis emanates from the properties of these two key ideas, therefore, it is reasonable to assume that it must be coming less from a weakening in the appeals of the idea of the nation than from a lessening in the cogency (normative or practical) of the idea of the state.

Crisis at the periphery

There are two main doubts about the state, both certainly as old as the concept itself, and each clearly foreshadowed in the historical experience of the miscellany of large-scale political units which preceded its full formulation and to which the concept has since been regularly applied (cf. chapter 4 above). The first is a doubt about the intentions of those who at any given time direct state power: a scepticism that these intentions are in the case in question (or usually, or often, or ever), as benign as they are fulsomely proclaimed to be. We can be confident in the face of this doubt, that there remain ample grounds for entertaining it; but we can be at least equally confident that the chances of the doubt's being in general better founded now than it has been for the last three and a half centuries are slight.[7] The second (and perhaps even weightier) doubt concerns the state's efficacy in relation to its expressed intentions: above all as a device for furnishing security to its subjects. Here too, while there continues to be massive reason for entertaining the doubt, it is inordinately unlikely that the grounds for doing so have strengthened greatly since the seventeenth century.

Certainly the concept of state is applied more widely (and perhaps more promiscuously) to political units in the world today than it was in the days of Hobbes: not least for its convenience in imposing a minimal framework of order on social interactions and economic transactions which bind human populations ever closer together. In the settings of modern international law and international relations the sufficient conditions for applying the concept manifestly do not at present entail a level of practical efficacy in state performance adequate to guarantee the security of anyone.[8]

---

[7] Compare the darkest suspicions which can be plausibly entertained about the purposes of state elites in France and Spain today with Elliott (1984); and consider the haunting English Civil War fear of 'a German devastation' (Underdown 1987, p. 154).

[8] For the importance of this predicament see Dunn (1994).

Some portion of the sense of crisis in the nation state today, accordingly, may well derive in this way from two types of threat to state legitimacy. The first, stemming principally from the diffusion of a variety of secular rationalist theories of political value and political possibility (cf. chapter 14 below; Dunn 1984; Dunn 1993, Conclusion), foments excessively high political expectations, and vents its disappointment at the failure of history to live up to them on the state powers which are (in fantasy at any rate) the most concrete facilities for at least attempting to realize them. It is inherently difficult to pin down a relation of this character (cf. Habermas 1976). But it remains a plausible diagnosis of anomalies within the modern understanding of politics, albeit more convincingly seen as a permanent dimension of vulnerability than as an at present especially dynamic source of novel hazard. As we have already noted, the second variety of threat to legitimacy, arising from the overextension of the category of the state, its relentless application to what are often grimly inappropriate referents, occurs principally at the periphery of the world political and economic system. The dismal realities to which the term 'state' frequently refers in these settings (President Mobutu on his river boat), do nothing for the majesty of the idea of the state. (They are not what Hobbes or Hegel had in mind.) But it is hard to believe that they inflict much damage upon its standing or authority closer to the centre of world political economy. (What would you expect of the Heart of Darkness?)

Crisis at the centre

If there really is a contemporary crisis of the nation state, it must in the end be a crisis not of the periphery but of the centre. At that centre, too, there is good reason to suppose that it must stem not from diminishing intrinsic powers on the part of particular nation states[9] but from a growing gap between the causal capabilities of even the more advanced nation states and the effective demands placed upon those powers. This is as we should expect. All power is relational. It is apparent enough that in many concrete ways the powers of advanced states today to carry out particular actions vastly exceed those of their predecessors. They can move their armed forces far more rapidly from place to place. They can communicate with (and spy upon) each other with a speed, intensity and amplitude which are wholly unprecedented. They can shift earth, raise buildings or unleash explosive power on a scale which no past ruler could

---

[9] Or even from diminishing powers in relation to one another: cf. Kennedy (1988) and Nye (1990).

have seriously imagined. But these awesome powers are not focused on fixed and stable targets. Indeed, now that the Cold War is over, they are no longer even aimed crucially at the rapidly rising powers of other human agencies. Instead, they need to be assessed (and to an increasing degree they are already coming to be assessed), in relation to a range of formidable new threats to human security of which we are belatedly becoming aware (cf. Hurrell & Kingsbury 1992). If there really is a contemporary crisis of the nation state (and not merely a transitory, quasi-cyclical decline in political self-confidence, prompted by recession or by reaction to the brief euphoria of 1989), this is where it must emanate from.

There is no reason to assume any clear relation between the degree to which human populations at any time are aware of the threats which they face and the scale of those threats themselves. Neither political theory nor political science offers much special aid in judging that scale (see chapter 10 above). But, between them, they may reasonably hope to capture some aspects of the structures from which the threats arise. Two of these structures are essentially external to state agency: a product of global economic dynamics and ecological degradation. But one is itself in part a consequence of state action: not an immediate product of state agency itself, but an interactive effect between states, generated by the extremity of the challenges now posed by global economic dynamics and ecological pressure.

It is hard to judge the acuity of all three threats, but easy to appreciate how each could readily exacerbate the others. Because of these two features of the situation, we can be reasonably confident at present that no one is in a position to assess accurately quite how severe the contemporary crisis of the nation state really is (or even whether the term 'crisis' is genuinely appropriate). But none of us should have much difficulty in seeing that the sense of crisis, however frivolously generated or insecurely grounded, may well turn out to be all too apposite.

The economic threat has been most extensively explored. We can catch the subjective flavour of it clearly enough in the petulant tones of M. Balladur at the obsequies of the *franc fort*: 'We can't allow a situation to continue where so much money can change hands in a very short time and threaten a nation's security' (*Financial Times*, 13 August 1993, p. 1). (Those who live by the market need not be surprised if they prove to die by the market.) It is still difficult to judge the full impact of the vast expansion in trade flows, the dramatic increase in the scale and speed of capital movements, or the dizzy volatility of currency markets, on the capacity of state elites to realize their own purposes; not least because the starkly unintended consequences of market liberalization will certainly continue to promote vigorous attempts to reverse many of the changes that have produced these outcomes. The accents of M. Balladur are those of a humiliated (and politically exposed) representative of a peculiarly proud state. But they serve to epitomize the discomforts of an entire political class. We can trace the resulting stigmata of impotence already in many prominent political processes: the effective blunting of the social democratic project (cf. Esping-Anderson 1985); the recoil from European monetary union;[10] the faltering of the Uruguay Round of the GATT (contrast Winham 1986); the sharpening (though ultimately contained) challenge under the Clinton presidency to the NAFTA agreements between Canada, Mexico and the United States.

The central challenge of global economic liberalization is to the Keynesian conception of the welfare state; the promise, reaching back at least to Lorenz von Stein, to take full responsibility for the economic welfare of a given population through the deft exercise of the power of its state. The existing and anticipated unemployment levels of the OECD countries, and of western Europe in particular, are a notable setback not merely to Keynes's own hopes and expectations in the aftermath of the *General Theory* (Clarke 1988), but also to the variety of expedients eventually deployed by other western governments in face of the Great Depression (cf. Barber 1985; Hall 1989), and still more to the levels of employment achieved and welfare publicly provided across most of western Europe over most of the period since the Second World War ended. Since there is such a clear elective affinity between the Keynesian conception of macroeconomic management to deliver popular welfare and the idea of the nation state (with its claim to embody a relatively intimate relation between ruler and ruled), it is unsurprising that these experiences should have spread anxiety well beyond the ranks of career politicians or state officials. Insofar as the political formula of the welfare state proves to be economically unsustainable (or even insofar as it proves to be unsustainable in the competitive political conditions of modern representative democracy (cf. Dunn 1992, Conclusion)), doubts about the normative legitimacy of capitalism which have dogged it throughout its history (and which have never been fully resolved even at a purely intellectual level – see chapter 7 above) will press against it once more, and with increasing force (Dunn 1990b, esp. Introduction and Conclusion). While they are most unlikely to place the state as a political format objectively in jeopardy, there is far greater likelihood of their disturbing the comfort of political incumbency (and thus of sharpening a sense of political crisis, not least against incumbents).

A less immediate, but potentially more profound, threat to state viabil-

---

[10] Compare the oversanguine expectations of chapter 11 above.

ity is already beginning to arise from the challenges of environmental degradation. In the spheres of economics, the threat to the political standing of the nation state comes essentially from the tension between a national framework of sovereign authority and government responsibility and an uncompromisingly international field of economic causality. In the sphere of ecology, the national framework of sovereign power and government responsibility is also in some tension with ecological causality. (Acid rain, the ozone layer, still more global warming, are no respecters of boundaries.) But the principal residual obstacle to effective action in face of ecological hazard (over and above the key elements of sheer expense and painfully limited scientific comprehension) is less an incapacity on the part of governments to meet locally generated ecological threats within their own borders than a difficulty in cooperating effectively together to guarantee one another against the involuntary importation of pollution from elsewhere. Their problem, in this context, is not a deficiency in domestic power but a disinclination or incapacity for effective collective action. Even domestically, the ecological threat to state viability may in the end prove quite formidable. The scale of cost already palpably involved in any attempt to reverse many major instances of environmental degradation,[11] the bitter conflicts which will certainly arise over distributing the costs of any such reversal, even the widespread doubts whether states can readily be equipped to find out what should best be done over matters where powerful interest groups are so drastically at risk, all ensure severe pressures on the state's capacity for effective agency.

But the main ecological challenge to state viability is likely to come not from domestic limits to the state's power, but from the difficulties of securing effective and trustworthy international cooperation (Hurrell & Kingsbury 1992). The problem of collective action (Hardin 1982) permeates all politics. It is at least as easy to pick up in the domestic politics of the United States[12] as it is in the general assembly of the United Nations. But the problems of collective action are peculiarly intractable where there is little realistic prospect of creating an effective enforcement agency and where the rational appeal of seeking to ride free is often devastatingly apparent. It is a complicated and unobvious question about many ecological issues whether or not the structure of costs and rewards of cooperation yields a clear balance of advantage for state actors to cooperate or to defect (Heal 1993): to form binding collective agreements to

---

[11] Already heavy enough to imperil the future of the oldest surviving international insurance market.
[12] For the historical antecedents of this feature of the American state see Stephen Skowronek's exceptionally illuminating book (Skowronek 1982).

restrict environmental damage to one another and abide strictly by their terms, or to participate, in the spirit of Callicles,[13] like skulking brigands, in the complex processes of global negotiations, affix their signatures slyly to such treaty documents as emerge from them, and resolutely ignore their terms thereafter, whenever it is more convenient to do so. One element of this complexity lies in the prospective costs and rewards of punctilious observance of the agreements themselves. But a second, which may in practice be every bit as important, lies in the strategic dilemmas delineated in the theory of games. What might be starkly irrational in the case of a single pay-off Prisoner's Dilemma could well be strategically optimal in a frequently repeated game, with no definite terminal point, and with conspicuous relations to many other concurrent repeated games.

If human beings are to re-establish control over the ecological dangers of which they are now becoming aware, they will certainly need to act together more deftly and patiently than they have usually contrived to do in the past. For the present, there is no serious possibility of their either discovering or fashioning a discrete new instrument of action which can supplant the nation state in this struggle against the recalcitrance of nature. If they do eventually learn how to behave in a consequentially less self-destructive manner, there is little reason to expect that the sites of their learning will have any especially intimate relation to states as such. But the agencies required to implement this learning in the last instance are likely to continue for the foreseeable future to be states. *Faute de mieux*: either states or nothing.

If states fail, by and large, to make, enforce, or abide by effective international agreements restraining the environmental destructiveness of modern economic activity, it may be an analytical error to blame them for this failure (Dunn 1990a, chapter 12). The fault may lie principally elsewhere: in the cognitive limitations (or intemperate and inveterate greed) of their subjects – the ultimately ruling *demos* – or in the fundamental features of the pay-off matrix of environmental costs and damage. But their subjects are unlikely to be prepared to acknowledge the former; and most of them will usually be unequipped to recognize the latter.

At the receiving end, therefore, the consequences of state inaction or breach of faith are likely, as they come out, to appear both avoidable and discreditable. While this need in itself have no instantaneous effect on the material or organizational components of state power, it would quite rapidly impair the residual normative appeal of states as such. Every state is many other things too; but the key feature of each state is that it is a

---

[13]   Plato, *Gorgias*, 507e, cf. 483a–4b; 1979 edn, pp. 56–7, 86.

potential structure for political action. Damage to the normative appeal
of a state is not merely damage to an idea. It also impairs (and can at the
limit simply eliminate) the capacity of a state to serve as a structure of
political action. If there is a crisis of the nation state today, it cannot result
merely from speculative guesses about future possibilities. But even if it is
right to conclude that there is no clearly delineated crisis of the nation
state today (no objective feature of its location which explains why it must
now be in crisis), that is no guarantee that there will not be such a crisis
tomorrow. We do not yet know that the political challenge of arresting
environmental degradation is any threat at all to the nation state as a
format for political life or political action. But just in case it does prove to
pose such a threat, we would be well advised to consider that possibility in
advance. That at least would give us an opportunity to see why exactly it
might do so, while there was still time to do something about it.

REFERENCES

Anderson, B. 1983. *Imagined Communities*. London: Verso
Barber, W. J. 1985. *From New Era to New Deal*. Cambridge: Cambridge University
     Press
Bracken, P. 1982. *The Command and Control of Nuclear Forces*. New Haven: Yale
     University Press
Buchanan, J. 1986. *Liberty, Market and State: Political Economy in the 1980s*. New
     York: New York University Press
Calder, K. E. 1988. *Crisis and Compensation*. Princeton: Princeton University
     Press
Clapham, C. 1969. *Haile-Selassie's Government*. London: Longman
     1988. *Continuity and Transformation in Revolutionary Ethiopia*. Cambridge:
     Cambridge University Press
Clarke, P. 1988. *The Keynesian Revolution in the Making*. Oxford: Clarendon Press
Cruise O'Brien, D., J. Dunn and R. Rathbone 1989 (eds.). *Contemporary West
     African States*. Cambridge: Cambridge University Press
Dunn, J. 1978 (ed.). *West African States: Failure and Promise*. Cambridge:
     Cambridge University Press
     1980. *Political Obligation in its Historical Context*. Cambridge: Cambridge
     University Press
     1984. *The Politics of Socialism*. Cambridge: Cambridge University Press
     1985. *Rethinking Modern Political Theory*. Cambridge: Cambridge University
     Press
     1989. *Modern Revolutions*, 2nd edn. Cambridge: Cambridge University Press
     1990a. *Interpreting Political Responsibility*. Cambridge: Polity Press
     1990b. *The Economic Limits to Modern Politics*. Cambridge: Cambridge
     University Press
     1992 (ed.). *Democracy: The Unfinished Journey*. Oxford: Oxford University Press
     1993. *Western Political Theory in the Face of the Future*, 2nd edn. Cambridge:
     Cambridge University Press

1994. *The Nation State and Human Community: Obligation, Life-chances and the Boundaries of Society* (in Italian). Edizioni Anabasi, Milan

Elliott, J. H. 1984. *Richelieu and Olivares.* Cambridge: Cambridge University Press

Esping-Anderson, G. 1985. *Politics against Markets: The Social Democratic Road to Power.* Princeton: Princeton University Press

Gellner, E. 1983. *Nations and Nationalism.* Oxford: Blackwell

Gray, J. 1984. *Hayek on Liberty.* Oxford: Blackwell

Greenfeld, L. 1992. *Nationalism: Five Roads to Modernity.* Cambridge, Mass.: Harvard University Press

Habermas J. 1976. *Legitimation Crisis,* trans. T. McCarthy. London: Heinemann

Hall, P. A. 1989 (ed.). *The Political Power of Economic Ideas.* Princeton: Princeton University Press

Hardin, R. 1982. *Collective Action.* Baltimore: Johns Hopkins University Press

Hawthorn, G. 1994. 'The crises of southern states'. *Political Studies* 42, 130–45

Hayek, F. A. 1973–9. *Law, Legislation and Liberty,* 3 vols. London: Routledge
   1978. *New Studies in Philosophy, Politics, Economics and the History of Ideas.* London: Routledge

Heal, G. 1993. 'Formation of international environment agreements'. *Economics and Politics,* July, 191–211. International School of Economic Research, University of Siena

Hobsbawm, E. 1990. *Nations and Nationalism since 1780.* Cambridge: Cambridge University Press

Hurrell, A. and B. Kingsbury 1992 (eds.). *The International Politics of the Environment.* Oxford: Oxford University Press

Johnson, C. 1982. *MITI and the Japanese Miracle.* Stanford: Stanford University Press

Kennedy, P. 1988. *The Rise and Fall of the Great Powers.* London: Unwin Hyman

Makiya, K. 1993. *Cruelty and Silence.* London: Jonathan Cape

Nye, J. S. Jr. 1990. *Bound to Lead: The Changing Nature of American Power.* New York: Basic Books

Okimoto, D. I. 1989. *Between MITI and the Market.* Stanford: Stanford University Press

Olson, M. 1982. *The Rise and Decline of Nations.* New Haven: Yale University Press

Plato. *Gorgias,* trans. T. Irwin (1979). Oxford: Clarendon Press

Skinner, Q. 1989. 'The state'. In *Political Innovation and Conceptual Change,* ed. T. Ball, J. Farr and R. Hanson, pp. 90–131. Cambridge: Cambridge University Press

Skowronek, S. 1982. *Building the New American State.* Cambridge: Cambridge University Press

Underdown, D. 1987. *Revel, Riot and Rebellion.* Oxford: Oxford University Press

Vincent, R. J. 1990. 'Grotius, human rights and intervention'. In *Hugo Grotius and the Theory of International Relations,* ed. H. Bull, B. Kingsbury and A. Roberts, pp. 241–56. Oxford: Oxford University Press

Weber, M. 1980. 'The national state and economic policy' (Freiburg address). *Economy and Society* 9, 428–49

Winham, G. 1986. *International Trade and the Tokyo Round Negotiation.* Princeton: Princeton University Press

13 Political and economic obstacles to rapid collective learning

How should human beings respond to the dawning recognition that they may well for some time have been destroying the fundamental conditions of their own existence? This is, paradigmatically, a question which must be explored and thought through carefully *together*, rather than prejudged and dogmatized about by particular individuals.

In essence, it is an issue of the viable basis for practical cooperation; and it depends upon the existing beliefs and sentiments of immense numbers of human beings, and on the degree to which these can in practice be modified over a reasonably short period of time and by means which may actually prove to be available. At its core, it is an issue of feasibility, human beings being taken as they are (and where and when they are) rather than as we might prefer them to be. What is feasible for us to do to restrain or reverse the damage which we have been doing depends on many different considerations, most of which I am wholly unequipped even to assess for myself. It depends, plainly, on how rapidly and how accurately we can identify the *nature* of the damage we are inflicting, and on how speedily we can learn the scope and limits of our purely technical capacities to restrain and eventually reverse the harms in question. In both dimensions, there will be an important political component to determining the outcome, simply because of the resource implications of the cultivation of greater vigilance or of more widespread and active inquiry into the relevant causality (chapter 10 above). But the principal elements, plainly enough, will be matters of natural scientific research.

In some ways we are still at a very early stage in thinking through the question of how we *do* have good reason to respond to recognizing the harm which we have been doing and few, if any, even of its main aspects have yet been identified with real precision or dependability. I cannot pretend to have a personal judgement of the slightest value either about the fields in which the relevant natural scientific inquiry most needs to be undertaken, or even about the palpably political question of the relative weight we should give to such inquiry as a whole, over against the many other more or less urgent calls on public expenditure in each of the more prosperous states in the world, from the provision of the most basic welfare to the maintenance and deployment of effective forces of coercion. All such questions are political. All of them are complicated; and there is little that can be said informatively about them except in considerable detail and in very carefully delineated contexts.

What I should like to focus on instead is the interface between the grossly general question of how human beings now have good reason to respond to recognizing that they are drastically harming their own habitat, and a set of far older questions about how they have long had good reason to understand the nature of their political relations with one another. On an alarmist view (which may very well prove a scientifically correct view), what human beings now practically need to do is to learn fast and accurately that they *must* change many of their existing habits and styles of behaviour, from the most domestic to the most intractably national or even civilizational, and do so rapidly, drastically and permanently.

One of the central preoccupations of the history of political thinking, in the west but also in a number of other ancient political traditions, has long been with exploring the scope for, and hazards of, attempts to alter human habits and styles of behaviour rapidly, drastically and durably (or even permanently) through the amassing and exercise of political power and authority. One whole strand in the human effort to comprehend politics has been devoted precisely to pressing this question à l'outrance, just as another has been devoted to assailing the spiritual queasiness, aberration of judgement and practical futility of attempting anything of the kind. Some of the greatest interpreters of the peculiar burden and menace of politics – Plato and Locke, Machiavelli and Kant – have plainly felt the full force of each viewpoint.

I take it (perhaps a bit presumptuously) that the core ecological thought at present is, roughly, that it is wildly imprudent to behave as *greedily* as we now do, to appropriate and consume so much and so heedlessly (because doing so is so wasteful, and because it has proved to have such ghastly negative externalities). *Amor sceleratus habendi*, as John Locke put it (Locke [1689] 1993, II, para. 111, p. 172), a criminal desire to possess, lurks permanently in the motivation of all human beings, can be kept under firm control only by the utmost care and force of will, and is somehow not merely connived at but actually sanctified by the fundamental organizational logic of the civilization to which we belong. (For the central importance of this fact see Dunn (1990b).) The way the most potent and consequential of large-scale interactions between human beings and the rest of nature, and of groups of humans with each other, are now articulated presupposes a firm acceptance of the legitimacy and indispensability of effective appropriation and accumulation. The dominant value of contemporary political culture across the western world, and increasingly also in other wealthy countries like Japan, the value which Constant christened modern liberty (Constant [1819] 1988, pp. 313–28), the right to live as one pleases, reiterates this underlying economic and political logic at the level of explicit personal commitment, vindicating, and indeed *celebrating*, the way our societies in fact function, as though this was in itself a sort of civilizational achievement.

The view that this commitment is a major spiritual error, a form of avowed public depravity, is as old as modern political culture itself (and the values *behind* that view, of course, are considerably older still). Even the view that it must in the end be instrumentally imprudent at a collective level to be quite so openly licentious at an individual level goes back almost as far. The ecological theme today thus recapitulates a central cultural critique which effectively long predates the triumph of capitalism; and it does so in terms which those who have always found capitalist economic relations pretty repulsive are likely to find reassuringly familiar and invigoratingly evocative (Dunn 1993). But what it is essential to remember at this point is the massive cumulative discredit which, in the meantime, has befallen the political tradition of resistance to *amor sceleratus habendi*, the tradition which Filippo Buonarroti in the 1820s christened 'the order of equality' (Buonarroti [1828] 1957, I, p. 25), and later speakers have tended to refer to as socialism or communism. On one view, this discredit can be isolated in two distinctive blemishes of the tradition – its penchant for authoritarian political solutions, and its trust in the efficacy of large-scale overall economic coordination from the political centre (Dunn 1984). Both of these imaginative propensities retain some appeal; and in my view we cannot confidently anticipate that either will prove to have been comprehensively expunged from the human future. What we certainly *have* learnt, however, and learnt quite incontrovertibly since the days of Buonarroti, is the extraordinary danger, and the severely limited potential benefit, of dabbling in this line of thought and conduct: the murderously unpromising balance between the most that one can reasonably hope to gain from doing so, and the worst one should reasonably fear from the same line of action.

But if the order of equality offers no convincing remedy for the insistent destructiveness of modern production and exchange, what remedies, if any, might actually be compatible with the persistence of its ghostly enemy (what Buonarroti christened 'the order of egoism')? A civilization founded on the systematization of greed and appropriativeness is necessarily a trifle unprepossessing. But, as modern history has shown, it is in many ways staggeringly effective; and the practical, and even moral, case in its favour does not have to be at all a shallow one. Indeed it is a perfectly defensible view that we not merely have at present no practical alternative of the least eligibility to this civilization (a matter of some practical importance), but also at present have no sound reason to believe that there could even be (history being taken as it now is, and human beings being taken as they really are capable of becoming) an alternative of the least eligibility. In the face of this potentially awesome predicament of growing ecological peril, therefore, it is of the utmost urgency to identify accurately just what the resources of the order of egoism really are for handling it effectively on our behalf (cf. chapter 12 above; Hurrell 1994).

Its simplest remedy, already formally espoused by the British government (and by the governments of most other reasonably prosperous countries in their public self-characterization) is essentially technocratic: that all we really need to do is to ascertain how to *price* ourselves back into a less destructive relation to our habitat, and then to implement this new understanding in a prompt, precise and systematic fashion. There are two principal drawbacks to this proposal. The first is that it relies more heavily than we have any inductive grounds for doing on the learning capacities, prospective convergence of judgement, and political cogency of economists themselves. It is entirely reasonable to believe that some improvement in technical economic understanding is a necessary condition for a less hazardous form of collective life; but it would be bewilderingly ingenuous to mistake it for a potential sufficient condition (Dunn 1990a, chapter 12; Dunn 1990b). The second limitation to the proposal follows from the first. Technocracy – the perfect alignment of power with technique – is a very old and rather deep political fantasy. The main suspicion levelled against it throughout its long historical career is that it rests in the end of a resolute imaginative repression of politics itself, on an obdurate refusal to acknowledge the practical importance, and the irreducibility, of disagreement in judgement and conflict in sentiment within and between human populations. Economists do have some real standing over the question of just what price relations are right, what combination of taxation, subsidies and outright orders and prohibitions, will most readily, reliably and expeditiously emend modern economic activity into a mode which no longer is cumulatively destructive. But these price relations will certainly not be a unique and rigid set. And they could scarcely in principle prescribe just how the costs and benefits of the emendation are to be allocated: who will get what out of them and at whose expense. Deciding this is an intractably political task. The question I wish to address is essentially: how ought we to *think about* this task? What really is its *character*?

A purely technocratic answer to it could hope to be relatively simple.

The question is how to align the relevant techniques with the requisite degree of authority: how to achieve, in effect, government by economists and ecologists, with their full panoply of specialist natural scientific advisers, and how to make sure that the economists and advisers in question are the right economists and advisers and not the wrong ones. (The importance of this last proviso is one which economists and scientists will be the first to underline.) The cumulative lesson of the history of political thought and practice is that this solution by itself is vastly less determinate than it sounds, and that – not least just because it *is* so indeterminate – its prospects of political success in practice are exiguous. Seen very abstractly, the problem is encouragingly simple – how to integrate judgement, subject it reliably to the way the world really is and works, and lend it in its resulting form decisive power to implement itself. But to formulate the solution in this way is flatly incompatible with the ruling doctrine of state of the great majority of civilized and prosperous countries in the world today: with the theory, or if you will, the ideology, of the modern representative democratic republic (Dunn 1992; Fontana 1994). Today we never knowingly and voluntarily surrender final and lasting authority to choose for us to any determinate set of claimants to know just how to do so. The people are sovereign. The people choose who is to exercise their authority for them; and they choose just how long that authority is to be exercised for. All this, of course, is very simplified and laundered as a description of what is actually going on in any modern state. But it is not an aspect of what is going on which can simply be ignored if we wish to think about how we, in the societies of Europe, North America and the Pacific rim, can reasonably hope to confront the threat of ecological catastrophe effectively and in the long run.

If the main obstacle to averting such catastrophe were simply the difficulty of identifying technically how most simply, cheaply and reliably to do so, the political or social, or even economic, impediments to doing so would be a comparatively minor part of the story. But that is emphatically *not* the main obstacle.

It is not, in my view, yet clear just what the main obstacle really is. But what is already very clear indeed is that there is more than one major obstacle, above and beyond those posed by our limited existing comprehension of the natural scientific causalities at work. It is also clear that these distinct sources of constraint on our possible responses interact permanently and dynamically with one another, so that the prospect of reaching a practically illuminating holistic grasp of the implications of their interactions in the near future is pretty slight. Let me list, very cursorily, a few of the more important obstacles. One is the simple difficulty of communicating intelligibly to one another an accurate understanding of the natural threats in question – the threats to our biological survival – and of our own options in responding to them. A second is the difficulty of *coordinating* even such actions as we all have, in some plain sense, good reason to undertake in response (cf. Dunn 1990a, chapter 12). A third is the difficulty, individual by individual and collective agency by collective agency, of deciding just what risks to run and just what costs to accept in the intrinsically competitive process of allocating the burden of adjustment between us. A fourth, still more disobliging but most unlikely to prove simply dispensable, is the difficulty of deciding whom or what exactly we can trust to enforce on ourselves, and still more on the more recalcitrant amongst our fellows, the appropriate degree of adjustment. (For the central importance of this issue in politics at all times, see Dunn (1990a, chapter 3).) (Being forced to be free is a paradoxical idea and the paradox was always precisely the rhetorical point of so expressing it. But there is nothing inherently paradoxical about being forced to retain the practical option of biological survival. On a shorter time horizon, shouldering precisely that task is a prominent instance of parental responsibility within the individual life cycle of the great majority of human beings, and has fairly plain analogies in those of numerous other animal, and indeed bird, species.)

A fifth obstacle is the more spiritual and perhaps also more engaging task of discerning how far we really do have good reason to remould our imaginations to accept the limits open to us and the responsibilities that follow from those limits: to see our destiny as the ground of our responsibilities. This fifth obstacle, to speak a bit grandiloquently, is above all a condition of the psyche, a matter of the complex web of beliefs and desires in every human individual and across every human society. One remedy for our predicament – a very old and very widely explored and interpreted remedy for human predicaments across time and space – is essentially a change of soul, a reordering of imaginative and ultimate purpose to a more chastened, edifying, coherent and steady, a less erratic and myopically and hastily desire-driven, mode of life.

Even this remedy, essentially a complete and permanent victory over, or at the limit an *elimination* of, *amor sceleratus habendi* (human greed) would not be a full and immediate remedy for our present predicament (at least as I understand this). But, of course, if it were available, it would make the identification and implementation of the residue of expedients required relatively effortless. I think it remains reasonable to see the principal site of obstruction to averting ecological catastrophe as the human soul, and that in this sense rather archaic spiritual diagnoses (Christian, Buddhist, Jain, perhaps Confucian, Hindu, Judaic or even Islamic) remain eminently to the point.

But if there is one thing which is politically harder on a world scale than communicating intelligibly, coordinating rapidly and accurately, deciding what to accept in the distribution of the massive costs of adjustment, and judging to whom or what to entrust the degree of coercion which will be required to secure the coordination and enforce the distribution of costs, that one thing would certainly be a rapid and worldwide changing of souls through public collective action. The conjunction of political power with projects of large-scale and rapid transformation of souls has seldom been a felicitous one. But in the twentieth century it has plumbed new depths of barbarism and horror (Dunn 1989; Dunn 1990a, chapter 6). In the face of these grim stories, we have every reason to fear any direct relation between highly organized, large-scale, coercive power and any such task of spiritual reconstruction.

Each of us can safely think of our *own* souls as a site of obstruction to the realization of a better world, if we choose to do so. But any hasty identification of the souls of others as the site of such obstruction – especially of others about whom we know almost nothing and comprehend even less – is a sound recipe for political stupidity, as well as a ready source of quite unwarranted spiritual self-regard. Spiritual narcissism and political stupidity are scarcely the main obstacles to averting ecological catastrophe. But they definitely are formidable impediments in their own right to doing so; and they are impediments which lie to a large degree within our own control. We can all do something effective to limit them, if only we try hard enough. And if we did all try hard to do so for a decade or two, the human world in which we then lived would be a very different world from that of today, and the problems of reproducing it would stand a far better chance of falling within the reach of the congeries of professional agents – career politicians and bureaucrats, and natural scientists – whom our societies employ to handle such problems for us: the stewards of modern liberty (Dunn 1990a, chapter 5, p. 70; Constant [1819] 1988, pp. 313–28).

The characteristic political and social division of labour of modern societies has in many ways proved astoundingly successful. But it has always carried a danger of marginalizing and politically infantilizing the majority of the population in the residue of purely amateur roles which it leaves open to them (Dunn 1985, chapter 7; Dunn 1990a, chapter 12). The massive frictional force of what one might think of as essentially *spiritual* inertia in face of the task of remoulding our collective global way of life is a power inherently beyond the capacity of the modern professionalized division of political and social labour to overcome. All of us are part of that friction to greater or lesser degrees. We cannot sensibly hope for our leaders or technicians to overcome it for us. We can only hope to overcome it, severally and together, by modifying our own selves and learning a more historically adult, patient and generous style of living with one another. It is a very old task, but also one with a quite new urgency. In essence, as I have tried to argue, the most helpful way to see it is as a task of surmounting the political, economic and personal obstacles to rapid collective learning.

REFERENCES

Buonarroti, F. M. [1828] 1957. *Conspiration pour l'égalité dite de Babeuf*, 2 vols. Paris: Editions Sociales
Constant, B. [1819] 1988. *Political Writings*, ed. B. Fontana. Cambridge: Cambridge University Press
Dunn, J. 1984. *The Politics of Socialism*. Cambridge: Cambridge University Press
  1985. *Rethinking Modern Political Theory*. Cambridge: Cambridge University Press
  1989. *Modern Revolutions*, 2nd edn. Cambridge: Cambridge University Press
  1990a. *Interpreting Political Responsibility*. Cambridge: Polity Press
  1990b (ed.). *The Economic Limits to Modern Politics*. Cambridge: Cambridge University Press
  1992 (ed.). *Democracy: The Unfinished Journey*. Oxford: Oxford University Press
  1993. *Western Political Theory in the Face of the Future*, 2nd edn. Cambridge: Cambridge University Press
  1994 (ed.). *Contemporary Crisis of the Nation State?* Special issue of *Political Studies* and Oxford: Blackwell (1995)
Fontana, B. 1994 (ed.). *The Invention of the Modern Republic*. Cambridge: Cambridge University Press
Hurrell, A. 1994. 'A crisis of ecological viability? Global environmental change and the nation state'. In *Contemporary Crisis of the Nation State?* ed. J. Dunn. Special issue of *Political Studies* and Oxford: Blackwell (1995)
Locke, J. [1689] 1993. *Two Treatises of Government*, ed. M. Goldie. London: Dent

14   The heritage and future of the European left

To inherit, one must be alive. The heritage of the European left depends not merely on its own past but also, and intractably, on its own future. Inheritance is not a naturally grateful category for the left, as it would be, for example, for a feudal aristocracy. The left cannot hope to draw its legitimacy essentially from its past, however grand or inspiring that past may sometimes have been. Indeed it is in evident danger of being supplanted as soon as it attempts at all strenuously to do anything of the kind. In the organized routine politics of the modern capitalist democracy, the most immediate threat which the left at present faces is having this heritage filched from it by more agile, more locally perceptive and less encumbered antagonists. The key question which confronts the European left for the moment is not what its short-term prospects may prove to be, here or there, within the routine politics of individual states or the EEC or in wider arenas, it is whether it really has a distinctive future of its own at all, whether it can hope to remain alive and to reproduce itself effectively as a political force across the generations to come.

In the nature of the case, short-term prospects in routine politics are massively contingent: predicated on the timing of electoral cycles, on the factional stability or instability of immediate enemies and on their recent triumphs or debacles. Such prospects are drastically affected by raw political skill or nerve, and even more drastically affected by sheer luck. This is not, of course, to say that they are inconsequential. At least in the modern world, routine politics at any time is always (however bumpily) a direct outcome of routine politics immediately beforehand. But that does not make the interminable accumulation of narrative histories the best way (let alone the only way) in which to develop political understanding. Even in relation to routine politics, it is always necessary as well to stand further back and to identify the broad forces which have shaped the content of routine political conflict and still establish the limits within which it must take its course. In the near future in Europe the left can be confident that it will fare distinctly better in some settings than it will in others; and it is not hard to make an educated guess as to which these settings are likely to be. An educated eye, accordingly, is readily liable to gratuitous optimism over the left's longer term prospects just because of its palpable resilience in particular settings in the short term.

To have great achievements amongst one's presumed ancestors is no guarantee of inheritance. To be an heir one must be seen by others as their lineal descendant (or as being as close to a lineal descendant as subsequent history has left). It must be agreed that the ancestors in question are genuinely one's own – or more one's own than those of any other claimant. And for what they have left to be worth inheriting it must be agreed that their achievements (the assets they leave behind) exceed their crimes (their debts or liabilities). With claims of ancestry, as with other types of political pretension, contenders for political authority seek with some vigour to split the good from the bad, claiming credit for, and intimate association with, the good for themselves, and attributing blame for, and even more intimate association with, the bad often quite brazenly to their opponents. Determining what the heritage of the left truly is is not an exercise which will be entrusted solely to the latter's own adherents. By the time the assessment has been completed, the left is still for the present in real danger of much further demographic attrition. Routine politics, of course, goes on all the time; and it would be monumentally injudicious for any political contender to ignore it – to leave it to the tender mercies of their opponents. But the greater risk for the left at present is precisely the opposite. Because it is so hard to see clear and encouraging outlines of a future for the left, the overwhelming temptation for its adherents is not to look too hard: to attend instead to the sometimes rewarding immediacies of political struggle, to draw encouragement from the successes it affords and sustain identity within it by fond, if increasingly air-brushed, memories of the past.

Does the left then *have* a future? Can it reasonably hope to remain alive on a scale, at a level of practical coherence and with a degree of vitality sufficient to equip it to inherit anything worthwhile in a political space which will certainly continue to be intensely contested? I do not myself know the answer to that first blunt question. But I am sure that if one wishes to try to answer it, it would be prudent to attend first to the second, and somewhat more elaborate and concrete, query. The encouragement available to the left within routine politics for the moment comes principally from the existing scale of – in the broadest sense – socialist *survival*. In most settings (perhaps in every setting), as of now, this scale of survival is less encouraging than it has been at some points in the near or more distant past. But it is substantial enough in several settings to confer governmental power on parties that describe themselves as socialist, and to give real prospects there or elsewhere of enabling such parties to win governmental power again in the future. This may not be the movement of which past socialists dreamed. (I doubt if anyone in the past ever dreamed of existing christian democrat or conservative regimes in other parts of Europe either.) But it is, in any case, scarcely a movement slinking quietly and shamefacedly from the European political stage. What does that mean for the future of socialism, or, indeed, for the future of the left more capaciously envisaged? I would say, nothing whatever. On its own in politics mere demographic survival at one time is palpably insufficient for any future at all. It is the form in which it survives – and above all the practical coherence and vitality of that form – which is crucial for the future of a political organization or movement. Here the present state of affairs in any country of which I know enough to make a serious judgement is appreciably less encouraging for socialists. Some socialist parties, in opposition or government, show a measure of practical coherence and some show a degree of vitality. But in none of which I am aware is there a close and steady relationship between vitality and practical coherence; and such coherence as there is seems increasingly to have been imposed by the political and economic power of less equivocal and ambivalent defenders of the capitalist order itself. (I do not mean to suggest that this fact in itself is in any sense a criticism of that practical coherence (Dunn 1984).)

There are two ways in which one could look at this predicament – historically, in terms of the broad rhythms of the world economy and geopolitical relations, and analytically in terms of the imaginative and theoretical basis of socialism's inherited pretensions. I am not equipped to do the first. But although I cannot do it and will make no attempt to do so, it is important to underline its emphatic relevance and its potentially overwhelming causal weight. I have never been a Marxist. But I have not the slightest doubt of the validity of the central Marxist tenet – that it is the historical development of human productive powers and the ferocious causal force of the rhythms of the global economy which these powers have created which now dominate the life of the species to which we belong (cf. Dunn 1990). In this respect, political movements and actors propose, and it disposes. It is therefore of the utmost importance that the present practical incoherence of socialist political organizations in and out of office, along with their wilting *esprit de corps* and capacity for inspiration, are themselves in substantial measure a product of the geopolitical shock of the collapse of what was comically (if briefly) labelled the World Socialist System, of the painful discoveries about the hazards of economic planning that precipitated that collapse, and of a belligerent politics of marketization pressed by opponents virtually across the world. It would be easy to exaggerate the intellectual quality or insight of this often victorious movement, or the efficacy of the techniques which it has hawked around the world. But it is difficult for its severest critics to deny either its vitality over the past fifteen years or the core of common purpose which it has pursued over this timespan.

Proponents of the movement throughout have naturally been inclined to attribute the pace and scale of their victory to the intellectual quality and insight of the ideas which they adopted. But it is unlikely in retrospect that this will prove any more comprehensive and cogent an explanation for their triumph than the intellectual quality and insight of putatively Keynesian ideas appears to have been of their somewhat more sporadic advance in the aftermath of the Great Depression (Clarke 1988; Hall 1989; Barber 1985). A comparably simple but more promising approach to explaining the political success of the economic projects of the Reagan and Thatcher years would start off not from the regnant conceptions of economic causality themselves (which have proved pretty volatile: cf., in the British case, Gilmour (1992)), but from the determination to avoid some of the more prominent unintended consequences of the styles of economic policy that immediately preceded them. These widely advertised (and plainly unintended and unwelcome) consequences were closely associated with the deteriorating real profitability and economic dynamism of the major capitalist economies, however these may have been disguised by artificial short-term booms or bubbles that temporarily obscured them. It is extremely important that the left still has no distinctive and minimally plausible conception of how to rectify these deficiencies at all dependably. But it has become blisteringly obvious by now, not least in the United Kingdom, that neither, for the present, do its existing opponents to the right. Unlike the latter, furthermore, the left has a relatively convincing commitment at least to try to remedy the more massive and humanly disagreeable unintended consequences of the rule of less inhibited defenders of the need of capital to reproduce itself. If the outcome of the Reagan and Bush presidencies, the Thatcher and Major premierships, the reunification of Germany (six million employed in the east by 1992, in contrast to ten million at the time of reunion (Peel 1992)), and the Japanese bubble economy proves to be, as it is already well on the way towards being, a really substantial slump, this will almost certainly in the short term favour in most settings the political fortunes of broadly social democratic forces (though it will do so, of course, in relation to the position which they occupy at the time within the history of local political conflict and which may therefore already have been rendered so weak by recent political performance to be beyond the reach of aid from more global political rhythms). But even such short-term aid as the left does receive will accrue to it essentially in the medium of routine politics; and it

is sure to be speedily squandered unless and until social democratic
regimes recapture a coherent conception of what they might reasonably
hope to achieve in the longer term which goes beyond the Abbé Sieyes'
eventual boast in face of the French Revolution: survival itself.

For these reasons the question of whether the left really does have a
future, not as a broad on-going stream of perception and sentiment, but
as a relatively integral and buoyant political movement, with real
prospects of exercising power and achieving substantial and durable
goals, can now be best addressed at some imaginative distance from
immediate political circumstances. Let us agree for the present that the
past of the left, despite the stunning indiscretions and horrors which it has
incontestably contained, remains a heritage worth surviving to inherit:
Liberty, Equality, Fraternity, indeed Sorority, Democracy, Justice within
and between human societies, a world in which these societies come
increasingly to make rational sense to their inhabitants and the latter
come to choose freely together how their society should in fact operate.
These have always been easy dreams to mock. But I do not think that,
simply as dreams, there is even now the faintest reason to apologize for
them. The left has no monopoly on all the best tunes: no proprietary right
to be seen by others as the true exponents of all these fine words and
ideas. But it is not on the whole its desires or hopes which have betrayed it
so cruelly, so much as its often hapless conceptions of what is to be done.
One might indeed say, less its theories than its practices, had it not
insisted so fecklessly on constructing its most ambitious, striking and historically consequential theory firmly on the claim that certain varieties of
practice were inherently trustworthy (cf. Harding 1992).

I take the socialist movement in all its historical and imaginative heterogeneity as still the core of the left, principally because no subsequent
claimant of comparable scope and political determinacy has yet emerged.
(Feminism, for example, plainly has immense force, depth and potentiality. But it is still remarkably inchoate as a political theory, let alone a political movement. And no one has yet given the least reason to suppose that
it could ever, in and of itself, offer a coherent approach for human beings
as a whole at a particular time to coping with the world which they will
have inherited.) It may help to sharpen the issue of the left's future to contrast what first made socialism such a formidable political movement with
the features of its present embodiments which render the latter in
comparison so palpably debilitated. I take this to have been most decisively a distinctive combination of three components: a schedule of
emotive and sometimes inspiring values and goals, a presumed (and
eventually quite richly specified) set of techniques for constructing and
managing an economy which were taken to be decisively more effective

than those in principle available to the political custodians of capital, and an immediate and dependable relation to privileged and predictably potent types of agency. The principal reason why the issue of the left's heritage is so inflammatory at present, and the reason why it is so inextricably involved with the question of its potential future, is quite simply that only the first of these three components is still at all plausibly to hand. And if, of course, only the first – the goals or purposes or intentions – is at all plausibly to hand, what could be easier or prospectively more menacing than for immediate political enemies to profess an equally poignant concern for exactly the same goals, or indeed, if they are shameless enough, to profess virtually identical intentions. Politics, soberly considered, is a fairly dirty business. (Perhaps on reasonably intimate inspection most businesses are.) The tendency of socialists at present promiscuously to expand their schedule of purposes or good intentions is not inherently damaging. Better, wider, more generous, less inadvertently gender-bound or chauvinist, aims are plainly more edifying than their opposites. But it is extremely dangerous in politics to expand one's goals in a swift and weakly coordinated *fuite en avant*, without at the same time equivalently expanding one's causal capabilities, the political resources or effective expedients at one's disposal for achieving intended effects.

Here the legacy of the left is very exposed indeed, and its future correspondingly imperilled. The types of agency which have been regarded as having a special affinity with the left – the industrial working class, the rather larger range of adults who do not own their own means of production or livelihood and must therefore sell their labour (in some cases today for quite handsome rewards), the autonomous and belligerently anti-parliamentary or even anarchist revolutionary syndicates, the Leninist or post-Leninist revolutionary parties – are either so drastically discredited by their historical record, so obviously weakened, or so tenuously or unreliably linked to representative political organizations of the left that to ground hopes for its future principally on any of them can now only appear an exercise in gratuitous credulity. To assume eventual historical triumph because of a privileged relation to a social group which was thought to be compelled to expand relentlessly into an immense majority by the core mechanism shaping an entire way of economic and social life may have been a catastrophic misjudgement. But at least, while the assumption could be credibly sustained, it made an emphatic sort of sense. The somewhat sluggish and diffuse 'laws of motion' which can be reliably picked up in contemporary societies offer no such reassuring promises to the left. They do so neither in the form of assurances of growth in its natural allies or clients, nor in the shape of dependable allegiance on the part of these elements in society which do indeed appear to be growing.

More decisively perhaps, the special set of expedients for organizing and developing an economy, the expedients which putatively carried the clear potential gain in rationality and efficiency for socialism over capitalism, appear to be no longer to hand. This is least contestable, perhaps, in the case of socialism's boldest claims to special practical potency. The slow, reluctant but increasingly undeniable discovery of the sheer intractability of the obstacles to the rational planning in practice of an economy founded on public ownership of the major means of production, the learning curve above all of eastern European (Brus & Laski 1988), and then Soviet, and by now certainly of Chinese and perhaps even North Korean and Cuban, economists, have by this stage alerted even the more torpid observers of modern politics to the fact that socialists for the present possess no grand and coherent alternative approach to managing a modern economy to those deployed, more or less haphazardly, by incumbent OECD governments which would certainly not choose to describe themselves as socialist. It is hard to exaggerate the imaginative and orientational significance for the left of this unpleasant discovery.

The absence of any such dependable and potent instrument for realizing its own distinctive goals breaks socialism's privileged relation to the future (its bland assumption of being History's chosen heir), and makes it apparent that any major and sustained political advance for it will have to be secured by more conventional and blatantly contingent political factors: by improvisatory skill and alertness, nerve, luck and cumulative rhetorical prowess, an altogether too Machiavellian (or Paretian) vision of the determinants of socialist political success to appeal to socialists themselves.

Even within routine politics, always the favoured habitat of social democracy (Lichtheim 1961; Przeworski 1985; Dunn 1984), the bare minimum programme of socialism throughout my own political lifetime, the defence of the welfare state as indispensable palliative to the irretrievably ugly logic of a society grounded systematically on exchange value, has become an increasingly herculean task, chastened in virtually every society in the world and effectively abandoned in not a few. The cause of this abandonment is naturally controversial. But even those who regret it most bitterly can hardly dispute that one major causal factor behind it is the potentially crippling cost in a savagely competitive global market of the tax burden required to fund it. If socialists have no strategy at all for replacing an essentially capitalist system of production and exchange, they will not necessarily lose a certain reactive appeal that issues essentially from their patent regret at the intrinsic licentiousness and the sometimes inadvertent cruelty of a market society. But they will have little real capacity to avert that cruelty at all durably and not much chance even to restrain the licence that routinely accompanies it.

In this perspective, it is all too easy to make sense of the common profile of socialism in face of the routine politics of reasonably advanced capitalist societies today. Increasingly, putatively socialist political parties which stand a chance of governing (and still more, socialist parties which happen to *be* governing) present their projects not in terms of special identities or uniquely available forms of agency, still less in terms of distinctive techniques of economic administration and strategy, but as expressions of a fluent and alert pragmatism, guided by the very best of intentions. In routine political competition they are naturally under harsher competitive pressure over the claims to fluency, alertness and pragmatic efficacy. But it is instructive how far even those of their socialist critics who find themselves at a greater distance from the pleasures and frustrations of governmental office choose to press against them, not a clearly specified and carefully assessed set of alternative techniques, but simply a richer and spiritually more tasteful schedule of intentions. In face of the exigencies of routine politics – especially the merciless presence of better funded opponents with superior access to the more influential media of mass communication – neither of these two orientations looks at all promising. There is nothing politically irrational in espousing a pragmatism with the very best of intentions. But it will hardly prove a royal road to power. Pragmatism itself is scarcely a prerogative of the left; and those of the expressed intentions that prove to be at all electorally winning and that are even partially compatible with the requirements of pragmatism are most unlikely to remain a prerogative of the left either.

Do I conclude, then, from these (I trust) moderately astringent considerations that socialism palpably *has* no future? The short answer is that I do not. But what I do conclude, at least when expressed frankly and intelligibly, may not appear to many on the left to be notably more attractive. What I conclude is that at present socialism has no *palpable* future: that if it does have a future remotely commensurate in scale and human promise with what it still likes to think of as its heritage, then for the present it has not the haziest idea what that future is going to be, what form, even in the broadest of outlines, it is going to take. For myself, trivially, I wish it a future. Not out of indolent sentimentality, but out of what might be optimistically thought of as a judicious blend of fear and hope.

The fears are obvious enough. First amongst them is the devastatingly complicated challenge of preserving a habitat which we are already straining so brutally and over which we will need to learn to cooperate with the greatest skill and patience and self-restraint if we are to have the slightest hope of preserving it. Second is the game-theoretically bemusing challenge of reproducing a worldwide framework of trading relations by sustained political choice, let alone the moral and political enormity of the global historical task of making that framework less starkly unjust. Third is the appalling potentiality for regressive barbarism latent in modern instruments of war wherever they are to be found and permanently on active display in one area or another of the world.

The core of the hope is that human beings are in principle capable of such cooperation and that they must learn how to carry it out if they are to have the slightest chance of averting these fears. It must be said that this core itself is blazingly optimistic (perhaps ludicrously so). But it is also the minimum condition for any real hope at all over time for the species as a whole and for huge numbers of its present or future members. Around this core there is a virtually infinite proliferation of more luxurious and cheering hopes, drawn in effect from the unsteady but irrepressible movement over time of the moral understanding of the species at large (cf. Dunn (1992) or, in a very different vein, Parfit (1984)).

This increasingly ample periphery of civilized aspirations is probably at present of greater importance for the identities of most of those who today think of themselves as being socialists or on the left. But I suspect myself that it is the core itself – the central practical challenges of modern human existence – on which it would be wisest for socialists to focus their main attention. Only if they can grasp these more clearly than their political opponents can socialists at present have any reasonable hope of learning how to meet them more effectively. And even if they do grasp them more clearly, there can be no prior guarantee that the problems themselves admit of solutions which are even minimally friendly to socialist values. To understand might be to *have* to abandon hope. But, as Lady Thatcher used to say in the days before her ennoblement, there *is* no alternative. To secure the heritage which they have promised themselves for so long socialists today must learn how to win it – and win it not by ingenious, indefatigable and ruthless manipulative struggle, but by the intellectual mastery of the most pressing problems of practical life.

Socialism (or the left more broadly) will have no integral future unless its exponents can make one for it, and do so most crucially by their own creative practical intelligence. The first step towards making one would be to recognize as sharply as possible where we now are and why we have come to be here. But, of course, that first step would do nothing for socialism's future if it also proved to be the last. *Faites vos jeux, Mesdames et Messieurs.*

REFERENCES

Barber, W. J. 1985. *From New Era to New Deal.* Cambridge: Cambridge University Press

Brus, W. and K. Laski 1988. *From Marx to the Market.* Oxford: Clarendon Press

Clarke, P. 1988. *The Keynesian Revolution in the Making.* Oxford: Clarendon Press

Dunn, J. 1984. *The Politics of Socialism.* Cambridge: Cambridge University Press

   1990 (ed.). *The Economic Limits to Modern Politics.* Cambridge: Cambridge University Press

   1992 (ed.). *Democracy: The Unfinished Journey.* Oxford: Oxford University Press

Gilmour, I. 1992. *Dancing with Dogma.* Hemel Hempstead: Simon and Schuster

Hall, P. A. 1989 (ed.). *The Political Power of Economic Ideas: Keynesianism across Nations.* Princeton: Princeton University Press

Harding, N. 1992. 'The Marxist-Leninist detour'. In *Democracy: The Unfinished Journey,* ed. J. Dunn. Oxford: Oxford University Press

Lichtheim, G. 1961. *Marxism.* London: Routledge and Kegan Paul

Parfit, D. 1984. *Reasons and Persons.* Oxford: Clarendon Press

Peel, Q. 1992. 'German economists see gloomy outlook'. *Financial Times,* 28 October, p. 2

Przeworski, A. 1985. *Capitalism and Social Democracy.* Cambridge: Cambridge University Press

Index